Agency and Patronage in Eastern Translatology

Agency and Patronage in Eastern Translatology

Edited by

Ahmed Ankit and Said Faiq

Cambridge
Scholars
Publishing

Agency and Patronage in Eastern Translatology

Edited by Ahmed Ankit and Said Faiq

This book first published 2015

Cambridge Scholars Publishing

Lady Stephenson Library, Newcastle upon Tyne, NE6 2PA, UK

British Library Cataloguing in Publication Data
A catalogue record for this book is available from the British Library

ISBN (10): 1-4438-7416-7
ISBN (13): 978-1-4438-7416-8

This volume is dedicated to

His Highness Sheikh Humaid bin Rashid Al Nuaimi
Member of the Supreme Council and Ruler of Ajman
United Arab Emirates

CONTENTS

India

Iran

Turkey

Arab World

ACKNOWLEDGEMENTS

The editors would like to thank the contributors to this volume. The chapters were first presented at the Fifth Asian Translation Traditions conference (ATT5) held in November 2012 at Ajman University of Science and Technology in the United Arab Emirates (UAE). Particular gratitude and thanks are due to His Highness Sheikh Humaid Bin Rashid Al Nuaimi, Member of the Supreme Council and Ruler of Ajman, for granting his patronage to the ATT5 conference and for his wise directives for pursuing professional academic work in the universities operating in the UAE.

It was a delight and privilege to welcome all the participants and then to work with them on their contributions to this volume—to all, thank you. Thanks and gratitude are also due to Dr. Thomas Hochstettler (Provost in 2012) and Mr. Salem Al Qaseer (Vice Chancellor for Public Relations), both of the American University of Sharjah.

The editors would also like to acknowledge the support and generosity of Ajman University of Science and Technology. Particular gratitude and thanks go to the Presidency of Ajman University, to the late Mr Thamer Salman, Vice President of the University, to Dr Khaled Al-Khaja, Dean of the College of Information, Communication and Humanities, and his colleagues Dr Sahab Abdul Azeez Salih and Dr Aboudi Hassan, and to the many colleagues from the departments of Finance, Information Technology, and Public Relations for all their cooperation and the great work they did in gathering all the contributors together at the international conference in November 2012.

Ahmed Ankit and Said Faiq
Ajman and Sharjah
(United Arab Emirates)
July 2014

PREFACE

That translation studies has witnessed a phenomenal shift since the 1980s is axiomatic. The focus in translation has shifted from (un)translatability to the cultural, political and economic ramifications of translation; away from concerns with translated texts (matter vs. manner), to treating translations as social, cultural and political acts taking place within and attached to global and local relations of power and dominance. It should be noted that this shift has, not surprisingly, been precipitated by work on orientalism, post-colonial and cultural studies, and by the questioning of the transparent and fluent strategies and practices of translating (representing) others (Faiq 2004). But the problem for translation is that it has been framed almost exclusively by and within Western discourses. One of the two editors (Said Faiq) recalls the surprised faces and perplexed looks when he added Arabic translation studies to a graduate course on translation studies at a UK university back in the 1990s. He also recalls the same reactions in 2002 when he added Arabic translation studies to a course on translation theory in a graduate program in Arabic/English translation and interpreting at a university in the Arab World—"this should go under history, area studies, heritage, oriental studies ..." were some of the comments. It may not be far from the truth to say that this situation prevails globally.

With a few exceptions here and there, the discourse of translation has been largely Western-oriented—in the wider sense of the term—covering Western European and North American discourses on translation. "Western" here does not necessarily refer to particular geographies, but rather to intellectual tendencies, paradigms and conceptions. There have been challenges, albeit not very vocal, to the so-called positivist take on what translation is and what it entails (restricting translation to one fixed definition). These challenges have mostly been initiated by scholars working within non-Western circles with a view to exploring the rich and diverse nature of other discourses and practices (traditions) of translation, and have on the whole emanated from the East (Asian traditions of translation, for example). There have also been voices within the Western discourse calling for the treatment of translation as an open concept to accommodate the various traditions.

The aim of such calls is to go beyond the often conflictual situation of Western vs non-Western discourses on/of translation to a situation whereby translation is seen as encompassing characteristics of different cultures in their representation, regulation, production and consumption of translation products as cultural goods. To this end, voices from non-Western discourses on translation need to be heard, promoted and diffused.

It is within this context of complementarity rather than opposition that this volume is located, as one of very few publications on translation traditions in/from the East. The theme cutting through the chapters is agency and patronage in Eastern Translatology (translation studies/traditions). Each in its fashion, the ten chapters explore agency and patronage, with the problematics of power as inevitable, in the examination of the interface and relations between agency and agents and patronage and patrons, including political leaders, commissioners, authors, translators, editors, publishers, and audiences.

The chapters, contributed by some of the world's leading scholars on Asian Translation Traditions, examine the common theme from different theoretical frameworks (framing of translation), methodologies, and special national (cultural) perspectives. Thus, from Japan in the east of the East, to Korea, China, Malaysia, India, Iran, Turkey, and to the Arab world, the west of the East, the authors explore issues that range from official patronage, shifting loyalties, the power of the translator, the role of the commissioner, the translator as a dis-unifier of cultural groups of one seemingly united nation, to the legitimization of patrons, authors and texts, women and agency in translation, power relations between translators and editors, and the agency of translation in nation-building.

Patronage, agency and power have become the subjects of important debates in translation studies, as affecting both macro and micro dimensions of translation and translating (socio-cultural and textual practices in/of a culture/nation). Patronage may include "a religious body, a political party, a social class, a royal court, publishers, and, last but not least, the media, both newspapers and magazines and larger television corporations" (Lefevere 1992: 15). Patrons affect decisions about what texts are chosen, translated and published. They also directly and indirectly affect the views of individual agents, including policy and decision-makers, translators, critics, media outlets and workers, and influential figures (for example philanthropists), as well as issues of stereotyping, ethnocentricity, racism, and prejudice. As such, patronage and agency within a web of power relations continue to be fascinating topics in translation studies, under whatever guise in which they may be explored (such as the sociology, politics and/or ideology of translation).

Currently, there are calls for "new turns" in translation studies to perhaps jolt the field/discipline, and the chapters in this book will contribute greatly to such calls, since they offer a gateway to the rich and diverse traditions of translation emanating from the East. The book also goes a long way to contributing to a truly burgeoning discipline of cross-cultural and global translation, while providing insights into the complex network of power relations between patrons and agents (patronage and agency) that hugely affect the state and status of translation.

This volume will be of great interest to students (graduate and undergraduate) and researchers in *all* areas of translation studies. It will also provide a unique input for those studying and researching history, geopolitics, intercultural studies, globalization, and related areas—the surprised faces and perplexed looks.

Ahmed Ankit and Said Faiq
Ajman and Sharjah (United Arab Emirates)
July 2014

References

Faiq, Said, 2004. "The Cultural Encounter in Translating from Arabic", in Said Faiq, ed., *Cultural Encounters in Arabic Translation*. Clevedon (UK) & New York: Multilingual Matters, 1-13.

Lefevere, André, 1992, *Translating Literature: Practice and Theory*. New York: Modern Language Association of America.

JAPAN

IMPORTS AND INSTITUTIONS: OFFICIAL PATRONAGE AND (NON-)PUBLISHING OF TRANSLATIONS IN EARLY MODERN JAPAN

JUDY WAKABAYASHI

1. Introduction

Official patronage of translations of European works on the part of central and regional government authorities played a significant role in Edo-period Japan (1603–1867), since private patronage during this time was limited in scale and influence.[1] The most important patronage of European knowledge goods emanated from government authorities, and it is this nexus between power and knowledge transfer that is the focus here. This official patronage is analyzed through two aspects. The first is the imported European works, some of which were subsequently translated— i.e., the focus is on books as physical objects and what they tell us about Japanese readers' interests under those particular social circumstances. The second aspect examined here is the official institutions that sponsored translations and trained translators. I argue that official patronage functioned to promote the production of translations while simultaneously restricting their dissemination to a narrowly-prescribed circle of readers because of the potentially destabilizing effect of these translated works on society and the power hierarchy. In terms of the "archaeology of translation" (St-Pierre 1993: 63), the focus here is on the 'what' and 'who' of translation history in Edo Japan. The specific timeframe is the century

---

[1] Publishing houses played virtually no role in backing translations from European languages (unlike the situation with translations of Chinese vernacular novels, which had far greater marketing potential). Nor did religious authorities play any role in sponsoring translations of European works. Some wealthy merchants, although at the bottom rank of the four main tiers of Edo-period society, did provide financial support for scholars of 'Dutch Learning' (i.e., knowledge about the West).

from 1754, a few years after the reading of Dutch books had become allowed, to 1854, when Japan's national seclusion came to an end.

Methodologically, this paper is situated at the intersection of translation history, book history and institutional history. The first part analyzes the demand for and supply of European books[2] from two angles—i.e., the book orders submitted by various Japanese officials who were authorized to make such requests, and the books that were actually imported. These did not always coincide, and of course not all imported books subsequently underwent translation. Moretti (2005) has argued that counting books helps reintegrate the 'lost' archive of non-canonical works. Concentrating solely on well-known translations overlooks the broader picture of the far more numerous non-canonical translations that, while individually of less importance, were significant in their collective impact on society. (An emphasis on translations also ignores the influence of imported works that were read in the original, without being translated, but that is beyond the scope of the present study.) This section also examines the role of the state and regional officials involved in ordering these works and commissioning translations of some of them. The second part of the paper explores the role of official institutions that were engaged in translating these works and training translators, focusing on two different timeframes in the nineteenth century.

The historical background to these book imports was that by 1639 Japan had become a 'closed' country because of fear of potential external threats, mainly from Europeans who were making their religious and commercial presence increasingly felt in Asia. It was precisely because of these fears, however, that it was important to keep a small 'window' open for the Japanese authorities to learn about Europe and its more advanced science and technology. This was why the central military government (shogunate) gave permission to the Dutch, whose interests were confined to the commercial, to maintain a small trading post on the island of Dejima in the harbour of Nagasaki. They were the only Europeans allowed in Japan for over two centuries, and their movements were highly restricted. Each trading season brought a small number of Dutch ships, which arrived at Dejima with cargoes that often included some European books. The first Japanese to lay hands on these were usually the official hereditary

---

[2] European works were in fact outnumbered by imported Chinese works (works originally written in Chinese as well as Chinese translations of European works). Chinese works also contributed to Japan's incipient modernization and the formation of a modern lexicon, and there was, for instance, official sponsorship of translations of Chinese scientific works. The focus here, however, is on European works.

translators known as *tsūji*. Employed by the government to act as translators-cum-interpreters as well as customs officials, and even as spies on the Dutch, the bilingual *tsūji* had privileged access to imported works, and for about a century, this gave them a virtual monopoly on European knowledge. Although the core of their day-to-day work was trade-related translation and interpreting duties, some of the more scholarly-minded *tsūji*, over time and on their own initiative, also took on the translation of European scientific works (*not* literature or works from the humanities). The linguistic expertise and scientific knowledge acquired in the course of their work meant they accrued influence well beyond their lowly official position. From the mid-eighteenth century, and in order to access this valuable knowledge, some scholars from the capital Edo (present-day Tokyo) studied Dutch under the *tsūji* and took up translation. The shogunate and provincial domain authorities increasingly commissioned and/or sponsored scientific-technical translations by both groups of translators, so as to use advanced European knowledge to protect and, within limits, modernize Japan or their own provinces.

Official patronage of translations in Edo Japan constituted an attempt by the secular authorities to centralize and monopolize information from abroad as part of foreign and domestic policy. Thus the translation process became highly politicized, with translations used as an effective vehicle of *circumscribed* change. There was a utilitarian focus on knowledge goods, rather than cultural works, much less on instigating widespread social change. Unlike in the subsequent Meiji period (1868–1912), therefore, these translations did not lead to a "thorough-going intellectual re-orientation" (Jansen 1957: 592). Nevertheless, they laid the grounds for a gradual yet influential shift in thinking and in the practice of science and technology in Japan.

2. Book orders and book imports

2.1. Pull-driven demand as reflected in Japanese book orders

The fact that Dejima was the sole channel for orders and imports of European books allows us to track the pull- and push-driven demand for foreign works. Here, 'pull-driven' demand refers to book orders submitted to the Dutch on Dejima by various Japanese entities, while 'push-driven' refers to works imported by the Dutch themselves as gifts for Japanese officials or in anticipation of what might interest (and be purchased by) the Japanese. The primary source (in both the sense of the main source and that of a source originating in that historical period) of information about pull-driven demand on the part of the Japanese is the order forms submitted to the Dutch up until 1857. These orders by the Japanese are a better indicator of actual demand than official gifts from the Dutch or imports by the Dutch based on assumptions about Japanese interests. As Chaiklin (2003: 69) points out, these orders "illustrate the quest for knowledge in a restricted society." The order forms (*Eisch Boeken*)—41 of which are extant[3] although more existed—reveal the interests of specific Japanese parties in a range of European items, including books. The orders probably began around 1765 or earlier (Ōmori 1988: 233), even if at that stage they were not yet properly formalized. Existing studies of these order forms include those by MacLean (1974), Ōmori (1988), Chaiklin (2003) and Nagazumi (2008). The orders show that some requests were submitted repeatedly by the Japanese without being met. The reason remains unclear, as these works do not seem to have been particularly sensitive in nature. Censorship of foreign works—the reverse side of patronage—was certainly in place during this period, particularly with regard to works that mentioned the banned religion of Christianity, but no thematic pattern is discernible in these unfulfilled repeat requests. Nor is there any indication of censorship on the part of the Dutch. It is possible that the requested works were simply not available in the home country at that time or that the Dutch did not regard the importation of these particular works as commercially viable, although it is just as likely that the reasons for not fulfilling these orders were largely haphazard. Overall, however, it seems that most orders were indeed met, even though it often took a few years for the items to arrive.

The orders mention seven ranks of officials who were permitted to submit orders, from the shogun down to the *tsūji*. Broadly classified, those eligible fell into two categories: (1) officials in the central government; and (2) officials involved in the administration of Nagasaki or in relations with the Dutch (Ōmori 1988: 240). Orders by the latter regional group outnumbered those by the former group at the centre of government. The books ordered included dictionaries in various European languages, encyclopedias, astronomical calendars, and specialized works in a range of fields. As an example of the content of these orders, Table 1, which draws on Ōmori (1988: 237–8) and MacLean (1974: 27), shows the book orders that were submitted in 1809.

---

[3] The order forms are kept in the General State Archives in The Hague.

Table 1: Orders for European books submitted in 1809

Title of person submitting the order	Books ordered
Shogun	Almanacs; Pieter Marin's *Woordenboek*, 6th ed. (three sets); English-Dutch dictionaries (three sets); an English grammar; *Trap der Jeugt*; *Spelkunst*; Russian-Dutch dictionaries (three sets); a book on writing the Dutch almanac; book by E. Kaempfer (possibly *De Beschreijving van Japan*).[4]
A Nagasaki commissioner (Tsoetia Kie no Cammi Samma[5])	Books on artillery and the preparation of gunpowder, bombs, shells and combustible substances.
A senior Nagasaki town official (Takashima Shirobei)	Book on various kinds of birds.
Another senior Nagasaki town official (head burgomaster, Gotto Sotaro Samma[6])	Two books on astronomy (Pybo Steenstra's astronomical table).
Tsūji	Book on botany; two sets of Noël Chomel's encyclopedia (*Huishoudelijk woordenboek*; 9 vols); Jérôme Lalande's *Astronomie* (5 vols); Kaempfer's book; new world atlas; François Valentijn's *Beschrijving van de hele wereld* on geography; English-Dutch dictionary; Marin's dictionary and two sets of the 6th edition; Lorenz Heister's *Chirurgie* on surgery; book about Russia; Steenstra's *Beschrijving der Stuurlieden* on astronomy; François Halma's Dutch-French dictionary (two sets) and one set of the 4th or 5th edition of Egbert Buys' *Woordenboek*. Also writing materials, scientific instruments, and items for use in medical treatment.

---

[4] Engelbert Kaempfer (1651–1716) was a German doctor who visited Japan in 1690 and 1696, passing himself off as Dutch in order to gain entry. After his departure, he wrote a book about Japan titled *De Beschreijving van Japan*. Its appendix included a chapter in which, after listing several of the disadvantages of national isolation, Kaempfer concluded that isolation was not necessarily a problem, since Japan was self-sufficient. This outsider's views on Japan's seclusion were clearly of potential interest to the shogun.

[5] This is the Dutch spelling of the name of Tsuchiya Ki-i no Kami.

[6] Gotō Sōtarō.

What is most striking about this is that out of the ranks eligible to submit orders, it was the lowly *tsūji* who were the most keen to acquire these sources of European knowledge. Not only did they order more works than the higher-ranking officials, but these books were also more wide-ranging in content, indicating the intellectual curiosity of the *tsūji*.

The orders submitted by or on behalf of the shogun (who was the most powerful figure in Edo Japan, not the emperor) constituted interest from the very top. They were, however, largely limited to almanacs (which were included in every order and hence not shown below) and linguistic rather than scientific works, as indicated in Table 2. The different shoguns also evinced interest in how Japan was perceived by Europeans, as indicated by the four items in bold type below.

Table 2: European works ordered by various shoguns

Year	Works ordered by the shogun
1757	Dutch translation of Heister's book on surgery
1791	Valentijn's *Oud en Nieuw* (8 vols); Buijs' *Woordenboek* (10 vols)
1794	Valentijn's *Reysebeschrijving*; Jacob Buys' *Werken* (works)
1801	**Kaempfer's *De Beschreijving van Japan***
1814	English-Dutch and Dutch-English dictionaries (2 vols.); a book on the sextant; ***Kaempfer on Japan*** (1 vol.)
1817	Lalande's *Astronomie*, 8 vols.
1818	Russian and German grammar and dictionary
1825	Four dictionaries (German, Dutch, French, Portuguese)
1826	Three dictionaries (German, Portuguese, Spanish)
1830	Set of German-Dutch dictionaries
1833	Chinese and French dictionary, with supplement; Italian and French dictionary, 2 vols. (into Dutch); Portuguese and French dictionary, 2 vols. (into Dutch); Spanish and French dictionary, 2 vols. (into Dutch); German and Dutch dictionary, 2 vols.; Russian and German dictionary (into Dutch)
1834	**Hendrik Doeff's memoir *Herinneringen uit Japan*; Overmeer Fisscher's *Bijdragen tot de kennis van Japan***
1844	Merkus. *Vestingbouwkunde*; *Exercitierreglement der Veldartillerie*; *Aanhangsel op idem*; *Uitrustingsstaat*; De Bruyn. *Voorlezingen voor de artillerie over buskurid, gieterij etc.*; Scharnhorst. *Mil. Zakboek*; Incomplete **work by Philipp Franz von von Siebold** (*Koloniën*, no. 717, no. 9)

The shoguns were not the only important officials who ordered European books. From 1820, the names of certain provincial lords (*daimyō*), along with those of other high-ranking officials, also appear on the book orders as purchasers of European works. However, of the 60 or more *daimyō* in Edo Japan at any given time, the extant orders include orders from only five *daimyō* during the period under examination, and only two *daimyō* submitted more than one order (Chaiklin 2003: 62). Because these feudal lords represented potential 'competition' to the shogunate, they needed special permission, at least for certain purchases. But, as discussed below, some *daimyō* were active in patronizing the translation of European knowledge works. The ranks of the other high officials who ordered European books included *rōjū* (members of the council of ministers), *wakatoshiyori* (junior councilors), *daikan* (governors), commissioners and *machitoshiyori* (city elders).

By far the most numerous orders, however, came from a group outside the main official circles—i.e., Het Collegie (College of Interpreters). This was the *tsūji* guild, which ordered dictionaries, medical and military works, and other Dutch works. Their day-to-day contact with the Dutch, especially the surgeons stationed on Dejima, made the *tsūji* keenly aware of the ways in which European learning was superior to Japanese knowledge at that time. They ordered certain key works repeatedly (e.g., Dutch/French dictionaries by Halma and Marin), so it is possible or likely that over time all or most of the *tsūji* came to have access to their 'own' dictionary, rather than having to share around these valuable but initially scarce resources.

2.2. Actual book imports

My task was made easier by the fact that earlier researchers (notably MacLean 1974) have already done the groundwork in compiling and translating into English the lists of items imported by the Japanese in this period (which included not just books but a wide range of scientific instruments, household goods, and animals, to mention just a few categories). Hence all that was necessary here was to identify and extract book-related items and compile a spreadsheet to be used as the basis of the analysis.

As noted earlier, not all book orders were filled by the Dutch. The orders for 1825 are one example of the compliance rate. In that year a total of 618 items (not just books) were ordered by the shogun (24 items), 19 other individuals, and the *tsūji* guild (74 items) (Ōmori 1988: 245). Of these 618 items, only 44.3 percent were actually imported in the next trading season. (The round trip took two years, so they might have arrived later.) However, Chaiklin (2003: 51) has disputed Ōmori's findings on the compliance rate, arguing that the "documents support the assumption that the orders were filled to the best of the Company's (VOC) ability, just not always with the alacrity the Japanese desired", and that "Ultimately, the statistics will be arbitrary".[7]

Since not all works ordered by the Japanese were supplied, it is important to make a distinction between the book orders and actual imports. Ordered books did not always arrive the following year or at all, so although orders are an excellent indicator of Japanese demand for European works, it is also important to focus more narrowly on actual arrivals—i.e., those that had the potential to exercise an impact in Japan. Here, the Dejima records of imports are an important source of information. They show that in some years, no ships arrived from Europe or the ships carried no books. This would have made those books that did arrive even more valued. The first book imports listed by MacLean (1974) were in 1754,[8] but a handful of books had already been imported and translated prior to that. The records show that in the entire Edo period, about 6,000 volumes of Dutch books were imported (Ōmori 1991: 207), including multiple volumes of the same work on numerous occasions. Imports of these multiple copies were often spread out over time, but they also often arrived on the same ship (e.g., 12 copies of Marin's *Méthode familière, pour ceux qui commencent à s'exercer dans la langue française* arrived on the *De Dortenaar* in 1834), indicating the demand and the possibility of passing these works on to other interested readers in some form or other. Moreover, some works were multi-volume sets (e.g., a 37-volume set of Linnaeus' *Kruidkunde* for the *tsūji* guild in 1824), indicating the thirst for knowledge, as well as the magnitude of the task of reading and translating these works or even part of them. Hence the number of discrete works imported was considerably less than 6,000. Of particular note is the preponderance of bilingual dictionaries in which Dutch was the target language—particularly French-Dutch dictionaries, but also from other languages such as Latin. The imported works also included many *woordenboek* (glossaries). The many imports of grammars were mostly grammars of Dutch, but a Latin grammar was imported in 1814. The imports even included spelling books, indicating the basic level of *tsūji* needs even a century after the first encounter with the Dutch language (a level that makes their achievements in producing scientific translations even more noteworthy). Certain authors were repeatedly imported.

---

[7] VOC stands for Vereenigde Oostindische Compagnie, the Dutch East India Company, which was in charge of trade with Japan.

[8] MacLean (1974: 56) suggests that it was not until after 1745 that the reading of Dutch texts was permitted.

It is essential to note that 'imported' did not necessarily mean 'translated'. I have no complete statistics as to the proportion of imported books that were eventually translated into Japanese. An 1852 catalogue of translated Western works lists 174 printed books in 756 volumes and 288 manuscripts.[9] Focusing on medical works, Cullen (2003: 15) claims that "A total of 189 works, either medical or containing medical knowledge, were translated from Dutch into some 473 books or manuscripts (the latter sometimes recopied)." He does not specify any timeframe, but seems to be referring to the period from the late eighteenth century into the early nineteenth century. Caution is needed, however, when dealing with such statistics because of their incomplete and often subjective nature. Despite the lack of precise statistics as to the proportion of translated works, it seems reasonable to assume that some imported works were read in their original language without immediately (or ever) being translated into Japanese. This presents a methodological problem. On the one hand, focusing solely on translations overlooks the broader interest in and impact of imported works. On the other hand, focusing on the big picture—i.e., the impact of imported European works on Japanese society—makes the study unmanageable, and we lose sight of the specific role of translation as a vehicle for introducing knowledge from outside Japan. Although no ready solution to this problem presents itself, it is important at least to keep this distinction in mind when drawing conclusions about the role of European works in Edo Japan.

One route by which the imported works reached a broader readership than the officials who were authorized to submit orders was through the private trade (*kambang*) that flourished alongside these official imports. This private trade involved items ordered by people other than the shogun, and it was greater in quantity and diversity than the official trade. Despite its unofficial status, from 1685 the Japanese authorities permitted and encouraged this side trade, which was a profitable source of income for the *tsūji*, and books constituted an important part of this. However, after 1820 when foreign trade was subjected to stricter regulations, a quota was imposed on private trade. As noted earlier, the Dutch themselves acted as agents of push-driven imports and also as a 'filter' for the types of books selected to be sent to Japan. After the imposition of the quota in 1820, the Dutch organized their own Personal Trade Association for a short period

---

[9] *Seiyô gakuka yakujutsu mokuroku* [Bibliography of translations of Western writings] was compiled by the 'Master of the Grainear Pavilion' (Hotei shujin). It was completed in 1852 and published in 1854 (Miyashita 1975: 9). The catalogue records the names of 117 translators. The focus was on medical works, but it also includes works on other sciences, such as astronomy and geography.

between 1826 and 1830, motivated mainly by the potential to greatly supplement the incomes earned from the Dutch East India Company. In 1827, for instance, over 40 books were imported via this route (Nagazumi 2008: 16).

3. Institutional support for translations

3.1. The first wave

During the nineteenth century, a growing awareness of Western nations as a potential threat to national security and of the knowledge gap that placed Japan at a technological disadvantage led to certain institutions lending their support to the production of translations of European works. To avoid potential colonization, it was vital for Japan to catch up with European knowledge, so these institutions had a vested interest in patronizing translations of scientific and technical works in order to contribute to the production of Japanese modernity. Yet although these institutions supported the translation of such works, they also regulated the inflow of foreign knowledge and restricted its dissemination to a narrow circle, at least initially, so as to retain control over this valuable information.

Growing concerns about the possible European encroachment led, in 1803, to the establishment of the Waran shoseki wage goyō [Office Dedicated to Translating Western Books][10] within the Astronomical Observatory (Tenmondai) in Edo, and the first works translated there were on geography. Since scholars in Edo were not yet capable of translating European works, some veteran *tsūji* were sent from Nagasaki. This marked the establishment of the first full-time official translator positions in the capital. It also marked the start of government patronage of translations, since previously-published translations were private efforts, even when commissioned by shogun or *daimyō*. This move integrated the *tsūji* into "the traditional framework of scholarly studies operating under State patronage" (Horiuchi 2003: 169), and new information networks were formed (Jannetta 2007: 68). This translation office helped legitimize the translation of 'barbarian' works and extended Dutch Learning beyond the narrow circle of *tsūji* and the scholars in Edo.

In 1811, the Bansho Wage Goyō [Office for the Translation of Barbarian Books] was established within the Bureau of Astronomy (Tenmonkata) to translate Dutch works, because relying on the *tsūji* in

---

[10] Fukuoka (2012: 44).

Nagasaki for translations was too slow in emergencies. This office had predominantly utilitarian goals, rather than an interest in translating works revealing European thought. The initial aim was specifically to translate a Dutch version of Chomel's 7-volume *Dictionnaire Oeconomique*. This undertaking continued until 1840 and constituted the largest translation project in Edo times. The Bureau of Astronomy enjoyed a near-monopoly on government-supported translation projects, and had a particular focus on military works. In 1841, the perceived need to boost coastal defences led a member of the Council of Elders to order the translation of Dutch books on military matters. There was still little concern for fostering the 'civilization and enlightenment' that later became a feature of the early Meiji period. Nevertheless, translations did help broaden the common intellect as ideas of and about European culture seeped in. For instance, in the 1840s, the same Elder ordered translations of the Dutch Constitution, Criminal Code and Code of Criminal Procedure—documents containing difficult and unfamiliar legal concepts that must have presented considerable challenges to the translators. Unlike more directly practical works, these legal translations were intended for the private use of the Council of Elders, because they might spark "politically dangerous ideas", and nothing is known about what happened to them after presentation to the authorities (Verwaijen 1996: 66). It is reasonable to assume, however, that they helped shape the views of the influential Council of Elders.

Patronage of translations occurred both within and outside the centre of government, and these different kinds of patrons offered different advantages. The shogunate could enlist the services of specialists from around the nation, thereby facilitating larger-scale translations, but the smaller budgets of the provincial domains led to more concentrated and efficient translation efforts (Jansen 1957: 574). Until the rule of shogun Tokugawa Yoshimune[11] (1716–45), there had been little domain patronage of translations of European works except in the fields of medicine and gunnery. After Yoshimune relaxed his policies on the study of the West in 1720, studies of the Dutch language commenced on a more formal footing, and some *daimyō* became keen financial supporters of scholars of Dutch Learning. Again, they were pragmatically motivated by a desire for practical knowledge. They provided financial support for their scholars to study Dutch and Dutch Learning in Nagasaki, and some of these scholars went on to translate various works.

One notable *daimyō* patron of translations was Matsudaira Sadanobu (1758–1829), who began collecting Dutch works around 1792. Dutch

---

[11] Japanese names are written with the family name first.

Learning was at its height during his lifetime, and he employed people to translate Dutch documents that would contribute to Japan's welfare. He wished to acquire this knowledge, but also to restrict its spread. He was behind the first domain-sponsored translation of a Dutch work, when *Dodoneusu sōmokufu* [The Western herbal of Dodonæus illustrated] was translated by Ishii Tsune'emon. Herbalist Yoshida Masayasu subsequently spent 38 years revising and completing this undertaking, and their combined half a century of work resulted in 35 volumes in 1842, representing one of the largest and most important Edo-period translation projects. Another notable patron of translations was *daimyō* Shimazu Nariakira (1809–58), who "commissioned translations of Dutch books on steamships, steam engines, telegraphy, gas-lighting and photography, inviting some of those who carried out the translations to join a kind of science institute in the grounds of his Kagoshima castle, where they supervised production of the equipment their books described" (Beasley 1995: 49). Shimazu employed nearly all of the leading Dutch scholars at one time or another (Goodman 2000: 158). Another domain that patronized translations was the small but progressive Ōno domain, whose Yōgakukan institution, established in 1856 for teaching Dutch and translating works on navigation and military matters, attracted students from around the nation.

The 1850s were a time of concurrent patronage of and restrictions on translations. The growing need for training in Western technology and military science to ensure national survival boosted official patronage of translations. The shogunate did not, however, want the public (particularly *daimyō*) to have direct contact with Western knowledge, especially knowledge about guns. Hence *daimyō* wishing to have books on defense translated had to obtain permission and then present a copy of the completed translation to the shogunate. Anyone selling or translating European books that had not been inspected in Nagasaki was punished.

3.2. The second wave

The second wave of institutional support of translations occurred in the late nineteenth century when Japan was pressured into ending its self-enforced national seclusion by the arrival of the American Commodore Matthew Perry in July 1853. The following month, Katsu Kaishū *(1823–99)*, an expert on European military science, proposed the establishment of a school to teach the sciences (including military science) and to translate and publish Western works. Until then, what had been known as Dutch Learning and then Western Learning had been placed under strict control, but now the government itself introduced Western Learning. This was partly motivated by a desire to remove the translation of military and political secrets from the hands of the Bureau of Astronomy, which was ordered to stop translating in 1856 (Jansen 1957: 578–9). The shogunate made the Office for the Translation of Barbarian Books independent in 1855 and moved it to Kudanzakashita, where the Bansho Shirabesho (Institute for the Study of Barbarian Books) opened in 1857. This became the main government-sponsored institution of Western Learning and centralized the translation of Western works, providing the shogunate with a practical monopoly by attracting most of the outstanding scholars of Dutch. Its focus was on *translating* books on foreign affairs, military matters and other urgent affairs, *collecting* existing translations, and *training* translators and interpreters. Most of the students were samurai from provincial domains, and all of them were funded by the shogunate. At first they studied only Dutch, but English, French, German and Russian were added from 1859 into the early 1860s. The main works translated were Dutch scientific works and news articles, and writings on practical matters and technical manuals were also translated.

At the Bansho Shirabesho, institutional activities and norms intersected with the translation work of individual instructor-translators. Instructors also sometimes helped out with translations for the Office of Foreign Affairs. The position of official translator in the foreign affairs office was established in 1859, and diplomatic documents were supposed to be translated by assistant foreign affairs commissioners. However, when there were important documents or just too many to handle, they were translated by Bansho Shirabesho instructors, who were obliged to show their translations to the junior elders, although it is debatable whether these officials had the linguistic competence necessary for genuine monitoring of the translations. Conversely, outside scholars were also used as translators by the Bansho Shirabesho when necessary.

Although power was at work more in the *products* (the selection of source languages and texts) than in the *process* (the translation approaches adopted), translation and teaching were intimately-related functions at the Bansho Shirabesho, and this helped shape translation norms. Article 6 of a revised memorandum dated June 1855 represents an early codification of ethical principles, stating that secrets learned in the course of translators' duties must not be divulged to others and that a pledge to that effect must be submitted.

Although the Bansho Shirabesho was initially created to produce translations and train translators, over time, it also came to *regulate* translation. An 1856 order stated that translations of Western works had to be examined and approved by the Bansho Shirabesho. After commercial treaties with Western powers came into effect in 1859, this institution became responsible for supervising all imported books, so as to guard against politically- or religiously-subversive material.

In May 1862, the Bansho Shirabesho's name changed to Yōsho Shirabesho [Institute for the Study of Western Books]. In the following year, its fields of translation expanded to include the natural and social sciences, as well as works on industrial problems (machinery, smelting, etc.), and in response, the name changed again in August to Kaiseijo [Institute for Development]. It became a more comprehensive institute aimed at providing a wide-ranging education for samurai, not 'just' a language/translation institute, and it grew rapidly. In 1861, there had been only about 100 students (accepted from around 1,000 initial applicants) in the whole Bansho Shirabesho, but by October 1866 the number had grown to 150 students just for English, and this figure doubled to 300 by December. For French, the numbers rose from 60 in October to 100 in December. This growth was evidence not of an intrinsic interest in these languages, but of a desire to learn about Western matters (Tōkyō daigaku hyakunenshi henshū iinkai 1984: 41). Until then, the main focus of Western Learning had been on practical matters such as medicine, astronomy and gunnery, but instructors such as Nishi Amane, Tsuda Mamichi and Katō Hiroyuki were interested in the humanities and social sciences and expanded the institute's range of interests.

The shogunate's attempts to control foreign learning in the closing years of the Edo period were not altogether successful. The importation and dissemination of books by the domains was increasingly beyond the shogunate's ability to control, and foreign merchants also sold books. Nor could the Kaiseijo any longer handle the work of instruction and translation alone. Eventually the knowledge contained in translated works became broadly available, contributing to the end of feudalism and the beginning of Japan's modernization. In that sense, these translations played a subversive role, despite having been sponsored by the authorities.

After the Meiji Restoration of 1868, which brought the Edo period to a close, the Kaiseijo was taken over by the new government and became the Kaisei Gakkō [Kaisei School]. Its instructors continued to produce translations for the government. Since most people who were competent in foreign languages were based there, government ministries and bureaus would ask the Kaisei Gakkō for translations. It also translated the imported books on geography and physics that were needed as school textbooks. Many Kaiseijo instructors went on to become influential cultural leaders (e.g., Nishi, Katō, Tsuda, Kanda Kōhei, Mitsukuri Shūhei).

This institute was renamed the Daigaku-kō in 1869, and in the following year, it underwent yet another name change to become the Daigaku Nankō. The Daigaku Nankō's translation bureau (*Han'yaku-kyoku*) had been established to translate practical and beneficial Western books to assist the government and promote enlightenment. Its regulations provide a glimpse into the translation norms and professional expectations of this government translation bureau:

- *Regulation 2*: Translations must be straightforward and clear, and any display of floweriness is prohibited.
- *Regulation 3*: If there is something the checker does not understand, he should consult with the translator, and he must not make unnecessary alterations.
- *Regulation 7*: In the case of urgent translations, the translators should work diligently, showing up for work early and leaving late, regardless of the time. (Tōkyō daigaku hyakunenshi henshū iinkai 1984: 172)

So what was the legacy of these different incarnations of the official translation bureau in the late nineteenth century? The Bansho Shirabesho's successors outlived the government that had founded them and evolved in unforeseen directions. In 1877, after three more name changes and reorganizations, Daigaku Nankō joined with the Tokyo Medical School to form the University of Tokyo. Today the University of Tokyo is Japan's most prestigious university, yet the official translation bureaus that were its predecessors did *not* inspire a modern translator-training scheme at this university or lead to translation studies as a field of research there. This can be explained in part by the fact that as translation became less a matter of urgent national need, it moved from centre stage. Further, the growing number of people able to read imported works in the original languages, while still small, to some extent, diminished the importance of translations.

4. Conclusion

Summing up, it can be said that Official patronage of translations in Japan during the period under examination played an ambivalent role. It enhanced the status of the translators (both *tsūji* and scholars) involved in these activities, but also restricted their freedom of text selection (leading to some self-monitoring) and the circulation of the translated texts. The information contained in these translations lent them a value to be controlled and restricted to certain circles, so the finished translations were not always published or disseminated. Thus official patronage of translations was simultaneously *reformist* and *conservative* in that it channeled translation and knowledge transfer in line with national and local interests. Although these translated works challenged and revised existing scientific notions, they were appropriated by the authorities in line with the prevailing ideology of protecting Japan against outside threats or protecting regional interests. This was an effective centralization of information while also fostering talented people.

So what is the contemporary relevance of all this? This case study highlights the role that official patronage can play in promoting, channelling, and controlling knowledge transfer through translations. It also illustrates yet again the close link between translation and national needs. Further, it demonstrates the powerful impact that translators can have on knowledge transfer and production, particularly when supported by political leaders. This Japanese case also emphasizes the importance of not overlooking non-literary and non-canonical translations and the value of focusing on books and institutions as material objects. It also highlights anew the fact that translations need to be contextualized against the broader picture of imported works and foreign influences.

References

Beasley, W. G. 1995, *Japan Encounters the Barbarian: Japanese Travelers in America and Europe*, New Haven and London: Yale University Press.

Chaiklin, Martha 2003, *Cultural Commerce and Dutch Commercial Culture: the Influence of European Material Culture on Japan, 1700–1850*, Leiden: Research School of Asian, African and Amerindian Studies, Leiden University.

Cullen, Louis Michael 2003, "The 通事おらんだ: Interpretation and translation in Nagasaki, 1641–1868", *IJET-14 Conference Proceedings*, 17–18 May 2003, Dublin, Ireland, 13–17.

Goodman, Grant 2000, *Japan and the Dutch, 1600–1853*, Richmond, UK: Curzon Press.

Fukuoka, Maki 2012, *The Premise of Fidelity: Science, Visuality, and Representing the Real in Nineteenth-Century Japan*, Stanford CA: Stanford University Press.

Horiuchi, Annick 2003, "When science develops outside state patronage: Dutch Studies in Japan at the turn of the nineteenth century", *Early Science and Medicine*, Vol. 8 no. 2, 148–172.

Jannetta, Ann Bowman 2007, *The Vaccinators: Smallpox, Medical Knowledge and the 'Opening' of Japan,* Stanford CA: Stanford University Press.

Jansen, Marius B. 1957, "New materials for the intellectual history of nineteenth century Japan", *Harvard Journal of Asiatic Studies,* Vol. 20, 567–97.

MacLean, J. 1974, "The introduction of books and scientific instruments into Japan, 1712–1854", *Japanese Studies in the History of Science,* Vol. 13, 9–68.

Miyashita, Saburo 1975, "A bibliography of the Dutch medical books translated into Japanese", *Archives internationals d'histoire des sciences,* 1975, 8–72.

Moretti, Franco 2005, *Graphs, Maps, Trees: Abstract Models for Literary History,* London and New York: Verso.

Nagazumi, Yōko 2008, "Personal trade at the Dutch Factory in Japan: the trade society organized by Chief Factor Meijlan (1826–1830)", *The Memoirs of the Toyo Bunko* 66, 1–44.

Ōmori, Minoru 1988, "Edo jidai ni Nagasaki Dejima Oranda shōkan ni shukō sareta chūmonsho ni tsuite", in Yanai Kenji, ed., *Sakoku Nihon to kokusai kōryū: Gekan,* Tokyo: Yoshikawa Kōbunkan, 220–49.

Ōmori, Minoru 1991, "The *Eisch Boek* in Dutch-Japanese trade", in Karl Reinhold Haellquist, ed., *Asian Trade Routes,* London: Curzon Press, 199–208.

St-Pierre, Paul 1993, "Translation as a discourse of history", *TTR* Vol. 6 no. 1, 61–82.

Tōkyō daigaku hyakunenshi henshū iinkai [Editorial Committee for One-Hundred Year History of the University of Tokyo] 1984, *Tōkyō Daigaku hyakunenshi: Tsūshi* [University of Tokyo One-Hundred Year History: General History], Tokyo: Tōkyō Daigaku Shuppankai.

Verwaijen, Frans B. 1996, *Early Reception of Western Legal Thought in Japan 1841–1868,* Leiden: Leiden University.

KOREA

CHANGING PARADIGMS, SHIFTING LOYALTIES: TRANSLATION OF CHILDREN'S LITERATURE IN COLONIAL KOREA (1900-1940) AND NORTH KOREA (1940-1960)

THERESA HYUN

1. Introduction[1]

During the period from the end of the nineteenth century through the 1960s, shifting patterns of patronage and agency can be identified among literary translators in Korea. Korean translators at the turn of the twentieth century focused on importing foreign works which would enlighten young people and prepare them to build a modern nation. Under Japanese colonial domination in the 1920s, the government policy of cultural appeasement permitted the publication of translations, and children's literature flourished.

After the liberation from Japanese rule in the late 1940s, the government, which was established in the North, promoted the translation of foreign works of children's literature in order to train future citizens of the socialist society. This paper compares the situation of the translation of children's literature during the colonial period with that of North Korea in the early years of the socialist regime in an effort to gain insight into the roles that translators play in the shifting of national identities.

---

[1] I would like to express my appreciation to Professor Yoo Im-Ha, Professor Jeon Young-Sun, Ch'oi Jin-I and Han Joung-Sik for their advice, and Yi Son-Kyong and Hwang Eo-Jin for their help with this research.

2. Translation of Children's Literature during the Japanese Colonial Period

2.1. Overview

In Korea, the period from the 1890s through the 1910s is known as the Enlightenment (*kyemong*), when the society opened up to modernization and foreign influence. At this time, interest arose in the situation of children. In order to establish a modern nation, one of the most important matters was the producing of members, and deciding how to define the concept of "citizen". One aspect of this process was the recognition that children (*adong*) belonged to a distinct category of members of the nation. As part of the conflict between "new" (*shin*) vs. "old" (*ku*), "civilization" (*munmyong*) vs. barbarism (*yaman*), and young people (*sonyon, ch'ongnyon*) vs. old people (*noin*), the innocence and the potential of "children" (*adong*) became an expression of the new direction of the enlightenment project.[2] Therefore there was an increased focus on the need to train children to become citizens of this imminent modern nation, and newspapers, magazines and publishing companies were involved in their education.

The translation of foreign literature was deemed to be particularly useful for this purpose, and in this regard, one of the most important publications at the time was *Sonyon* [Boys], a magazine edited and published by Ch'oe Namson, which first appeared in 1908. This publication provided a space in which to circulate discussions about the experiences of youth as independent members of a modern nation. Through the introduction and translation of foreign works, Ch'oe Namson sowed the seeds of the desire to head towards modern civilization through science and learning. The Russian Emperor, Peter the Great, was taken as an example of leadership, while Robinson Crusoe and Napoleon were presented as models of heroism, and Aesop's *Fables* were translated for their moral and ethical lessons.[3] Between 1909 and 1918, Ch'oe Namson continued to translate a number of works, including *Gulliver's Travels* and *Uncle Tom's Cabin*, with the aim of educating young people.

These translations of foreign works, which went on the market at a low price, aimed to awaken young people to the necessity of going beyond the

---

[2] The connection between the increased interest in "the child" and the development of the modern state in the early twentieth century in Korea is discussed in an article by Seo Dong-Soo (2008: 243-248).

[3] Kim Byong-Ch'ol (1988: 280-302) gives a detailed analysis of the underlying translation norms and attitudes in *Boys* magazine.

narrow confines of their own borders and preparing themselves for the task of building a modern nation. During the 1920s, the publication of material for children increased greatly. Pang Chong-Hwan's collection of translated children's stories, *Sarang ui sonmul* [Love's Gift] (1922) was one of the best-selling books of the time. In 1935, Chon Yong-T'aek published a collection of translated children's stories *T'ukson segye tonghwa chip* [World Fairy Tales]. This volume, which included fourteen stories by Hans Christian Andersen and several by the Brothers Grimm, contributed to the formation of children's literature in Korea. The number of children's magazines also increased in the 1920s, and by the early 1930s there was a wide selection of materials available.

2.2. Key Examples of the Translation of Children's Literature

2.2.1. Aesop's *Fables*

During the early twentieth century, various Korean translators produced versions of some of Aesop's fables. These translations mostly appeared in text books, newspapers, and periodicals such as *Boys* published by Ch'oe Namson. These translators were new intellectuals who were promoting enlightenment, and rather than regarding Aesop's works simply as fables, they saw them as a means of awakening young people to the dangers which their nation was facing from the threat of Japanese imperialist domination. Through these brief stories, the translators aimed to deliver messages about moral values, social responsibilities, and political realities. Aesop's *Fables*, which were useful for enlightening the population in general, came to occupy an important place in the education of children. In particular when socialist ideology was being established in North Korea, Aesop's *Fables* were recognized for their applicability to a wide variety of educational purposes.

2.2.2. Pang Chong-Hwan's *Sarang ui sonmul* [Love's Gift]

Pang Chong Hwan's collection of translations of foreign children's stories was first published in 1922 by Kaebyok Publishing Company. Pang chose ten foreign stories by Hans Christian Andersen, the brothers Grimm, and others, and adapted them for consumption by young Korean readers. Notes were provided for words which would have been difficult for children to understand, such as an explanation for the Chinese character form of the country name "Italia" used in the translation of a story by the nineteenth century Italian author Edmondo De Amicis. Pang Chong-Hwan also introduced the use of the honorific term "Orini" to show respect for children who were sometimes mistreated in traditional society. He was the first to establish Children's Day on 1 May 1923.

In the same year, he founded *Orini* [Children], the first magazine in Korea aimed exclusively at children. This publication provided an outlet for a variety of children's stories and songs. In the brief preface to his book, Pang states that the work is a gift that expresses his sympathy and affection for the children of his country, who had to endure abusive treatment and difficulties. (Pang Chong-Hwan 2003: 15) There are some distinctive differences between Pang's work and that of other translators of children's stories at the time, including the large number of sales of copies of his work. First, widely differing types of stories were included in Pang's book: traditional and more recent tales, as well as fantastic and realistic stories. Second, he made fundamental contributions to the establishment and expansion of children's literature through his translations of foreign stories. For example, while traditional Korean tales tended to focus on events which happened long ago, Pang's stories recount the adventures of particular young boys or girls, thus putting the spotlight on their activities, and creating a sense of their identity.

This marked the beginning of a new individuality for children.[4] Youm Hee-Kyung distinguishes two aspects of the creative world of *Love's Gift*. First, Pang Chong-Hwan transmits a message of liberation for the Korean people who were suffering under Japanese colonial domination. Of the stories in the collection, the first ("Nanp'a son" [Shipwreck]) and last ("Kkot sok ui chakuni" [Rose Fairy]) symbolize this process. The first story, "Shipwreck", based on the original by the nineteenth century Italian author Edmondo De Amicis, reveals the modern concept of nation as an ethnic and linguistic unity, and emphasizes the importance of ethnicity in the face of the sinking ship of Korea under colonial domination.

The final story, "Rose Fairy", was written by Hans Christian Andersen, who was inspired by Boccacio's *Decameron*. Pang highlighted the aggressive traits of the villain in a way which mirrored the atmosphere of Korea under imperial domination. While the conclusion of the original highlights the rose fairy in a concise and suggestive way, Pang's version emphasizes the death of the villain. If we consider that Pang might have consulted an intermediate Japanese translation, then his intention to emphasize Korean nationalism becomes clearer. Another aspect is the embodiment of the ideas of the Ch'ondo religion, a nationalistic

---

[4] The ways in which Pang Ch'ong-Hwan's translations of foreign fairy tales have contributed to the creation of a modern image of children are examined by Jang Jeunghee (2011: 343-363).

organization which had its roots in nineteenth century Korea. Pang translated Oscar Wilde's "Wangja wa chebi" [The Happy Prince], a story which reflects the Christian Socialist movement associated with John Ruskin and the opposition to the growing materialism of Victorian England.

It is revealing that Pang's story first appeared in the monthly bulletin of the Ch'ondo Church, and it reflects the idea that happiness comes from spiritual fulfillment, rather than the approval of the corrupt world. Pang's version did not contain the original's criticism of the vanity of the ruling classes because of the Ch'ondo religion's attitude of surpassing class distinctions. (Youm Hee-Kyuong 2007: 162-181)

3. Translation of Children's Literature in North Korea

3.1. Establishment and Principles of Production

3.1.1. Establishment

In 1946, the North Korean Artistic Federation (Pukchoson Yesul Ch'ongyonmaeng) was formed and this became the foundation for literary and artistic policy. Members of the Korean Artists' Proletarian Federation (KAPF), which had been active since the 1920s, came to North Korea and participated in the process of establishing children's literature (Ch'oi Jin-I 2002: 224). They emphasized the distinctive characteristics of children's literature as opposed to literature for adults, and held that the principle of "rewarding good and punishing evil" should be inserted into every work of children's literature. *Adong Munhak* [Children's Literature] was a monthly magazine published by the Central Committee of the Choson Writers' Union. An examination of this publication, in the mid- to late 1950s, reveals the extent to which children's literature was subject to political control. Literary forms in this magazine, such as narrative poems (*kasa*), nursery rhymes (*yuhui tongyo*), lyric epic poems (*sojong sosa si*), and fairy tales (*tonghwa*) reveal characteristics of North Korean literature. Nursery rhymes reflected the emphasis on communal participation in North Korean society.

Lyric epic poems were first introduced in the May 1957 issue and became an important aspect of North Korean children's literature. This type of poetry aimed to strengthen the ideological unity of North Korean children and followed the cultural policies of the communist party. Narrative poems were written as the lyrics of songs and displayed regular rhythms. They were divided into subgroups, such as worker songs and fighting songs, which reflected the political trends of North Korean society. Fairy tales praised individual sacrifice, pitied the people of South Korea and depicted the necessity of struggle against the North-South division. These works aimed to build a successful socialist society through strengthening the party and educating the masses. (Sun An-Na 2008: 80-94)

3.1.2. Principles of Production

I Won-U's 1956 volume, *Adong munhak ch'angjak ui kil* [Writing Children's Literature] provided detailed guidelines for those wishing to enter this field. Two major points were stressed. First, the author criticized bourgeois writers of the Japanese colonial period, like Ch'oe Nam-Son, Yi Gwang-Su and Pang Chong-Hwan, who conceived of children's literature as a way of making young people conform to adult interests. In his view, proletarian literature suggested ways for children and adults to live together in society. These works should not only describe positive things, but also arouse animosity towards negative aspects of society.

Second, writers of children's literature should quote foreign authors in order to justify their own points of view. An important writer in this respect was Maxim Gorky, who satisfactorily brought out both the thought and artistry of proletarian children's literature. One of the main points of I Won-U's book was that children's literature should educate children in the ways of socialism according to Gorky's theories. The works of other foreign writers such as Maupassant and Gogol were also cited. (I Won- U 1956: 41-51)

3.2. Translations in *Adong Munhak* [Children's Literature] Magazine

3.2.1. The Work of the Writer / Translator Paek Sok

The writer and poet Paek Sok became interested in translating children's literature in the late 1940s after the end of the Japanese colonial period, and wrote about Aesop's *Fables*, the works of Gorky, and other socialist writers. He suggested how the works of foreign writers might be helpful in finding the path for the development of children's literature in North Korea. Paek Sok's ideas on children's literature were based on the concepts of socialist realism.

He praised Gorky's contributions to the Russian revolution and the development of new Russian culture. In his article "Maksim Korikki"

[Maxim Gorky] in the March 1956 issue of *Children's Literature*, Paek Sok pointed out that Gorky's novel *The Mother* was a first-rate work which clearly revealed the principles of socialist realism (Paek Sok 1956: 65). However, even in this context, Paek Sok emphasized the importance of literary qualities, claiming that it was more important to emphasize the role of children in linking the past, present and future of cultural history than to focus exclusively on socialist thought. Thus, his article "Marusyak'u ui saengae wa munhak" [Marshak's Life and Literature] in the November 1957 issue of *Children's Literature* examined how the Russian writer Marshak contributed to the development of Soviet humanitarianism with his poetry for children (Paek Sok 1957: 67-72).

Paek Sok's literary translations deal with socialist ideology, but at the same time display an intense concern for literary form. In 1957, there was a debate about children's literature in North Korea. The idea that rather than emphasizing class consciousness, it was more important to produce literature to suit the needs of children; was characterized as a remnant of bourgeois thought, and Paek Sok was criticized on this basis. Although Paek Sok's 1958 publications in *Children's Literature* reflect socialist ideology, the following year he was exiled from the capital city of Pyongyang.[5] It is clear that even children's literature could not escape political influence.

3.2.2. Tendencies in the Translation of Children's Literature

3.2.2.1. Translation of Well-Known Works

It is worth noting that many of the works which were translated during the colonial period were also translated in North Korea according to the principle that literature should educate children about society. Some of the authors whose works were translated in *Children's Literature* from the mid-1950s to the mid-1960s include the Brothers Grimm, Tolstoy, Aesop, La Fontaine, De Amicis, and Marshak. In some cases, the translation process involved a degree of re-interpretation and adaptation to emphasize revolutionary socialist ideology and criticize the bourgeois class.

The Brothers Grimm

In a *Children's Literature* article in July 1962, entitled "Chakka sogae – Kurim hyongje" [Introduction to the Brothers Grimm], Ch'oe Tong-Hyop comments that the two Grimm brothers wanted to make the German

---

[5] Kim Je-Gon points out that Paek Sok's writings on children's literature at this time praised Kim Il Sung strongly (2007: 87-89).

people aware of their good qualities by searching for interesting stories from their traditions. By listening to these tales, they would become more impressed with the diligence of their own people. The brothers therefore collected stories from the different regions of their country, and in 1812, published a book of these fairy tales. In their efforts to arouse patriotism, the Brothers Grimm did not stop their collecting of stories. They also undertook research in an attempt to improve the German language, and published a dictionary and a book on German grammar (Ch'oe Tong-Hyop 1962: 92).

At a time when North Korean national identity was under threat, this reconsideration of fairy tales was seen as a way of boosting national pride. Thus, by translating Grimm's tales, the North Korean translators were suggesting the goodness and diligence of their own people. The intention to emphasize the traditional principle of "kwonson chingak" [reward good and punish evil] was one of the reasons for selecting Grimm's tales. Since good people tended to be poor, weak and pitiable, while evil ones were rich and powerful, the conflict between good and evil was extended to the class and power struggle. For instance, in the Grimm tale "Metchellitcha halmoni" [Mother Hulda] translated by So Song-U in the October 1954 issue of *Children's Literature,* the stepmother's two daughters are contrasted as good and evil. The good and diligent step-daughter is rewarded, while the evil, lazy biological daughter is punished, thus illustrating the principle of rewarding good and punishing evil. The story "Kananhan saram gwa puja" [The Poor Man and the Rich Man], which Pak Hong-Sok translated in the October 1964 issue of *Children's Literature*, contrasts the miserly and heartless rich person with the warm and diligent poor person.

The problem of good and evil also suggests the conflict between the bourgeois and proletarian classes. "Paran pul" [The Blue Light], translated by Pak Hong-Sok in the February 1962 issue of *Children's Literature*, portrays a king who is punished by a supernatural being for abusing the people. Socialist ideology is bolstered through this depiction of the class struggle and the misuse of power. I Pong-Sop's translation of "Nop'a ui yeon" [The Devil and the Three Golden Hairs] appeared in the December 1957 issue of *Children's Literature*. The North Korean version features an old lady whose role is to give wisdom to the hero, and she foretells his fate and helps him to escape from a difficult situation. The King's corrupt use of power is contrasted with the old lady's benevolent use of sorcery in order to bring out the theme of rewarding good and punishing evil couched in terms of the class struggle.

Edmondo De Amicis

The works of the nineteenth century Italian writer Edmondo De Amicis were translated by Pang Chong-Hwan because of their patriotic aspect, although when these works were translated in North Korea, the patriotic elements were given a socialist turn. In his article on "Rambadi ui sonyon ch'okhubyong" [The Young Soldier Scout of Rambadi] in the December 1962 issue of *Children's Literature*, the translator Chu Chong-Gil, commenting on the works of De Amicis, noted that while his works unfortunately reflected the limitations of the society of the time, De Amicis did display sympathy for poor people, and encouraged education about the contradictions of society and patriotic thought (Chu Chong-Gil 1962:88). The North Korean translators seem to have felt that the national situation in Italy at the time De Amicis was writing was similar to that of their own country.

The North Korean translation of "The Young Soldier Scout of Rambadi" emphasizes the tragic and revolutionary aspect of the youth facing death, and provides a lengthy description of the funeral of the soldier. Thus the value of self-sacrifice and patriotism is highlighted for the reader.

Aesop and La Fontaine

As was the case during the Japanese colonial period, in North Korea, fables were translated to educate young people. I Won-U's *Writing Children's Literature* lists fables as one of the principal genres of children's literature, along with stories, fairy tales, songs and poems, and he particularly valued the satirical and critical aspect of fables. In an article in June 1962 for *Children's Literature*, "Isop'u wa ku ui uhwa" [Aesop and His Fables], Paek Sok wrote that Aesop detested the oppression of the weak by the strong, the endless greed of the rich, and the fact that the dominant classes kept good people in a state of oppression. Since he hoped that people would live cleanly and wisely, he wrote interesting fables that would teach them the right way of doing things.

Through the actions of animals, he mocks the powerful and praises the virtue, wisdom and strength of innocent oppressed people (Paek Sok 1962: 96-97). Introducing Kim Byong-Kyu's translations of La Fontaine's fables "Sungnyangi wa Yang" [The Wolf and the Lamb] and "Sungnyangi wa Omi Yomso wa Saekki Yomso" [The Wolf, the Nanny Goat and the Kid] in the October 1963 issue of *Children's Literature*, the editors explain that in his fables, La Fontaine criticizes the powerful within his society, such as the king and nobility, for their inhuman actions and greed. At the same time, he has warm sympathy for workers, and he demonstrates this struggle through his satirical works. His fables sharply criticize the ruling classes, describing them as foxes or sick lions, and satirize the parasitic life of the bourgeois class. In order to produce his work, La Fontaine researched the cultural traditions of his country as well as the work of Aesop, and in doing so raised the level of fables (Kim Byong-Kyu 1963: 62).

As noted above, we can say that one of the major aims of the translation of fables in North Korea was to link the concept of "rewarding good and punishing evil" with the class struggle. La Fontaine's fables were considered useful as examples of socialist ideology, and for North Korean translators, the brevity of fables and the fact that a moral lesson could be attached at the end made them ideal for re-interpretation in the light of revolutionary thought. These translators seemed to have felt that the general applicability of fables meant that they were suited to being translated into many languages to fit in with the characteristics of each country. The translations of La Fontaine's fables emphasize class struggles and socialist ideology. In his "Sungnyangi wa Yang" [The Wolf and the Lamb], the relationship between the lamb and the wolf is a struggle between good and evil. The fact that there can be no peace, since the struggle against evil is permanent, dramatizes the socialist revolution. In North Korea, the wolf is taken as a symbol of the misuse of power by the bourgeois class, even in stories for children.

Tolstoy

The translation of Tolstoy's fable "Willipp'ok'u" by Song Tong-Gyu in the November 1954 edition of *Children's Literature* includes some explanatory notes about Tolstoy's way of depicting the oppression of the peasants and the corruption of the upper classes. The Soviet writer Maxim Gorky states that if you did not know Tolstoy, you did not know Russian culture. Certainly Tolstoy's many novels are known all over the world, and there is no library which does not contain his works. Tolstoy dealt with class conflict and the poverty of the peasants before the revolution. (Song Tong-Gyu 1954: 54)

3.2.2.2 Translation of Socialist Ideology

The translations mentioned above dealt with well-known works which were adapted to fit in with the North Korean socialist ideology. *Children's Literature* also published translations of authors who were acknowledged as proponents of socialism or who were from socialist countries. One of these writers was the Russian S.Y. Marshak, who mostly wrote children's poetry and received recognition for his ability to transmit both ideology and artistry through the creation of a children's language of Soviet humanism. North Korean translators appreciated the fact that young Soviet readers were taught to recognize that the class structure of capitalist society divides people into rich and poor.

4. Conclusion

This paper has given an overview of the connections between the translations of children's literature in the Japanese colonial period and those which appeared in North Korea in the 1950s and 1960s. During this formative phase of the regime, there was a certain amount of flexibility in the North Korean cultural world, and writers and translators introduced works from various foreign countries. In the late 1940s and early 1950s, many Korean intellectuals went to North Korea, among whom were writer-translators like Paek Sok who contributed to the establishment of children's literature as an important means of educating citizens of the emerging socialist society.[6] As this research progresses, it will be useful to examine how South Korean translators negotiated a very different set of constraints as they attempted to further the development of children's literature.

References

Primary Sources

Ch'oe Tong-Hyop 1962, "Chakka sogae – Kurim hyonje" [Introduction to the Brothers Grimm], *Adong Munhak*, July, 92-96.

Chu Chong-Gil 1962, "Rambaudi ui sonyon ch'okhubyong" [The Young Soldier Scout of Rambaudi], *Adong Munhak* December, 88-92.

I Pong-Sop 1957, "Nop'a ui yeon" [The Devil and the Three Golden Hairs], *Adong Munhak*, December, 57-69.

I Won-U 1956, *Adong munhak ch'angjak ui kil* [Writing Children's Literature], Pyongyang: Kukrip Ch'ulp'ansa.

Kim Byong-Kyu 1963, "Lap'ongt'enu" [La Fontaine], *Adong Munhak*, October, 62-65.

Paek Sok 1956, "Maksim Korikki" [Maksim Gorky], *Adong Munhak*, March, 60-71.

Paek Sok 1957, "Marusyak'u ui saengae wa munhak" [Marshak's Life and Literature], *Adong Munhak*, November, 67-72.

---

[6] Kim Jae-Yong (2011: 119-122) examines the tensions in Paek Sok's work from 1959 to 1962 in terms of his support for the emancipation of the people and his need to produce literature which supported the party ideology.

Paek Sok 1962, "Isop'u wa ku ui uhwa" [Aesop and His Fables], *Adong Munhak*, June, 96-99.
Pak Hong-Sok 1962, "Paran pul" [The Blue Light], *Adong Munhak*, February, 87-92.
Pak Hong-Sok 1964, "Kananhan saram gwa puja" [The Poor Man and the Rich Man], *Adong Munhak* October, 83-85.
Pang Chong-Hwan 2003, *Sarang ui sonmul* [Love's Gift], Seoul: Uri Kyoyuk.
So Song-U 1954, "Metchellitcha halmoni" [Mother Hulda], *Adong Munhak* October, 60-64.
Song Tong-Gyu 1954, "Willipp'ok'u", *Adong Munhak*, November, 54-56.

Secondary Sources

Ch'oi Jin-I 2002, "Pukhan ui adong munhak" [North Korean Children's Literature], in Mokwon Taehakkyo Kukokyoyukgwa, ed., *Pukhan munhak ui ihae* [Understanding North Korean Literature], Seoul: Kukhak Charyowon, 223-233.
Jang Jeunghee 2011, "Sop'a Pang Chong-Hwan ponyok tonghwa ui ch'angchak tonghwa ro ui ihaeng yongu" [Pang Chong-Hwan's Literature from Translated Children's Stories to Creative Children's Stories), *Tonghwa wa Ponyok* 21, 343-363.
Kim Byong-Ch'ol 1988, *Han'guk kundae ponyok munhaksa yongu* [The History of Modern Korean Literary Translation], Seoul: Ulyu Munhwasa.
Kim Jae-Yong. 2011, "Paek Sok munhak yongu, 1959-1962 nyon Samsu sichol ul chungsim uro" [Two aspects of Paek Sok's Literature in the Period of Samsu], *Hyondae Pukhan Yongu* 14-1, 118-143.
Kim Je-Gon 2007, "Paek Sok ui adong munhak yongu" [A Study of Paek Sok's Children's Literature], *Tonghwa wa ponyok* 14, 71-98.
Seo Dong-Soo 2008, "Adong ui palkyon gwa 'sikminchi kukmin" ui kihoek" [The Discovery of the Child and the Plan of 'Colonial People'], *Tonghwa wa Ponyok* December, 243-271.
Sun An-Na 2008, "1950 nyondae Pukhan adong munhak ui hyonhwang" [The State of Children's Literature in North Korea in the 1950s], *Tonghwa wa Ponyok* 15, 73-97.
Youm Hee-Kyung 2007, "'Neisyon' ul sangsanghan ponyok tonghwa, Pang Chong- Hwan ui *Sarang ui sonmul* e taehayo" [Tonghwa (Fairy Tales) as a Translation to Imagine Nation: Focusing on Pang Chong-Hwan's *Sarang ui sonmul* (Love's Gift)], *Tonghwa wa Ponyok* 13, 157-186.

COURT INTERPRETING OFFICIALS IN KOREA UNTIL 1392

KIM, NAM HUI

1. Introduction

Interpreting studies became established in the academic field after the founding of the first doctoral programme at ESIT[1] in Paris in 1974. Introductory books, various models and theories, handbooks, encyclopedias, and journals of translation and interpreting studies are indications of this, but what about the history of interpreting? How can we establish a present-day identity without understanding the past? The fragments of information that we do have are mostly about the European tradition, not Asian interpreters and much less about Korean interpreters. Ironically for translation and interpreting studies, it is once again the language barrier that hinders our knowledge of the history of interpreting in various countries. In his "Perspectives on the History of Translation", Baigorri-Jalon (2006: 102) notes the difficulties facing researchers in interpreting history due to a lack of sources: "those who embark upon the task of rebuilding the history of interpreting are faced with an additional challenge: that of the sources". This, of course, has to do with one of the most notable characteristics of interpreting: *verba volant, scripta manent* (spoken words fly away, written words remain). When we consider the history of interpreting in Korea, we have an additional obstacle in the form of the language barrier.

The second main section of the *Encyclopedia of Translation Studies* includes a short history of interpreting and translation in some selected countries and languages (Baker, 1998). Although Korean is a less widely used language than English, French and Chinese, it has more users than, for instance, Slovak and Finnish which do have entries, unlike Korea. In *Translators through History*, Delisle and Woodsworth (1995), who were aware of the Eurocentrism in their presentation of the roles and impact of

---

[1] *École Supérieure d'Interprètes et de Traducteurs (ESIT).*

interpreters on history, explained this as follows: "It is undeniable that the West in general, and Europe in particular, have been given preferential treatment, as it were, owing to the sheer number of historians in that part of the world [...]" (Delisle and Woodsworth 1995: 3). Thus it will be a welcome development for translation and interpreting studies to have scholars in interpreting studies who are interested in historical themes, so that we can expect a more balanced portrayal of the role and impact of interpreters in continents such as Asia and Africa. This will move historical research on interpreting a stage further.

With that goal in mind, this chapter takes a gentle step into the history of interpreting in Korea, based on existing research results from scholars in Korean language, history and historical documents, and taking into account previous research and the Database of Korean Classics, where historical source texts translated into Korean can be found. Since historical source texts in the Korean peninsula were written over a long period of time in Classical Chinese, they have remained almost incomprehensible to those who have not mastered the reading of the Classical Chinese texts written by the historians and literati of previous Korean dynasties. From the 1960s, scholars of Korean linguistics and Korean history who were able to read and work on Korean-Chinese source texts carried out research on interpreting officials, known as *yŏkkwan*, and their institutions, but until now, these studies have been introduced only sketchily to interpreting and translation studies, either in Korea or elsewhere. Since this brief overview cannot cover all the historical periods, it is confined in scope to the period up until the end of the Koryŏ Dynasty (918–1392).

Before going into detail, I introduce the terms that relate to interpreting officials. There have been many Sino-Chinese terms, mostly used since the Koryŏ Period, such as *yŏk-kwan* (譯官),[2] *yŏk-ŏ* (譯語), *yŏk-cha* (譯者), *yŏk-in* (譯人), *t'ong-sa* (通事), *t'ong-byŏn* (通辯) and *sŏl-in* (舌人). The lexeme *yŏk* (譯) means 'interpreting' or 'translating', while the lexeme *t'ong* (通) means 'go through' or 'communicate'. Lexemes such as *in* (人) and *cha* (者) mean 'human', *kwan* (官) means 'an office or official', while *ŏ* (語) originally refers to a language, but here signifies a person who is somehow involved with languages; while *sŏl* (舌) means 'tongue', so *sŏl-in* (舌人) means 'tongue person'.

The first appearance of any of the above-mentioned terms is *t'ong-sa* in the 22nd chapter, Koguryŏ 10th chapter, King Pojang (667 CE) in the

---

[2] The transliteration of Korean, including the names, into the Roman alphabet has been done according to the McCune/Reischauer system.

History of Three Kingdoms[3] (*Samguksagi* 三國事記, abbr. *SGSG*). The fact that we can find no other records before 667 does not necessarily mean that there were no interpreting officials until then. However, their acts or influence must not have been sufficiently important in the eyes of the historians who had written or compiled the histories up until then. Or perhaps the interpreters functioned without any problem, so they were not visible or worth mentioning. When Silla (ca. 57 BCE–935CE) started to maintain a close relationship with the Tang dynasty (618–907) in China, in order to defeat Paekche (18 BCE–660 CE) and Koguryŏ (37 BCE–668 CE) with the help of the Tang, the interpreters presumably became more visible after Koguryŏ had been defeated (King Pojang was the last King of Koguryŏ). *T'ong-sa* and sometimes *sŏl-in* were often used during the Koryŏ Period, while *yŏk-kwan* seem to have been used mostly after that period.

To avoid any terminological confusion, I use the term (royal court) interpreting officials when referring to the Koryŏ Period, while *Yŏk-kwan* is used to describe interpreting officials during the Chosŏn Period (1392–1910). The following section deals with the period prior to the Koryŏ Dynasty, and is followed by a discussion of the interpreting officials and various institutions during the Koryŏ Period (918–1392). Research results for *yŏk-kwan* during the Chosŏn Period are intended to be presented in a separate paper.

2. Interpreting-related institutions prior to the Koryŏ Period

It is difficult to find historical documents or research results regarding interpreting before the Three Kingdoms Period (i.e. before around 57 BCE). In his essay on "History of Interpreting and the Role of Interpreters", Pak Sŏngnae (1983) surmises that more or less primitive needs for interpreting would have existed. Even though there were

---

[3] *Samguksagi* is a historical record of the Three Kingdoms of Korea (Koguryŏ, Paekche and Silla). Compiled during the reign of Koryŏ's King Injong (r. 1122–1146), it is written in Classical Chinese. The government official and historian Kim Pusik (金富軾, 1075–1151), together with ten other scholars, undertook its compilation on the basis of historical documents and books from China and Korea. It was completed around 1145, and it is assumed that the woodblocks were first printed sometime between 1149 and 1174. This is the oldest extant Korean history (Encyclopedia of Korean Culture: http://encykorea.aks.ac.kr/Contents/Index). All the Korean translations used in this paper are from the Database of Korean History, and the Korean Classics Database.

exchanges among tribes with different languages before the period of the Three Kingdoms, due to basic social and political structures, communication must have taken place using just several hundred words, and such exchanges were probably not frequent. Paek Okkyŏng (2000: 1) mentions that diplomatic relationships with China during the Kojosŏn Period (?–108 BCE) and Proto–Three Kingdoms Period (300–57 BCE) were rather rare, but this claim is not supported by substantial evidence. Chŏng Kwang (1990, quoted in Kang Sinhang 2000: 3) assumes that there must already have been an institution for interpreting officials for the royal court before the Three Kingdoms Period, but since only a few historical documents from that time are extant, these assumptions by scholars of Korean studies and history must be viewed with caution.

We find in *SGSG* that "[Silla] established a friendly relationship with the Japanese (倭國結好交聘) (1st chapter, biographical sketch of the Kings of Silla, T'arhae (脫解, 尼師今reign ?~?) Isagŭm [King] [...] 59 CE, 5th lunar month). Other than that and until the third century, there are rarely any records regarding envoys from China and Japan. In another source, *Memorabilia of the Three Kingdoms* (三國遺事 *Samgugyusa*, abbr. *SGYS*),[4] the King of Silla (Naemurwang) sent his son to Japan following a request by the Japanese. From the fourth century, there were active exchanges with both China and Japan (cf. Chŏng Sŏnghae 2002: 287–288; Kang Sinhang 2000: 3). The lively cultural influence and exchanges from and with China started via the introduction of Chinese characters and the expansion of Buddhism, which then spread to Japan via Korea from the late fourth century. In *SGSG* we find mention of foreign delegations when Buddhism was introduced into the Korean peninsula. There is also a similar record in *Tongsagangmok* (東史綱目, abbr. *TSGM*),[5] according to which Buddhism was introduced into Koguryŏ (37 BCE–668 CE) in 372.

---

[4] *Samguk Yusa* was compiled by the Buddhist monk Ilyeon (一然, 1206–1289) in 1281 and published around 1310. It is a collection of legends and historical accounts relating to the Three Kingdoms of Korea (Koguryŏ, Paekche and Silla), as well as to other periods and states such as the Kojosŏn and Pre/Post-Three Kingdoms periods. Like *SGSG*, it is written in Classical Chinese. It is regarded more as literature than as a reliable source for history (cf. Encyclopedia of Korean Culture).

[5] *Tongsagangmok* (東史綱目) was written by An Chŏngbok (1712–1791), a Silhak scholar who studied practical matters in the Chosŏn Dynasty. It covers history from the Kojosŏn period to the Koryŏ period. An started to work on *TSGM* in 1756, completing it in 1778. It is written in Chinese (cf. Encyclopedia of Korean Culture).

In the first lunar Month, Paekche sent an envoy (朝聘) to China.[6] This was the first time that Paekche entered into a diplomatic relationship with China. [...] In the Sixth Month, Chin (秦 [221–207 BCE]) sent two Buddhist stupa (浮屠), [a] statue of Buddha/Bodhisattva (佛像) and Buddhist texts (经佛) to Koguryŏ. The King of Chin (秦王) Fú Jiān (苻坚)[7] sent an envoy with the Buddhist Monk Sundo (道顺)[8] who brought [a] statue of Buddha/Bodhisattva (佛像) and Buddhist texts (经佛) to Koguryŏ. As a reward, the King of Koguryŏ sent a [counter-] envoy with its local products (方物). Afterwards, the Monk Ado (阿道)[9] came from Chin, and this was the beginning of the introduction of the teachings of Buddha [Dharma] to the East of the Sea [Korea]. (2nd Year of Sosurim, King of Koguryŏ; 27th Year of Kŭnch'ogo, King of Paekche [...] Year 372) (see Database of Korean Classics).

During the Three Kingdoms Period, the kingdoms of Koguryŏ, Paekche and Silla were founded. Since there was lively trade and cultural exchanges with the Chinese and Japanese, historians assume that there must have been interpreters who belonged to relevant institutions (cf. Kang Sinhang 2000: 3). In the quotation above, the existence of an interpreting official is not mentioned, but the word 朝聘 (envoy) indicates that countries were sending official envoys,[10] so we can assume the

---

[6] [An] signifies An's footnote which he inserted, as per the above citation.

[7] "Fú Jiān (苻堅) (337–385), courtesy name Yonggu (永固) or Wenyu (文玉), formally Emperor Xuanzhao of (Former) Chin ((前)秦宣昭帝), was an emperor (who, however, used the title 'Heavenly Prince' (Tian Wang) during his reign) of the Chinese/Di state Former Qin, under whose rule (assisted by his able prime minister Wang Meng) the Former Qin state reached its greatest glory—destroying Former Yan, Former Liang, and Dai and seizing Chin's Yi Province (益州, modern Sichuan and Chongqing), posturing to destroy Jin as well as to unite China, until he was repelled at the Battle of Fei River in 383. For a variety of reasons, the Former Qin state soon collapsed after that defeat, and Fú Jiān himself was killed by his former subordinate, Yao Chang, the founding emperor of Later Qin, in 385." (Wikipedia, http://en.wikipedia.org/wiki/F%C3%BA_Ji%C4%81n, accessed 10 February 2013.)

[8] 順道 (shùndào): detailed information about Sundo's life is unavailable, although he is known as the monk who introduced Buddhism to Koguryŏ, and was probably from a country other than China (cf. Encyclopedia of Korean Culture).

[9] 阿道 (ādào): nothing is known about Ado's life. According to diverse historical documents, he was a monk in Koguryŏ or from India (cf. Encyclopedia of Korean Culture).

[10] Dictionary of Korean Classic Terminology:

existence of interpreting officials. We cannot be sure of the role of the court interpreters—i.e. whether they rendered only the words between the two parties (or only in one direction, e.g. from Korean into Chinese), or whether they acted as diplomats and were involved in various matters. Nevertheless, since the first record relating to an official interpreter dates from 667, it seems that until then, interpreters had played only a minor role. According to the 38th chapter, 7th theme chapter in *SGSG*, the office was changed in 621 from Yŏnggaekpu (領客府), which was actually called Waejŏn (倭典; Office for Japanese), into Yŏnggaekchŏn (領客典; Office for Guest Reception). Later on, the Waejŏn was again established separately. It has been assumed that the Yŏnggaekchŏn was in charge of the reception of guests from Tang China and that the later Waejŏn was in charge of Japanese envoys (倭使).[11] We can suppose that the sending and reception of official delegations from China and Japan implies the existence of a person in charge of intercultural communication—i.e., interpreting—and that presumably, there were interpreting officials in institutions such as Yŏnggaekchŏn and Waejŏn in Silla. Since we can rely only on the few extant historical records from this time—all written many centuries later—it is difficult to obtain a concrete image of and insight into the actual role of interpreters and their positions in the different dynasties.

The records in *SGSG*[12] state that in 714, the office for diplomatic writings (Sangmunsa, 詳文師) was renamed T'ongmunbaksa (通文博士) and that from then on it was in charge of diplomatic writing (in Chinese). We can assume that this office took orders directly from the king, since it was situated within the royal court. In 721, there were students in this office, which implies that its mission was not only writing diplomatic documents, but also providing language training.

---

http://terms.naver.com/entry.nhn?cid=85&docId=110396&categoryId=2644, accessed 10 February 2013.

[11] 領客府, *Yŏnggaekchŏn* (領客典) means Office for Guest Reception. 倭典 means Office for Japanese. Also refer to the 38th chapter, the 8th chapter of miscellaneous in *SGSG* and its annotation, in the Database of Korean History.

[12] The 8th chapter, the biographical Sketch of the Kings of Silla, the 8th thematic chapter, the King Sŏngdŏk (聖德王, reign 702–737) in *SGSG*. See also the 39th chapter, the 8th thematic chapter (subject: offices) and its annotations. During King Kyŏngdŏk's 景德王 reign (742–765), the name T'ongmunbaksa was changed again to Hallimdae (待翰林), and there must have been students too. The name and structure of Hallimdae were also adopted from the Tang Chinese. King Kyŏngdŏk renamed and restructured not only this office but also other offices, as well as the district structure, according to the Tang system.

We can find a similar record in the *TSGM*.[13] There was a royal institution and trainees who later were in charge of foreign affairs. Princes and high-ranked officials were also sent to Tang China as hostages and guards to the emperor; called Sugwi (宿衛), they then learned Chinese and played a role as messengers between Tang and Silla, and probably also functioned as interpreters. Because of its openness to foreigners, many students and monks were allowed to come from other countries (e.g. from Silla), to study the language and culture of Tang China. The most prominent Korean in Tang China was Ch'oe Ch'iwŏn (崔致遠, 857–?), who passed the Chinese imperial examination and returned home 17 years later. There were also active exchanges with other ethnicities such as the Khitan, Mongolian, and Japanese. These circumstances lead us to assume the existence of interpreting activities in the royal court. According to *Tongsagangmok*, a high-ranking official known as an Ach'an (equivalent to a deputy minister) paid an official visit to Tang China:

> On the first lunar month, the delegation [to Tang China] was sent and entered the court of Tang. [Silla sent] Ach'an Kim Sayang (金思讓) for an official visit to Tang. […] Afterwards yearly tributes were sent regularly, sometimes two or three times a year. Japan sent an envoy and visited [the court of Silla]. (*TSGM* 4th chapter, […], the 2nd year of King Sungdok […] 703) (Database of Korean Classics).

According to *SGSG* (50th chapter, historical biography 10th chapter, Kungye, Year 905), there was the Sadae (史臺) institution, which was in charge of language learning and interpreting in T'aebong (901–918). A similar record can be found in *Yŏllyŏsilgisul* (燃藜室記述, abbr. *YLSGS*),[14] which mentions the Sayŏgwŏn institution during the Chosŏn Dynasty (1392–1910) and also gives historical information for the T'aebong and Koryŏ periods. There is also a Chinese word 通譯 that has been used for interpreting until now:

---

[13] "On the 2nd lunar month, T'ongmunbaksa (通文博士) was established. The former name Sangmunsa (詳文司) was changed into this, and it is in sole charge of diplomatic matters. (*TSGM*, 4th Chapter, Year of Gapin, 13th year of King Sŏngdŏk […] Year 714)".

[14] *Yŏllyŏsilgisul* (燃藜室記述) was written by the Silhak scholar I Kŭngik (李肯翊, 1736–1806). This book deals with the history of the Chosŏn dynasty and is assumed to have been compiled around 1776. It is written in Chinese (cf. Encyclopedia of Korean Culture).

Sayŏgwŏn (司譯院): In T'aebong (泰封國) of Kungye (弓裔), Sadae (史臺) has been established and is in charge of all interpreting. In Koryŏ [this institution] is called T'ongmungwan (通文館) and renamed Hanmundogam (漢文都監). (*YLSGS* Annex 7th Chapter, Organization records, all offices) (Database of Korean Classics)

From the era of the Three Kingdoms onwards, after the dynasties had gained a firm foundation on the Korean peninsula, there were lively exchanges with the neighboring dynasties and tribes in China, Japan, and the Khitan. However, many questions remain unanswered for this period, such as how could one become a court interpreter; what was his role; did it correspond to the concept of an interpreting official in our modern understanding, or was it more like that of a diplomat; what was the social position and the power of an interpreter? However, more detailed information is available about interpreting officials during the Koryŏ Period, and this is discussed in the following section.

3. Koryŏ

The historical sources give us a better understanding of the interpreting officials in the Koryŏ Period, during which time there were many institutions involved with interpreting, including for example Yebinsŏng (Bureau for Guests, 禮賓省), Yŏgŏdogam (Interim Office for Interpreting, 譯語都監), Tongmungwan (Bureau for Interpreting, 通文館) and Sayŏgwŏn (Office for Interpreting, 司譯院). This gives us an insight into class relations, the social position of interpreting officials and their role in Koryŏ. In these institutions, languages such as Mongolian, Chinese, Jurchen and Japanese were taught and the officials there worked as interpreters.

To be a court interpreter in the Koryŏ Period, one must have been at least of the freeborn class (Misuk 2009: 214), but despite this regulation we can find historical documents stating that slaves (servants) could become interpreters. Nor was the hierarchical order in Koryŏ as strict as that of later Confucian Chosŏn society. According to a record from the *History of Koryŏ* (高麗史, *Koryŏsa*),[15] the Bureau for Guests held an

---

[15] The *History of Koryŏ* was edited by scholars in the Chosŏn Dynasty and was completed in 1451. From the first to the 46th chapter, it records chronologically the works and reigns of the kings of Koryŏ. The second part (47th to 85th chapter) which covers various themes, is followed by two tables, and ends with 50 historical biographies (cf. Database of Korean History).

examination to select interpreters in 1201. Promotion to a higher position was possible to some extent within the military ranks, while with a really good connection to the royal court or powerful politicians, one could become a general or even a highly-ranked civil functionary.

The Bureau for Guests (921–1298) was in charge of the reception of foreign guests. Its name changed many times: e.g., to Kaeksŏng (客省) in 995, and to Chŏn'gaeksi (典客寺) in 1298 and again in 1308.[16] Since there was an office that was in charge of foreign guests, it is assumed that interpreting officials belonged to the Bureau for Guests (Kim Sujin 1981: 10; Misuk 2009: 205). In *Koryŏsa* (94th chapter, 7th historical biography, the father of Hwang Poyu, Chŏng Yŏnu), we find that an official named Chang Yu (張儒) who was good at Chinese was posted to a position in the Bureau for Guests and received envoys. In addition, delegations from the Jurchens, Kitans and Parhae are mentioned in *Koryŏsa*. In the 21st chapter (5th year of King Sinjong, 3rd lunar month, 1202), the Bureau for Guests held a qualifying examination for interpreters.

It is not certain when the qualifying examinations first took place in the Koryŏ Dynasty, but since the imperial examination started during the reign of King Kwangjong (949–975), it can be assumed that the examination for interpreters must have commenced around or after the start of the imperial examination (cf. Kim Sujin 1981: 12ff.). We cannot find any details of the examination, but it is assumed that the contents and methods probably did not differ greatly from those of Chosŏn[17] (Misuk 2009: 223). In *Koryŏsajŏryo* (高麗史節要;[18] 2nd year of King Hyejong [1026]), we find

---

[16] Cf. Encyclopedia of Korean Culture.

[17] The examinations in Chinese, Mongolian, Jurchen (later Manchu) and Japanese during the Chosŏn Period are as follows: 1. *Imunbaegang* (臨文講書): reading the Four Books—i.e. Great Learning (大學), Doctrine of the Mean (中庸), Analects (論語) and Mencius (孟子)—in Chinese and translating them into Korean (in speaking). 2. *Paegang* (背講): firstly, learning by heart and reciting aloud in Chinese. The relevant books are *Nogŏldae* (老乞大), *Pakt'ongsa* (朴通事) and *Chikhaesohak* (直解小學). The next step was translating these into Korean and commenting on them in Korean. 3. *Saja* (寫字): The given text should be learned by heart and written down on paper (T'ongmungwangji 1998 75–78). 4. *Yŏgŏ* (譯語): Translating *Kyŏngguktaejŏn* (the Codes of Governance, 經國大典) from Chinese into Korean (Yang ŏjin 2007: 38). In the case of Mongolian, Jurchen and Japanese, candidates were tested only in *Saja*.

[18] *Koryŏsajŏryo*, edited by Kim chongsŏ, was compiled around 1452. This history of the Koryŏ Period consists of 35 volumes and is written in chronological order. Together with *Koryŏsa*, this is an important source for the history of Koryŏ.

a record of U Kwangyu (于光儒 n.d.), who was in charge of diplomatic affairs and belonged to Aegjeung-guk (掖庭局), which was situated in the court and served the King. Hence interpreters did not belong exclusively to one institution, but to various institutions (cf. Misuk 2009: 207–209).

The Mongolian invasion and the subsequent intervention in the Koryŏ Court by the Mongolians lasted for almost a century from 1231, and led to growing power on the part of people who could speak Mongolian. The relationship between the Yuan Dynasty (1271–1368) and Koryŏ was strengthened through royal marriages. We can be sure of the existence of 41 court interpreters, as there is detailed information in the historical records of the Koryŏ Period.[19] Misuk (2009) found six court interpreters in the first half of this period (T'aejo–Kangjong; reigns: 918–1213) and 35 interpreters (from King Kojong until King Kongyang; reigns: 1213–1392) in the second half of the Koryŏ Period, most of whom—around 70 percent of the enlisted interpreters—were active during the reigns of King Wŏnjong (reign: 1259–1274) and King Ch'ungnyŏl[20] (reign: 1274–1308), who cultivated close relationships with the Yuan court and actively engaged in cultural exchange and trade (cf. Misuk 2009: 150f.), something that happened naturally with interpreting officials.

An interim office called Togam (都監) was also established for interpreting activities as Yŏgŏdogam (譯語都監). It is assumed that this interim office was set up around the 18th year of the reign of King Kojong, which was the year of the Mongolian invasion (cf. Kim Sujin 1981: 16f.).[21] In the 123rd chapter, the 36th thematic chapter for the historical biography of the Mongolian interpreter Kang Yunso (康允紹, n.d.), where his greedy deed was condemned, we find a similar, but short entry about Chŏng Chajŏn (鄭子琠 or 鄭子璵, n.d.). Jeong had previously been a monk, had then learned Mongolian as a low-ranking official in

---

Chŏryo means a shortened explanation, but it supplements the *Koryŏsa* (cf. Encyclopedia of Korean Culture). It was written in Chinese. The translation used here is from the Database of Korean History.

[19] In I Misuk (2009: 223–226; especially 150f.), there is a list of 41 interpreters for Chinese (for reception and other functions for Song delegations, and later for Ming delegations); for Jurchen, for diplomatic affairs; and for Japanese and Mongolian, for escorting the delegation to Japan in the Yuan Dynasty.

[20] King Ch'ungnyŏl "was the first Koryŏ King, who tried to follow the Mongolian (Yüan) court voluntarily. As a crown-prince hostage from Koryŏ to the Yüan court, he was educated in the capital of the Yüan and married a daughter of the emperor, Qubilai" (Song Ki-Joong 2001: 4, n6).

[21] Misuk (2006: 176) assumes that it was after the 18th year of Gojong, i.e., between 1231 and 1259.

Yŏgŏdogam, went several times to the Yuan court, and was later promoted to a higher post. It is assumed that Chŏng Chajŏn must have been working at a similar time (i.e. between 1249 and 1308) as Kang Yunso who was from the lowest class (Misuk 2009: 209f.). In *Koryŏsa* (105th chapter, historical biography 18, Cho In'gyu (趙仁規, n.d.), Cho In'gyu, a court interpreter, is introduced as follows: "the young and clever sons (子弟) shall be selected for Mongolian language education, and Jo was selected too." A similar record is found in the *Koryŏsajŏryo*.[22] We cannot be sure of the age at which education for interpreters started, but the word for sons implies that they were young and at least from a commoner family. However, the same record mentions him as a person of lowly parentage.

Since most of the noble families regarded interpreting work as lowly, it is assumed that most interpreters came from a low family (Misuk 2009, 214). Apart from Mongolian, we can also assume that Japanese and Jurchen were taught, but this was before the foundation of Tongmungwan, so the institute for teaching these languages must have been Yŏgŏdogam (I Misuk 2009: 212f.).

In line with a suggestion by Kim Ku (金坵, 1211–1278), a high-ranking official in charge of the central administration, Tongmungwan was established in 1276.

> Tongmungwan shall be established, and let officials below the 7th grade of scholarly organization and under 40 years of age learn Chinese (漢語). Since the interpreters are mostly from a low class, they do not convey what they have heard as is, and there were many cases where they have cunning minds and act in their personal interest. These cases troubled the Minister, and Kim Ku, a secondary 2nd rank official, suggested the T'ongmungwan, and it has been established. (*Koryŏsajŏryo* 19th chapter, 1st year of King Ch'ungnyŏl 忠烈王 [...] 1276)[23]

---

[22] "Cho In'gyu is from the Sangwŏn county. From his childhood, he was bright and excellent. He learnt Mongolian, but was not superior to his colleagues, so he closed his door and studied day and night for three long years, and his name became well-known. Whenever there was an official matter for the Mongolian court, Cho was sent. He made more than 30 visits to Mongolia as a delegate, and he succeeded in making many great contributions through his wise answers." (*Koryŏsajŏryo* 23th chapter, 5th year of King Ch'ungnyŏl [...]) (Database of Korean Classics)

[23] More or less the same record can be found in *Koryŏsa* (76th chapter, 30th thematic chapter: all the government officials, T'ongmungwan).

Normally the word *Hanŏ* (漢語) stands for Chinese, but since this is during the period of Mongolian intervention, it might instead refer to Mongolian. Apart from T'ongmungwan, there was another institution called Hanŏ dogam (漢語都監, Interim office for Chinese) where Chinese might have been taught (cf. Misuk 2006: 180–183), since Yŏgŏdogam was in charge of Mongolian.

In 1389, in the late Koryŏ Period, a new institution called Sayŏgwŏn was founded. The same name was also used during the Chosŏn Dynasty. The power of the Yuan declined, and as the Ming Dynasty (1368–1644) became stronger, the importance of Chinese also grew. This might have been one of the reasons why a new institution for interpreting was established. *Ihak* (吏學) means the study of how to write administrative documents, and so the study deals with *Imun* (吏文) used specially for official diplomatic letters. *Ihak* affairs belonged to the Sayŏgwŏn.

3.1. Origins and Ranks of the official interpreters

To be an interpreting official, one had to be at least a commoner, but interpreters like Kang Yunso and Kang Chunjae (康俊才, n.d.) were from a lower class. Cho In'gyu might also have been from the same class, but because of his excellent language skills and the contribution he made, due to his "wise answers" during his visits, Cho In'gyu was promoted to the level of minister. Chŏng Chajŏn was a monk who returned to the secular world. Kang Suhyŏng (康守衡,–1298) was held captive by the Mongolians, during which time he learned their language, and he later served the Yuan court as interpreter (Kim Sujin 1981: 32–35). Kim Ku criticized low-class interpreters when he suggested the founding of the T'ongmungwan, so we can assume that the class to which interpreting officials originally belonged did not actually matter that much. Compared with the Chosŏn Period, when there were hardly any lower-class interpreters like the former servant Chŏng Myŏngsu (鄭命壽, 1653) and some others, interpreters were expected at least to be commoners, and unlike in the Koryŏ Period, this restriction was strictly adhered to. The names and some background information of 41 interpreters during the 474 years of Koryŏ history (918–1392) are known, but it is difficult to draw any conclusions about their original class. In the case of Chosŏn, especially in the second half of the period, we can observe commoner clans from which most of the interpreters, Yŏkkwan, were drawn. However, clan-building of this kind is not seen during the Koryŏ Period.

During this time, interpreters started from a low military position, and promotion to a higher rank was very limited. That was a main characteristic during the first half of the Koryŏ Period, but as time went on, especially during the years of the Koryŏ military regime and the Mongolian intervention, interpreters could reach higher positions, and some of them reached the primary 3rd rank (cf. Misuk 2009: 229). Cho In'gyu later became a general and minister (*Koryŏsa*; 105th chapter, historical biographies 18th chapter, Cho In'gyu). Interpreters might have been promoted to the position of general, but it remained difficult to become a high-ranked official as a civil administrator, although there were exceptions.[24] Interpreters could sometimes be promoted to become one of the central staff officials of the court, called Naesi (內侍), and during the second half of the Koryŏ Period, their role became more important. These promotions show the growing social position of interpreters (cf. Misuk 2006: 186).

3.2. The role of interpreters and their influences

In the *Sŏnhwabongsa-Koryŏdogyŏng* (宣和奉使高麗圖經, 8th chapter, prominent figures) where a delegate from the Song dynasty named Sŏ Kŭng (徐兢) came to Koryŏ and described his observations and illustrations in Chinese, there are positive remarks on the state structure and its officials, including interpreting officials. Although they cannot be regarded as representative examples of the role and work of court interpreters, from cases like U Kwangyu and Cho In'gyu, we see that these interpreters were not only in charge of escorting delegations or receptions, but that they also took care of diplomatic affairs, such as border conflicts and cultural subjects. When Ch'oe Ch'unghŏn (崔忠獻, 1149–1219), one of the leaders during the Choe regime, wanted to appoint the court interpreter U Kwangyu from a secondary 7th rank to an unprecedentedly high position, there were protests by civilian administrators. In response to a protest from a high-ranked official, Choe said:

> The diplomatic talent of Kwangyu, which has been shown during the investiture delegation from the Chin Dynasty [1115–1234] shall be valued, and therefore he will be especially appointed to an upper house position (叅職). Why are you insisting on the precedent regulations? […]

---

[24] According to I Misuk (2009: 228), we can find six official interpreters who might have played an important role in Koryŏ, but their close relation to the Yuan court was the key to their promotions.

(*Koryŏsajŏryo* 14th chapter, King Heyjong [...] 1206, [...] Database of Korean Classics)

Let us look at a record concerning the other interpreter, Cho In'gyu:

"My subordinate Cho In'gyu is good at Mongolian and Chinese, so he could translate the royal edicts without any mistakes. When I [King Ch'ungnyŏl] proceeded to the court of the Son of Heaven [the Emperor of Yuan], he escorted me all the time [...]. I wish, you[r Majesty] may bestow on him an honorary medal [...]." [...] So the Yuan court granted him a higher position and bestowed a golden medal. [...] "During the military expedition to Japan [the Mongol invasions of Japan] Cho In'gyu reported our situation very well to the Son of the Heaven. It is all thanks to his achievements that the Emperor appointed me as left senior minister in the royal court [...]" [...] At first, many Koryŏ people learned Mongolian, but there were hardly any people who could speak Mongolian. When the delegates entered the Yuan capital, the Royal Court of Yuan let Kang Suhyŏng, who was in charge of diplomatic matters with Koryŏ, interpret [...]. Sejo [Kublai Khan, reign: 1260–1294] praised his [Cho In'gyu's] answer and prohibited the gold colouring and commanded that ceramics coloured with gold should not be given as tribute. Also he says "A Koryŏan can speak Mongolian so well, so why do we need Kang Suhyŏng to interpret? [...] A Mongolian envoy who bore a deep grudge against Koryŏ tried to destroy our own custom and reported to the Emperor, so it was not possible to tell what would happen soon. At that time Jo went by himself to the Yuan court and had an audience with the Emperor. He was able to clarify the rights and wrongs so the situation could be settled. Regaining the border zones in the West and North was also Cho In'gyu's achievement, since he went as a delegate and was able to persuade the Yuan. Every time there was an affair to be addressed to the Yuan court, the King sent Cho In'gyu, so he went there 30 times as a delegate and worked hard for the country." (*Koryŏsa*, 150th chapter, Historical Biography 18th chapter, Officials, Cho In'gyu)

Due to the restrictions on promotion for court interpreters, they were not allowed to hold a position higher than the secondary 6th rank. However, U Kwangyu was ranked higher than this during the military regime of Ch'oe Ch'unghŏn, who supported his promotion. Apart from rendering speeches, interpreters played an important role in diplomatic affairs between Koryŏ and the Yuan court. Furthermore, they were in charge not only of the spoken language, but also of written documents. Thanks to their linguistic competence, they could maintain close relationships with the Yuan court (cf. Kim Sujin 1981: 50–55).

What influences could the interpreters have on Koryŏ society? For internal and external reasons, the military regime came to an end, and the Mongolian intervention period then began. During this time, interpreters like Kang Yunso and Chŏng Chayŏ played a politically, economically and culturally important role (Kim Sujin, 1981, 55–65). They contributed to a change in political orientation toward a pro-Mongolian stance, which meant that the pro-Mongolian interpreters could then be in a high position. The growing power of the Yuan court in Koryŏ was one of the factors weakening the Koryŏ court (Cho In'gyu, Yu Ch'ŏngsin (柳清臣, 1329), Ch'oe Ando (崔安道, 1240-1340)). From historical records, we can see that some interpreters accumulated great wealth thanks to their close relationships with the powerful[25] and also that they illegally acquired a great deal of land and drastically exploited the lower class (Kim Sujin 1981: 60–62). However, we cannot find any record that the interpreters could gain fortunes by trading with Chinese or Mongolians, as was the case in Chosŏn. They must have been in contact with the culture, customs and trends in Yuan and Japan and they must have been some of the importers of new trends from overseas; however, it is very difficult to find culture-related records.

This section has introduced interpreters and some general features of court interpreters during the Koryŏ Dynasty. Although it seems mosaic-like, it has been possible to sketch a picture of these interpreting officials on the basis of the scarce historical records.

4. Conclusion

Thanks to the lively trading and cultural exchanges during the Three Kingdoms Period, there were official institutions for the reception of guests from Japan and China. From that, we can assume that there must also have been interpreting officials. In the case of T'aebong, we could observe that there were official interpreters and a related institution, Sadae. The background historical sources were *TSGM, SGSG* and *SGYS*.

Researchers in the field of Korean history have been able to identify 41 interpreters for the Koryŏ Period, as well as their backgrounds and activities and their role as diplomats. There were also Japanese interpreters, but information regarding them is much scarcer than for Chinese and Mongolian interpreting officials. During the Yuan intervention period especially (13th century), Mongolian-Korean interpreters had very close relations with the Yuan imperial court and were able to gain great political power and wealth. Records from *Koryŏsajŏryo* and *TSGM* show that interpreters accompanied delegations to and from

---

[25] *TSGM* 13th chapter, […] the 34th year of King Ch'ungnyŏl […] 1308. Korean Classics Database.

China and were in charge of receiving delegations and, in some cases, solving diplomatic difficulties such as border conflicts and reducing cultural influences from the Yuan Dynasty on traditional Koryŏ customs. We can find records stating that interpreters were awarded for these achievements. Other sources tell us that some of the interpreters were used not only for their skills in the spoken language, but also for their work on official diplomatic documents. There are also records about interpreters accused of wrongdoing—e.g., illegally accumulating a fortune by depriving others of land or assets. Unlike Chosŏn, however, there was no mention of interpreters who traded with China and others.

On the basis of *TSGM*, *Koryŏdogyŏng*, *Koryŏsa*, *Koryŏsajŏryo* and *YLSGS*, we looked closely at court interpreters and the related institutions such as Yebinsŏng, Yŏgŏdogam, Hanmundogam, T'ongmungwan and Sayŏgwŏn, where an individual could learn Mongolian, Chinese, Jurchen or Japanese. During that time, even if from a low class, one could become a court interpreter, but promotion to a much higher rank was restricted. Yet every rule had its exception. Owing to close relationships with the military regime or the Mongolian court, some interpreters could become high-ranked generals or even civilian officials with high positions. Nor were the roles and functions of interpreters limited to rendering Korean into Chinese, Japanese or other languages, since interpreters also acted like diplomats, in our modern understanding of the role. We can therefore conclude that it was part of their work to deal with diplomatic affairs. On the economic side, some interpreters were criticized for exploiting the poor and accumulating a fortune illegally, but we could not find evidence of their trading-related activities.

It has already been more than 20 years since the 1992 Vienna congress was held under the theme "Translation studies, an interdiscipline". Since then, interdisciplinary research has been given greater importance, and interdisciplinary convergence is a new theme in Korea. Interpreting and translation studies are now firmly rooted in the academic field, as evidenced by the many introductory and theoretical works and encyclopedias. It is now time to take a parallel initiative by looking back to the past and studying interpreting and translating activities in earlier times so as to identify differences and commonalities, find influences that have been overlooked, and bring them to our present awareness.

As mentioned in the introduction, this chapter aimed to present a history of Korean interpreters. My understanding of history is of course not only a collection of names, dates and events in chronological order. Still, these can act as a starting point for connecting and understanding the implications of these names, dates and events related to interpreting, and will help us reconstruct the role and function of interpreting officials in various times and locations.

References

Baigorri-Jalón, Jesús 2006, "Perspectives on the History of Translation" in Georges D. Bastin and Paul F. Bandia, eds., *Charting the Future of Translation History*, Ottawa: University of Ottawa Press, 101-110.

Pak Sŏngnae 1983, "T'ongyŏgŭi Yŏksa mit T'ongyŏkkwanŭi Chungyosŏng Yŏkkwan" "통역의 역사 및 통역관의 중요성" [The History of Interpreting and the importance of Interpreters], *Oedaetongyeokhyeophoeji*, Vol. 1. No. 1. 15-22.

Paek Okkyŏng 2000, *Chosŏnjŏn'gi Yŏkkwanyŏn'gu Yŏkkwan 조선전기 (朝鮮前期) 역관연구 (譯官研究)* [Study of the Yŏkkwan during the first half of the Chosŏn Dynasty], Doctoral dissertation at Ewha Woman's University, South Korea.

Baker, Mona, ed. 1998, *Routledge Encyclopedia of Translation Studies*, London: Routledge.

Delisle, Jean and Judith Woodsworth eds. 1995, *Translators through History*, Amsterdam: Benjamins.

Kang Sinhang 2000, *Han'gugŭi yŏkhak 한국 (韓國) 의 역학 (譯學)* [Interpreting Studies in Korea], Seoul: Seoul National University Press.

Kim KuKim Kujin and I hyŏnsuk, trans. and eds. 1998, Kugyŏkt'ongmun'gwanji 국역통문관지 (通文館志) [Translated Tongmungwanji], Seoul: Sejongdaewang Kinyŏmsaŏphoe.

Kim Sujin 1981, *Koryŏyŏkkwan'go – Yŏwŏn'gwan'gyerŭl Chungsimŭro Yŏkkwan 고려역관고 (高麗譯官考) – 여원관계 (麗元關係) 를 중심 (中心) 으로.* [A Study of Koryŏ Court Interpreters–Focusing on the Relationships between the Yuan and Koryŏ Dynasty], Master's Thesis, Donga University, South Korea.

Yang Ojin 2007, "Chosŏnsidae Chunggugŏ Yŏkkwan Sŏnbarŭl Wihan Ch'uljesŏwa P'yŏngga Pangsik Yŏkkwan" "조선시대 중국어 역관 선발을 위한 출제서와 평가 방식" [Examination papers and the methods for selecting Chinese Yŏkkwan during the Chosŏn Period], *Chunggugŏmunŏnyŏkch'onggan*, 19, 32-49.

Misuk, I 2006, "Wŏn Kansŏpki Yŏkkwanŭi Hwaldong' Yŏkkwan" "원 간섭기 역관의 활동" [The Role of Interpreters during the Mongolian Intervention Period] *Sangmyŏngsahak*, combined Volumes 10, 11, 12, 171-200.

Misuk, I 2009, "Koryŏsidae Yŏkkwan Yŏn'gu Yŏkkwan" "고려시대 (高麗時代) 역관 (譯官) 연구 (研究)" [A Study on the Yŏkkwan of the Koryŏ Period], *Han'guk Sasanggwa Munhwa*, Vol. 46. 201-234.

Sŏng Kijung 2001, The Study of Foreign Languages in The Chosun Dynasty (1392–1910). Seoul and Somerset NJ: Jimoondang.

Websites

Database of Korean History
    http://db.history.go.kr (*Koryŏsa, SGSG, SGYS*)
Dictionary of Korean Classic Terminology
    http://terms.naver.com/entry.nhn?cid=85&docId=110396&categoryId=2644
Encyclopedia of Korean Culture
    http://encykorea.aks.ac.kr/Contents/Index
Korean Classics Database
    http://db.itkc.or.kr (*TSGM, Koryŏsajŏryo, Sŏnhwabongsa Koryŏdogyŏng, YLSGS*)
Wikipedia
    http://en.wikipedia.org

CHINA

THE GLOBAL AND LOCAL POWER OF A TRANSLATOR: A CASE STUDY

XIAOYAN WANG

1. Introduction

Language in modern society is no longer innocent. Rather, it is regarded as being representative of ideology and social politics. Volosonov proposed that "no utterance can be put together without value judgment" (1973: 55), and Graddol expresses a similar idea that "language is so intimately connected with social life and human behaviour that any model of language tends to embody assumptions and value judgements" (1994: 9). Echoing this point of view, Fairclough continues with the "social determination of language use" (1989: 19): noting that "language is a form of social practice" in being "a socially conditioned process, conditioned that is by other (non-linguistic) parts of society" (Fairclough 2001: 19). All this points to one conclusion, which is that language carries power and is formed by social power.

Translation as an advanced level of language use activity is a valuable skill that "requires knowledge of a foreign language at an advanced stage of learning" (Krings 1987: 160). This has been acknowledged by many scholars working conscientiously in the field (Catford 1965; Nida 1964; Krings 1987; Newmark 1981; etc.). Yet despite this fact, the labour of a translator has traditionally been considered as "secondary" to, or "less creative" than that of the author, and therefore translators have always been viewed as inferior or subordinate compared to the position of the original author (Bassnett 1996; Lefevere 1990, 1992; Venuti 1992, 1995, 1998; etc.). Thus, a translator's significance to the translated works and his/her position has been greatly ignored even marginalized (ibid). As Venuti has put it,

> Whereas authorship is generally defined as originality, self-expression in a unique text, translation is derivative, neither self-expression nor unique: it imitates another text (1998: 31).

Ironically, such a marginalized position was imposed on translators through the very criteria they accepted as good translations. Catford's (1965) linguistic approach (formal equivalence), Nida's (1964) functional approach (dynamic equivalence), and Chinese translation theorist Yan Fu's three principles of "Xin (faithfulness or fidelity), Da (fluency or comprehensibility), and Ya (elegance or polish)" (as cited in Chan 2004), all emphasize that the source texts should be used as the standard for the evaluation of the target texts, holding that the expertise of translation is to produce a "transparent" text, wherein the translator should achieve "self-effacement" (Venuti 1992, 1995).

Influenced by poststructuralist thinkers such as Foucault, Fairclough, Bourdieu, and Derrida, translation scholars brought their critical views of language use into the field of translation studies and began not only to re-think the role of translators and translations in situated social contexts, but also to re-consider the power and position that translations and translators possess, so far with fruitful results. In her critique on translation theory in Germany, Snell-Hornby (1990) calls for a culturally-oriented approach to translation theory to bridge the gap of all kinds of translations; Bassnett and Lefevere (1990), in response to this "cultural turn", established the school of Translation Studies, which deems translation as "re-writing", a kind of "manipulation" (Hatim and Munday 2004: 102); while Toury's descriptive translation approach views "norms as translation behaviour typically obtaining under specific socio-cultural or textual situations" (Toury 1995: 54-5, cited in Hatim and Munday 2004). Hermans (1996) emphasizes the translator's voice, believing that it is the translator's "discursive presence" (Hermans 1996: 27, cited in Hatim and Munday 2004) in the translated texts that makes the translation significant; Andre Lefevere "attempts a sketch of a genealogy of translation in the West", and explores "what the exercise of power means in terms of the production of culture, of which the production of translations is a part" (Bassnett and Lefevere 1990: 5). Venuti examines the "invisible force" that governs all translators and translations—ideology—and challenges the authors' authority by claiming that "a translation canonizes the foreign text, validating its fame by enabling its survival" (Venuti 1992: 7). In this way, the Poststructuralist approach of translation makes critical examinations of the ideological and social-cultural power that dwells in and shapes translations, highlighting translators' agency and influence on the final work.

This new approach has drastically changed the role of translators, who are no longer deemed merely as mimics but as manipulators—exerting their own unique power in the course of translation. The power of translators is viewed as involving that of "using language to 'include' or 'exclude' a particular kind of reader, a certain system of values, a set of beliefs or an entire culture" (Hatim and Munday 2004: 93). By bringing and adapting it into the target socio-literary contexts, translators use their translations to "canonize" the source texts (Bassnett and Lefevere 1990; Venuti 1992). Such a changed position of translators reveals the fact that translation academia has gained deeper insights into the nature of translation, the process of translation, and the recognition of the agency, power or subjectivity of a translator.

The frontier line of studies on translation agency is further expanded by Nord who, following a functional linguistics approach, put translation into the larger context of communicative interaction. With this perspective, Nord (2001) regards translating as a purposeful activity which involves the interactions and communications between various agents including the initiator, the commissioner, the source-text producer, the translator, the target-text receiver, the target-text user, etc. In addition, her depiction of the "interactive communication network" not only exemplifies the important roles that translators play in the entire enterprise of translation, but also specifies other substantial social cultural agencies that scope and shape the acts of a translator.

Research on the power and agents of translation have flourished ever since and achieved fruitful results from both macro perspectives (such as Lukits 2007; Milton & Bandia 2009) and micro ones (such as Haddadian-Moghaddam 2011), especially with the appearance of the volume *Agents of Translation* by Milton and Bandia in 2009, which includes a number of studies on translator agency from multiple perspectives and varied geographical spectrums. However, bulky contributions have also been made on theoretical and empirical studies of institutional agencies and various other external factors that may have influenced the translators and the translations (such as Borgeaud 2011; Merkle 2009; Milton & Bandia 2009; Nobrega & Milton 2009; Paloposki 2009; Zurbach 2009). Few have focused on revealing the trajectories of a translator's empowerment and their exercise of subjective power during the course of bridging contextual and cultural heterogeneities. Much less has been done on exploring the possible force behind this counterbalancing power of translators, especially through the combined lens of New Literacy Studies (Street 2003). But holding the central position in the translation process, translators probe the power of the source text and function like a "transformer station of potential high-power electricity" (Lukits 2007: 160). Given their vital position, it is necessary and enlightening to explore how translators are engaged in the transfer of power.

In addition, existing literature on agent and agency studies contains a few analytical cases from China. Chinese translators and their translations, with a strong tradition of aiming at larger readerships for mixed purposes and political concerns, deserve quiet exploration, both as an extension to the existing literature and as an important supplement to the mainstream translation metalanguages of Western origin (Tang 2007). Further, a hybrid method of blending ethnographic accounts may better situate the analysis into specific social cultural contexts and add perspectives to the current trend, hence raising the urgency and significance of studies on agency channels of Chinese translators' "knowledge dissemination and inheritance before heading towards centripetal participation in mainstream activities of knowledge production in the global academy" (Tang 2007: 371).

With the purpose of meeting the above-mentioned gaps in studies on translation agency in terms of scope, perspective and methodology, this chapter presents an ethnographical scrutiny of a famous modern Chinese translator—Zhang Guruo (1903-1994), in order to explore the trajectory of the translator's agency and exercise of power, and to discuss the driving force behind the translator's empowerment. Zhang is selected not only for his well-received translations of heavy volumes of Hardy's works into Chinese, but also for his significance as a prominent role-model in modern China's literary translation arena. It is also believed that the very extensiveness and thoroughness of his research in approaching the source texts (ST) and the ST's authors will have guaranteed the quality of his final translations. Through a detailed introduction to his translation idiosyncrasies and translation samples, the global and local perspectives of a translator's agency power are also analyzed. Two specific questions are addressed: a) What is the trajectory of the translator's agency during the meaning-making process traversing contexts, cultures, languages and space? b) What is the driving force behind his empowerment as a competent meaning negotiator with the source text author?

2. Zhang Guruo and his translations

Zhang Guruo, a professor in the English Department of Beijing University, was a modern Chinese translator of English literature who was best known for his translation of Hardy's works into Chinese. Born into an intellectual family on the small island of Zhifu, near Yantai city in the coastal Shandong province of eastern China in 1903, Zhang Guruo received systemic traditional Chinese education and graduated from the local primary school and the prominent Nankai high school of Tianjin with top scores. His diligent and extensive reading of traditional Chinese classics had built him a solid foundation of reading and writing in classical Chinese, and enabled his admission to the English Department of Beijing University in 1926 as the top candidate. In 1929, as a third-year English major student, Zhang Guruo set about his first attempt at translating Thomas Hardy's *The Return of the Native,* a novel he loved for its stories and its vivid depictions of English landscapes and society.

From that point, he became fascinated by the works of Hardy and other British writers, and was determined to introduce these great English novelists to a Chinese readership. His Chinese translations of *The Return of the Native* and *Tess of the d'Urbervilles* were first published by the Commercial Press in 1935 and 1936 respectively. Both became immediate successes and were lauded as one of the milestones of British literature translation in China (Sun 2004: 4). The two translations also established Zhang's position in China's academia as a prominent translator. In the ensuing half century, he revised the two translations several times, and their third editions, which both appeared in 1958, published by the People's Literature Press, are still reprinted and well-received today. Though translations of the two novels by others also appeared later, Zhang's translations have always been regarded as the best for their expressiveness, faithfulness and, above all, accuracy (Gu 2004; Li 2004; Sun 2004; Xiong 2005; Zhao 2005); this won him the title of the "Chinese expert on Hardy".

In addition to the two volumes, his other major translations include: Hardy's *Jude the Obscure* in 1958 (reprinted in 1981 with added annotations); Bernard Shaw's *Heartbreak House* in 1956; Charles Dickens' *American Notes* in 1962 and *David Copperfield* in 1980; and Henry Fielding's *The History of Tom Jones, a Foundling* in 1985. All of these became part of the canon of foreign literature in China and have influenced numerous Chinese readers ever since. His latest Chinese version of Fielding's *Tom Jones* won the National Award for Foreign Literature Translation in 1987, and he himself was awarded membership as an Honorary Fellow of the Hong Kong Translation Society in 1991 for his archetypal translations (Huang 1991; Sun 2004; Zhao 2005: 41). In short, Zhang is believed to have made "permanent and indelible contributions to the spread of British literature in China" (Zhao 2005: 241).

2.1. Idiosyncrasy of Zhang's translations

The novels translated by Zhang are part of Britain's literary canon, and are best known for their language feats and artistic achievements. Zhang's Chinese translations of them are nonetheless equally impressive and have always been praised as exemplars (Gu 2004; Huang 2004; Sun 2004; Zhao 2005). Compared with versions by others, Zhang's were the first to appear and have always stood out for the best preservation of the original sentences, stories, speakers, and styles (ibid). His accomplishment in Chinese has also enabled him to best represent both the artistic and linguistic values of these works.

One of the most remarkable features that distinguish Zhang's translations from others is the superb language feat demonstrated in his versions. As a master of the Chinese language, Zhang knew well how to use the aesthetic forms and rules of Chinese characters and rhetorical devices to reach expressiveness, and maintain accuracy while presenting the complexity, profoundness, and artistic feats of the works of Hardy and Dickens (Zhao 2005: 242). The accomplished language of Zhang's translations is best shown in his deft and deliberate use of Chinese parallelisms, especially his dexterity with classical Chinese four-character idioms as well as parallel structures. As a result of such effort, his Chinese translations are often impressive for their vivid descriptions, sonorous rhythms and intoxicating rhetoric (Sun 2004), which enabled him, through abundant creative adaptive measures, to best preserve the colloquial and/or even vulgar tones and styles that often appear in the source texts.

Another important feature of his predominance as a translator is the thorough research he carried out on the source texts and the source authors before, during and even after translating them. This made him a well-known literary researcher and translator in modern China's translation circles, and the results of his research were annotated and summarized, being either absorbed into the decision-making process of diction and revision as he worked, or compiled into the explanatory notes for the final versions to facilitate easy reading or comprehension. The annotations he produced for all his translations are unprecedented, and remain unparalleled by successive translators in terms of both quantity and quality. As summarized in Table 1, preliminary counting shows that for *The Return of the Native* (1958/1998 by the People's Press) he made 452 translational annotations; for *Tess of the d'Urbervilles* (1957/1991 by the People's Press) there were 436; for *Jude the Obscure* (1958/1995 by the same press) there were 403; there were 640 for *David Copperfield* (1989 by Shanghai Translation Press); and 1,356 entries for *Tom Jones* (1993/1995 by Shanghai Translation Press), amounting in total to 3,259 entries for these five books (as cited in Sun 2004: 82). The length of each annotation ranges from around 320 to 980 Chinese characters (ibid).

Table 1. Preliminary counting of Zhang's annotations

Name of the novels	Number of note entries	Published in	Publishing house
The Return of the Native	452	1958/1998	The People's Press
Tess of the d'Urbervilles	436	1958/1991	
Jude the Obscure	403	1958/1995	
David Copperfield	640	1989	Shanghai Translation Press
Tom Jones	1356	1993/1995	
Total entries	3259		
Length of entries	Ranging from 320 to 980 Chinese characters each		

Such a huge amount of research, all done manually, has never been reached or surpassed by any other translators working on the same books. In Zhang's opinion, exhaustive research enabled a translator to examine everything about the author and the source text—including the time and society into which the author was born, the cultural contexts of the ST, the author's formative life experiences, educational background, and even the readings that had influenced the formation of the source texts. For Zhang, it was also the prerequisite for accurate re-fabrication, or re-contextualization of these texts into Chinese. He also regarded it as a translator's responsibility to gain full comprehension of the source texts and to convey this understanding to the target readers. Thus, given the developmental stage of Chinese society in Zhang's day, when ignorance and poverty prevailed and many Chinese readers possessed little or no prior knowledge of foreign contexts or cultures, it was necessary for a translator to facilitate reader accessibility by including as much background information as possible into the translation by various means, including notes.

Furthermore, the quality of Zhang's translational annotations was even more distinctive, both in terms of scope and standards. His annotations can be relegated broadly into two categories: notes about the source texts and notes for the target readership, and each group can be further classified into six types of explanations: elaborations on the allusions, interpretations of obscured meanings, notes on the sources of quotations or sayings, explanations of the socio-cultural contexts, and notes on language skills (i.e., devices such as puns, partial tones, etc.) (as cited in Sun 2004: 81-102). His notes and annotations covered a wide range of proper names, geography, history, religion, legends, science, law, theology, etymology, customs and folklore, arts, even related writings, comments, rhetoric skills, and so on, inclusive of almost everything of the ST and the ST's author that could help him to approach an author's intentions in a similar manner or to make things easier for the target audience (Sun 2004; Zhao 2005). These solid annotations allowed him to dig thoroughly into the mind and soul of the source texts and their authors, and to extract every shred of meaning—even the contextual connotations hidden in the use of colloquial expressions, or puns spoken in dialect—for the target readers. Occasionally, skills or strategies adopted in translating puns, partial tones or sarcasms are also explained in the notes as a means of maximum exposure of and to the meanings of the source text.

Whatever the type of note, the prime principle was to lead the target readers to the intended meanings, social-cultural information or artistic skills of the source texts (Zhang 1982). Almost all the ST's contextual leads have been meticulously untangled, even a nursery rhyme that was familiar to local ears, being spotted and explained. An illustrative case of Zhang's translating can be seen in the following example from a section of Chapter 22 of *David Copperfield*, where there is an utterance by Miss Mowcher:

> "Well then", cried Miss Mowcher, "I'll consent to live. Now, ducky, ducky, ducky, <u>come to Mrs. Bond and be killed</u>!"

Zhang translated this directly into Chinese:

> "那样的话"，冒齐小姐喊道，我就答应活下去啦。现在，<u>小鸭，小鸭，小鸭，快到滂得太太这儿来挨刀</u>。"(as cited in Zhang 1982: 490).

But to explain to the readers why she uttered "ducky" and "Mrs. Bond" and "be killed" which seemed to make no sense within the immediate context, Zhang added a footnote to the underlined part, saying that "it comes from the first stanza of an English nursery rhyme" and then provided the Chinese translation of the nursery verse. With this note, readers would immediately understand that with this rhyme Miss Mowcher was joking with the two young men with whom she was conversing (Zhang 1982: 452). Annotations like this can be found in all their appropriate places in Zhang's translations, showing his meticulous spirit as a highly responsible and considerate translator.

This thorough and meticulous method of doing translation has much to do with the tenet upheld by Zhang throughout his translation career, and which forms another aspect of the uniqueness of his translations. Zhang's translational thought was best summarized in his article "Idiomatic source texts, hence idiomatic translations",[1] which was published in 1980 and is frequently cited by many researchers and papers. It details Zhang's philosophy of translation, and his understanding of the nature of translation. In his view, a good translation should be equivalent to the source texts in content (i.e., bearing the same idea/thought as the ST); in form (using similar or even identical words or sentence structures as the ST); in the nature of the diction (for instance, if the ST uses a slang expression, the target text (TT) expression should also be a slang word); and above all in style (by being as idiomatic to the target ears as it is to the source ears) (as cited in Sun 2004; Zhang 1982). Since the source text was written in idiomatic English familiar to and well-received by the ST readers, the Chinese translation should be equally idiomatic for the Chinese readers. Therefore, "idiomatic translation" was upheld by Zhang as the highest principle for the maximum preservation of the original meaning, flavour and style. Only in this way could target readers acquire a similar reading experience to that of source readers. For this purpose, a translator had to take the source texts, the author, and the target readers equally into consideration during the meaning-making of the target texts.

This precept also reflected Zhang's recognition of the nature and the process of translation. For him, comprehension (or re-conceptualization) and representation (or expression) were the two most important stages of translation. Instead of a simple mechanical replacement of one language with another, translation was meant to convey to the target readers not only the linguistic meanings, but also the author's thoughts, mind, and emotions intended in, or disguised under, the various language forms and devices of the source texts. Therefore, to ensure the accuracy of translation, a translator must "intrude into the inner world of the author, and capture the ideological vein and stylistic features of the source texts" (Sun 2004: 82). To this end, substantial research requiring extensive readings and investigations is necessary. As Zhang stated:

---

[1] "地道的原文，译文地道的", first published in 1980 in the first issue of *Translation Journal,* currently known as *Chinese Translators Journal.*

> A translator should read all the books that the ST author has ever read, or know all the things that the ST author has ever known. Or else his translation will be nothing but a parody or an impersonation (Zhang 1982: 455).[2]

A similar thought is also found in Neubert's (2000) discussion of translation competence:

> [R]eal translators ... make use of all resources including seeking advice from the experts, researching their texts, both parallel and background texts in the source as well as in the target languages to approach the source text author as much as possible for the benefit of faithful translation. In this sense, everything said and printed is their essential lifeline (p. 4).

Besides faithfulness, expressiveness is also highlighted in Zhang's tenets of translation, and is best shown in his consideration of the target readers and the target culture. On the one hand, with idiomatic expressions, the target readers can better understand the culture and society depicted in the original works; on the other, they can also experience the original language style used in the source texts. Many idiomatic expressions that are familiar and understandable to the target readers were reflected in Zhang's translations, so the target readers "can have the same reactions and/or responses as those experienced by the source readers" (Zhang 1982: 451).[3] Therefore, despite the prevailing practice of sacrificing expressiveness to faithfulness with rigid duplication of the ST forms and structures, followed by other major translators before the 1930s, Zhang insisted on achieving both expressiveness and faithfulness in his translations, which was why his versions were so successful.

However, his emphasis on the importance of idiomatic translations does not signify bending everything in the source text and/or source culture to suit the target text and please the audience. Indeed, target readers deserve a smooth-reading experience just as source text readers do, but equally, they deserve acknowledgement of the fact that these stories

---

[2] This is translated by the author. The source text is:
"译者也应该知，原作者所知道的。译者也应该读过，读过的书原作者所
　　。否则译时只能照猫画虎。道"

[3] This is translated by the author. The source text is:
"我认为译书主要是给不懂原文的。是我有意而为，译所以如此我之所
　　应该与读原文的人是一样，所起的反应、看译文的人所得的感受。人看的
　　。的"

are not happening on their native soil, but in a distant place. Therefore, the end of idiomatic translation does necessarily dictate the means of rigid enforcement of domestication. Rather, preserving meaning and form should be dialectical, and the balance between foreignization and domestication should be maintained for the utmost accommodation of both the source and the target cultures. Hence, in Zhang's translations there are frequent compromises, adaptations and innovations in the target language, for the purpose of reaching macro resemblance in terms of meaning, form and spirit, thus in effect re-canonizing the source works in the cultural context of the receiver. This balanced provision of both foreignization and domestication for macro faithfulness is another of the groundbreaking features for which Zhang's translations are so renowned. He explained this idea of faithfulness noting that:

> The thoughts and life-styles expressed with fluent and elegant Chinese should be all about the original source cultures: foreign society cannot be translated into Chinese society, nor can foreign folklore be transferred into Chinese tales, nor blue eyes turned into black eyes. With regard to language use or ways of expression, the style closest or identical to that of the source texts should be preserved. Prose should be translated into prose; and verses into poems. If elegant language of the noble class is used in the source text, such elegance should be reflected in the translation; if slang or rural dialects are used in the conversations of country people, rural accents and slang words should be adopted to reflect the same rustic flavour; Even if the source text contains a purposeful 'parody text', such a characteristic should also be responded to in the translation (Zhang 1980 cited in Sun 2004: 55).[4]

According to this principle, even the formative pauses, rhythms, variations of diction or structure deliberated on by the author and accompanied by particular tones or emotions were captured and best reflected in the translated texts by similar or alternative approaches (Sun 2004; Zhang 1982).

---

[4]This is translated by the author. The source text reads:
"…变成中国生活不能把外国的社会，和生活多是原有的译文反映的思想在语言。不能把蓝眼睛变成黑眼睛，不能把外国风俗改成中国风俗，方式用散，原作中的散文。尽量接近以至酷似原著的风格，上表达方式、文字原作用上层；翻译过来也必须是诗句，原作中是诗行的地方；文形式翻译、原作中乡民的对话用了俚语；翻译时要体现这个特点，社会典雅的语言原作如果故意是；译文也要选用劳动人民带乡土味的口语，方言"转文"。译文也要有相应的特点，的"

Zhang's notion of translation, in essence, echoes the fundamental idea of Nida's dynamic/functional equivalence theory (1964, 1993), especially its highlighting of the reconciliation between meaning and form, and the responses of the target readership. Though Zhang articulated this perception in his 1980 article, he had been practising it since the early 1930s, when he embarked on his first attempt at translating Hardy's works. His emphasis on both source and receptor cultures is also voiced by other western colleagues. As Munday (2001: 1) points out, translation "… by its nature, is multilingual and also interdisciplinary, encompassing languages, linguistics, communication studies, philosophy and a range of types of cultural studies."

Similarly, Zhang's combination of thorough research with translation can be also explained in the following view:

> A translation is not a monistic composition, but an interpenetration and conglomerate of two Structures. On the one hand there are the semantic content and the formal contour of the original; on the other hand the entire system of aesthetic features bound up with the language of the Translation (Levine 1991, cited in Bassnett 2002: 17).

With such thinking and understanding as to the nature of translation, and on the basis of Zhang's thorough investigation and meticulous reading of the life experiences, mind and ideas, stylistic features and language that brought his translations of Thomas Hardy's works to life, Zhang eventually emerged as a researcher on, and a successful translator of Hardy, which gave him the worthy title of "Expert on Hardy" (Sun 2004).

2.2. Process of Zhang's translation

Based on the scrutiny of Zhang's translational idiosyncrasies and thoughts, the process of Zhang Guruo's translation can be summarized as involving the following major steps, each with various activities and different goals which show how he could stride across linguistic and cultural heterogeneities.

Zhang began each of his translating works with a comprehensive reading of the source text. At this initial stage, thorough reading for complete comprehension of the original work was the primary goal. He did not read for the simple purpose of pleasure or pastime, but for the gaining of broader insights on both the macro- and micro-scales and structures of the entire original work, so that he could re-conceptualize it for the purpose of translation. From the macro-perspective, such comprehension would involve a clear understanding of the theme of the work and the author's thinking, alongside the historic and socio-cultural settings constraining both, etc. Viewed from a micro-perspective, it involved the capturing of the meaning of each sentence, the structural connotations of the syntactical devices and the discourse, and the threads of logic governing the lines, as well as the deliberations hidden in the author's careful choice of words, their sound, form, rhythm and combinations. This would have been a challenging reading experience for Zhang, since barriers of all kinds would arise during the entire absorbing process, given the scope and extensiveness of any of the original works he was attempting to translate.

The demanding task of comprehension for translation purposes compelled Zhang to undertake thorough research and investigation to clear away the difficulties imposed by the differences and distances between the two cultures. This constituted the second major step in the translation process. Researching the contexts and cultures of the source text and the author facilitated Zhang's thorough understanding of the contextual meanings of the English discourse, and also exposed him to the similar conceptualization experiences of the author. Being in essence dependent on and entangled with the previous reading comprehension, this step would involve more extensive reading around the socio-cultural and contextual settings of the source text, accompanied by numerous annotations clarifying the contextual clues. The purpose of this step was to confirm, modify, or even discard the preliminary re-conceptualizations gained through the previous reading comprehension. As noted by Zhang himself, the research and investigation had to be thorough and meticulous; it might even include reading all the books that the author had read, or learning about all the things the author had experienced, so that the translator would be conceptually well-prepared for the translating. With these two steps of reading and researching, Zhang could discover and re-conceptualize the meaning-making process achieved by the author during the writing of the original work, and reach accurate and adequate comprehension of the source text and the author for the benefit of translation.

Then followed the third step of transferring: i.e., using Chinese correspondence to represent the meanings—the explicit or the implicit, the denotative or the contextual, the formal or the intended—of the source text, on the basis of thorough comprehension and accurate re-conceptualization. Guided by his translation precepts, this step involved numerous moves such as weighing, selecting, translating, deleting, revising and experimenting with the target language, along with further and continuous reading and annotating for the purpose of choosing appropriate expressions in the target language or bridging the extreme gaps between the two cultures. While these selective moves would dominate and persist throughout the transferring movement, intermittent researching and investigating would also intermingle in the process, modifying or validating each attempt at meaning construction in the target language.

The fourth major step involved the reconstructing of the source text meanings with the transferred materials into a target text that would cater well to the targeted socio-cultural context and to new readers. Although selective moves would continue during this step, adaptations, compromises, innovations, and even reconciliations between notes and translations would have become the main focus as Zhang's concerns shifted from finding appropriate expressions in the TT to manipulating the target phrases for expressiveness. In this step the translator's weighing of possibilities would also be different, being very much slanted towards the seeking of balance between domestication and foreignization, and between faithfulness and expressiveness.

The fifth major step in Zhang's translation process involved polishing the final translation. Comparative readings were undertaken between the source and target texts to make sure the four-fold faithfulness was reached in the translation, especially in the parts where culture-loaded situations had been pondered. Careful proof-reading of the target text was also a major part of this step to ensure the text's expressiveness, to eliminate any possible mistakes or awkwardnesses, and to see whether the annotations best served the readers. For these goals, adjustments and modifications in the diction, structures, or note entries would be continued by the translator, but on a much milder scale, till the entire translation was regarded as satisfactory enough for publication. Upon completion of this step, Zhang would finally have traversed from re-conceptualizing the source text to re-constructing the target text, thereby completing his meaning-making journey across languages, cultures, and spaces.

However, for Zhang, it was not the end of the entire circle of the translation process. After the translation was published, responses and feedback from readers and critics would be collected. With the development of the target society and people, and with new experiences gained through other translations, some parts of the first version might be deemed as expedient, hesitant, or inappropriate in the new contexts, or better language solutions could be reached in the changed target situations. Having accumulated these reactions, the translator might choose years later to revisit the source and target books, and perhaps to initiate another round of meaning-making through all or some of the steps outlined above.

With this new edition having been accepted and published, the entire circle of Zhang's translation process would be officially concluded, and his efforts in reading and researching achieved. From the steps summarized above, one thing is clear, i.e., that Zhang's translation process was marked throughout by his constant return to reading and research, and the accompanying escalation in the quality of the final version.

3. Trajectory of the translator's agency

With the moves and goals in the steps described above, the trajectory of Zhang's exercise of agency power can be clearly traced. This section will therefore focus on examining how Zhang exercised his agency power and how his position changed in the power relationship with the source texts and the authors.

3.1. Empowerment of the translator

At the threshold of each translation, the source text and the author enjoy the supreme authoritative position in the enterprise of translation, while the translator, in this case Zhang Guruo, is merely a silent, passive but pious listener to the source text. Like any other ordinary English reader, he would know little of the content or the thoughts of the original work and would be full of curiosity. But unlike the English reader, he would know his mission and the huge challenges ahead of him in introducing the English canon to a Chinese readership. So he would have to conquer a huge linguistic and cultural Qomolangma[5] constructed by an author's recounting of life and society in a distant and completely different space. With determination and confidence, and through careful perusing of the source text, he would gradually make sense of the meanings between the lines. As the reading progressed, understanding would increase and his passiveness would begin to diminish. As his energy levels rose he would gradually start to participate in the mental and spiritual dialogue with the source text and the author. Therefore, the initial step of reading comprehension would see the change in the translator's position from that of a powerless, passive reader into an active dialoguer. The translator's agency would be best represented in his courage, determination, confidence, and persistent reading, and was also projected through his plans for approaching the work and the author, as well as through his knowledge of various means and resources for the mission. Upon the

---

[5] Known to the English reader as Mt Everest …

completion of this step, the source text would retain its authoritative status but the supremacy has been shaken, because the translator is no longer a passive or powerless audience but an active participant of the meaning-making activity.

The on-going second step would start with Zhang's emergence as an informed rather than an ignorant reader of the source text, and he would become more active than ever in his comprehension and annotations while making more resources available to himself, which in turn would further facilitate his dialogism with the original work and author. Continuing to ask about the 'how-and-whys' in order to ascertain the 'in-and-outs', he would note the research results for later reference. His mind would become increasingly active and powerful as he carried on synthesizing all the pieces into bigger conceptual frameworks for further comprehension and research. Gradually, the mist shrouding the source text would dissipate, and once the doubts and challenges blocking his thorough comprehension for translation had been resolved, the logic lines of the original work and the buried thoughts of the author would begin to emerge. At the end of the second step, when the entire macro- and micro-logic structures of the original work had fully emerged and clear links between various logic levels had been built, almost all myths surrounding the source text would have been broken, and an empathy towards the source text and the author would have been established in the translator, enabling him to see what the author saw and to feel what the author felt. Thus, the translator, having gained a complete re-conceptualization of the ST's meaning, would be ready with the conceptual framework for the next step of transferring.

Completion of the second step marks the upgrade of Zhang's status from an active reader of the source text to mastering its author's mind; it also sees the stepping-down of the source text and its author from the altar of supremacy. Void of all myths, the distance between the source text and the translator has been greatly shortened or even effaced, and the ST's meaning is now easily reachable and attainable by the translator. It is worth noticing that it is the translator's agency that prompts these changes. His agency is best represented in the conceptual frameworks he has vigorously formed while programming all the leads that have been researched for understanding cultural heterogeneities and the meaning-making processes of the ST. These mental frameworks, in recurring and spiral patterns, enable the translator consistently and progressively to negotiate the various meanings with the source text's author, until all doubts have been clarified and agreements reached.

With the ST's meaning and thought entirely under control, Zhang's agency would be fully unleashed in the third and the fourth steps of his translation. This could be directly observed in the entire process of assigning the ST meanings to Chinese expressions, and trimming the target sentence structures for accuracy and adequacy, and this powerful ability to cope with complexity and heterogeneity is something that was especially arresting in Zhang's translation competence. It was his knowledge of the complex nature and characteristic of the translation work that pushed him to be "constantly on the lookout for new ways of saying something" (Neubert 2000: 4). With a solid Chinese foundation, he related the ST's meanings through flexible diction and dexterous dispatches of various Chinese expressions, because maximum faithfulness and expressiveness, experiments or innovations with the target language would be initiated through creative combinations or segmentations of word meanings and forms. As a translator, Zhang's synthesis of the ST meaning and the target language bestowed a very subjective power on him.

Interestingly enough, this stage of representation of the source text meanings was marked by the dominant place of the translator in the foreground, with the source text and its author in the background. In the process of Zhang's reconstructing of meaning, the translator appeared to be the one controlling, concluding and conversing loudly, while the author and the source text remained reticent, static, or seemingly powerless to take any action apart from being cut up or exposed by Zhang while waiting to be translated for the target readership. Since the direction and development of the meanings of the translated text were still governed by the source text, the translator still had to revisit it to make sure that the translation was on the right track. Therefore, the translator seemed now to have become the spokesman or authorized agent of the source text and its author for the target audience. Though the source text and its author still administered Zhang and his translation, they could only do this silently and to a limited extent. The translator's position will have been achieved when he exercised his success over the Chinese language, translation skills and various meaning-making stunts to create the same story in the target language, because by then, he had become a potent story teller, or a writer—narrating the same story as the source text. This dominance of the translator continues throughout the whole revision stage, with a slight rise to the fore of the source text and its author during the proof-reading period.

The change of Zhang's power position as noted above reveals this fact: the process of translation actually witnesses the progressive empowerment of the translator. In the trajectory of Zhang's empowerment, he began as a passive and silent audience, but gradually grew into an active reader by reading and learning before he became an active participant in meaning negotiation with the source text. With more reading and research, his learning was further enhanced till he finally mastered the mind of the source text and its author. Upon completing the ST's meaning restoration, he embarked on the meaning re-constructing journey and eventually emerged as an authorized agent of the source text, a potent story-teller to the target audience. But what was the driving force behind his empowerment? How does that force enable his agency to traverse the meanings across contexts, languages and space?

4. The global power and the local power of the translator

For a better picture of the driving force underpinning Zhang's agency, it is necessary to make a distinction between the global and the local perspectives of a translator's subjective agency. The global perspective of a translator's agency, or the global power of the translator, is closely related to the translator's metacognitive knowledge (Flavell 1979, 1987; Wenden 1998). According to Wenden (1998), metacognitive knowledge, or metacognitive awareness, includes learners' "person knowledge", task knowledge, and strategy knowledge. Person knowledge is the general knowledge that learners have acquired about human factors which facilitate or inhibit learning. Task knowledge includes the purpose and nature of the learning task, and the demands of the learning task. Strategic knowledge includes knowledge about effective strategies and how to use them for particular tasks (Wenden 1998).

Inheriting the cognitive strand of language learning, the global power of a translator is defined as the translator's metacognitive knowledge toward translation. In a translation task, metacognitive knowledge includes the translator's awareness of *human factors*—what the self and other people can or cannot do to contribute to the translation; *the measurement of the task*—the scope, spectrum and difficulty level of the translation task at hand; and *corresponding strategies*—what measures or actions to take to arrive at various solutions both during the reading comprehension stage and the representation stage. More specifically, it includes the translator's knowledge or awareness of how to approach the meaning of the source text accurately and adequately; how to reconstruct it faithfully and expressively; what tenets to follow in planning, organizing, executing and evaluating the task and the translation; and above all, the translator's confidence about fulfilling the task. Therefore, the global power of a translator is concerned more with the translator's awareness of the macro perspectives of translation—the guiding principles, heuristic estimation, compensation mechanism and plan for action.

The local power of a translator, in contrast, is concerned with the local perspective of the translator's agency, and is defined as the various knowledge and actions that the translator adopts in the course of *doing* the actual translation under the guide of his/her meta-cognitive awareness. Specifically, it includes the various linguistic and non-linguistic resources of the translator, and/or actions adopted to enhance learning or efface the discrepancy between the current and required resources while proceeding with the translation task or seeking new translation solutions.

In the case of Zhang Guruo, this global power was best reflected in his awareness of utilizing contextual and/or prior knowledge (including non-linguistic knowledge) such as topic, genre, culture, and other schema knowledge stored in long-term memory to "build a conceptual framework for comprehension" (Vandergrift 2004: p. 4), and to guide and justify his choice of target words or structures for representation (that is, the using of top-down processes). The local power of Zhang could be observed in the moves and actions he took while approaching the source text meanings through extensive readings and meticulous research—clarifying every piece of doubt, disparity, and difficulty to construct the meaning. It can also be witnessed in his various attempts to play with the target words and expressions in order to preserve the meaning and style of the original work, as demonstrated in the meaning re-constructing stage.

In synchronizing the process of Zhang's translation and his empowerment, one important feature stands out—his extraordinary literacy ability, which is to say his ability to read for knowledge and interest, to write coherently and to think critically about the written word. With excellent literacy, Zhang learnt quickly and absorbed new knowledge fast. This learning, in turn, further enhanced his literacy. Such mutual enhancement of learning and literacy accompanied Zhang throughout his empowerment. In addition, both his global and local subjective powers were deeply rooted in his extraordinary literacy in both languages. It may therefore be assumed that, as an indispensable element of his accomplished translation and empowerment, Zhang's literacy was the true force behind the success of all his translations.

5. Driving force of the translator's agency power

5.1. Exercising the translator's agency power

With this inference in mind, three examples of Zhang's translation are examined to confirm the force of literacy accomplishment in his empowerment and in his translation. Three short pieces are excerpted from his Chinese translation of Hardy's *The Return of the Native*. These frequently cited and much lauded examples demonstrate Zhang's translation feat in dealing with long English sentences, rhetoric, and oral style. Using the sentence as the unit of translation, Zhang reveals how Catford's notion of equivalence can be achieved at sentential level (Xiong 2005: 254). Zhang's Chinese translation not only reproduces the source text meanings, but also observes the original structure and style as a whole. In light of this research, this is precisely where Zhang exercises his global and local power.

Excerpt 1

> **ST:** To recline on a stump of thorn[1] / in the central valley of Egdon,[2] / between afternoon and night,[3] / as now,[4] / where the eye could reach nothing of the world[5] / outside the summits and shoulders of the heath land[6] / which filled the whole circumference of its glance,[7] / and to know[8] / that everything around and underneath[9] / had been from prehistoric times[10] / as unaltered[11] / as the stars overhead,[12] / gave ballast[13] / to the mind adrift on change,[14] / and harassed by irrepressible New[15].
>
> **TT:** 从下午倒夜那段时间 [3]/ 就像现在说得这样 [4]/ 跑到爱敦荒原的中心山谷, [2] / 依在一棵棘树的残株上面 [1]/ 举目看来 外面的景物 一样也看不见 [5] / 只有荒丘羌阜四面排列 [6,7] / 同时知道 [8] / 地上地下周围一切 [9] / 都像天上星辰一样 [12] / 从有史以来一直到现在 [10] / 就丝毫没生变化 [11] / 那时候 我们那种随着人世的变幻无常而票白不定的感觉 [14] / 那种由于现代还无法制止的日新月异而受到烦扰的心情 [15] / 就觉得安宁稳沉 有所商托。 [13]

(As cited in Xiong 2005: 253)

The ST of Excerpt 1 is a long English sentence of 77 words in a heavily-embedded structure. Zhang's translation also preserves the form of the long sentence, but in a typical diffusive Chinese sentence pattern, with 179 Chinese characters. Preserving the same sentence structure in this way was unique in Zhang's time (the translation was done in the 1930s and revised in the 1950s), when the usual treatment would have been to split the ST into shorter Chinese sentences separated with full stops/periods, given the heaviness of the thoughts embodied in the ST. Close comparison reveals that the internal sense groups of the ST have been re-shuffled in the TT, in a manner that neither the ST meaning nor the force conveyed in its parallel structure is attenuated.

To illustrate this change, all phrases that constituted a sense group in the ST of Excerpt 1 were numbered, so that its reshuffled order can be observed in the change of the series number of the TT internal phrases. For example, the first phrase "To recline on a stump of thorn"[1] in the ST was shifted into the fourth segment in the TT, while the fourth phrase "as now"[4] in the ST was lifted into the second segment in the TT, and the sixth and the seventh phrases in the ST were combined into the sixth segment of the TT. Commas are used in the TT to join all these segments, which are arranged according to the temporal and spatial logic order of Chinese parataxis, but the global form of the ST remains the same and the meaning is also guaranteed with accurate diction.

In the light of this research, the skill of re-shuffling word order and using commas is precisely where Zhang's literacy accomplishment is disclosed and his agency unleashed. His good command of reading and writing in English enables him to perceive the force and meaning conveyed in the deliberated ST sentence structure. This perception, in turn, initiates his exercise of subjective agency to fulfill the translation. With the global guide of the four-fold faithfulness tenet, Zhang clearly knew that he was to produce a TT that would maintain both the intention and force of the original at the textual and sentential level. Locally, he dictates affluent diction choice and creative use of Chinese words to compensate for the loss of original meaning caused by the new cultural context. This local power can be observed in his Chinese treatment of the fifth to seventh phrases of the ST:

… [N]othing of the world[5] outside the <u>summits and shoulders of the heath land</u>[6] <u>which filled the whole circumference of its glance</u>[7], …

This was translated into the fifth and sixth segments of the TT as:

… 一样也看不见[5]，只有荒丘矮阜四面环列[6,7]，……"

In the TT segment, the double-underlined Chinese phrase "荒丘芜阜"[6] is creatively coined by the translator and carries exactly what is meant by the source phrase "the summits and shoulders of the heath land". Literally, "荒" means barren or desolate; "丘" means mound or hillock; "芜", overgrown with weeds; "阜", is a synonym of "丘". The new combination of the Chinese phrases not only represents the exact meaning of the ST, but also expresses the depressed feeling of fatalism that permeates Hardy's work, since each of the four choices carries the taste of a depressed emotion. In addition, all four of the Chinese characters are of formal use. The character "阜" (synonym of "丘", meaning mound, or hillock) is a rather formal word found only in classical writings. Without the blessing of literate accumulation and accomplishment, it would not have been possible for Zhang to reach such a word and combine it with the other three characters into "荒丘芜阜" a concise and vivid phrase that possesses both the felt meaning of the ST, as well as the beauty of the symmetrical cadence of Chinese expressions.

Excerpt 2

ST: A well-proportioned mind is one which shows no particular bias; one of which we may safely say that it will never cause its owner to be *confined as a madman, tortured as a heretic, or crucified as a blasphemer.* Also, on the other hand, that it will never cause him to be *applauded as a prophet, revered as a priest, or exalted as a king.* Its usual blessings are happiness and mediocrity. It produces *the poetry of Rogers, the paintings of West, the statecraft of Nurth, the spiritual guidance of Sumer;* enabling its possessors *to find their way to wealth, to wind up well, to stop with dignity off the stage, to die comfortably in their beds, and to get the decent monument which, in many cases, they deserve.*

TT:

中正平易的性情是不露特别的乖僻的；我们敢说 一个有这种性情的人，决不会叫人家当作疯子把他拘禁 认为异端把他用刑烤打，堪作亵渎神明把他在十字架上钉死。反过来讲 他也决不会让人家把他当得像先知，尊敬得像祭司，推崇得像国王。这种性情通常给人的幸福是快乐和平庸。露的诗歌 维持的绘画 呶司的政治手腕 素米的宗教指示，都是这种性情的产物 有这种性情的人 都能致富，都能有好下场，都能很稳当地从舞台下台，都能舒服地在他老死床上 都能得到体面的坟墓 本来这种东西 加在他们身上，倒他并不全不应该。

(As cited in Xiong 2005: 255)

---

[6] "荒" means barren, or desolate; "丘" means mound, or hillock; "芜", overgrown with weeds; "阜", a synonym of "丘". All four characters are of formal use.

What is essential for literary creation or recreation is the powerful use of rhetoric devices. This is also a major characteristic of Hardy's works (Sun 2004; Xiong 2005). Excerpt 2 shows the idiosyncratic use by Hardy of parallel devices (here in italics) at sentential, phrasal, and word level to add force and eloquence to his expressions. Obviously this rhetoric characteristic was correctly perceived by the translator, because it was successfully introduced to the Chinese readership by way of similar devices in the TT (as underlined) without any attenuation of the original thoughts or the perlocutionary force. In terms of structure, the parallel use of "part participle + as phrase" in the ST was replaced with the repeated use of the "把" structure and "… 得像…" structure in Chinese. Thus the TT not only maintained the smoothness and ornament of the ST, but also the exact word order of the ST. Similarly, the repeated use of "noun + of phrase" of the ST was replaced by the "的" phrases in Chinese; the "to do" parallels in the ST, by the repetition of "都能" in the TT, all illustrate the translator's excellent command of Chinese rhetoric structures. In addition, the use of Chinese four-word set phrases such as "酷刑拷打" (torture), "亵渎神明" (blaspheme), "冠冕堂皇" (with dignity), "抽身下台" (off the stage), and "舒舒服服" (comfortably) also adds much weight to the expressiveness of the TT in conveying the meaning and force of the original structure, which display Zhang's large stores of Chinese vocabulary and flexible use of Chinese diction and rhetoric devices. It also reveals Zhang's superb writing feat in Chinese. Consequently, the entire TT of this excerpt reads as eloquently and forcefully as the ST, which enables the target readers to appreciate the rhetoric charm of Hardy to the utmost.

It was not surprising for Zhang to have come up with a flow of expressions like these. In fact, he had been well-known for his writing accomplishment in classical Chinese since middle school, having entered the first modern middle school in China in 1922. As well as modern courses including English, physics, chemistry and mathematics, he finished reading many traditional Chinese classics and systematically studied the traditional Chinese exegesis and the philosophy of Zhuangzi. During this period of his education, his poems or prose, written in parallel metric style, appeared frequently in the school newspaper. With adept use of parallels, his article "A Comparison of Chinese and Western Cultures", written in traditional Chinese prose, won first prize in the school's writing competition and was highly praised by Dr Hu Shi, head of the judging panel. As one of the first batch of graduates from China's very first modern middle school, he was entrusted to compose the preface for the alumni memoir scroll, and his writing impressed all his fellow graduates with its rhetoric talent and parallel metrical accomplishment.

In a sense, without adequate literacy accomplishment in both languages, it would not have been possible for Zhang to exhaust the subtle but powerful force and feelings underpinning the author's dictions, structures, or other deliberate linguistic arrangements, nor would he have tapped the potential of the Chinese language to produce a target text that carried equal weight artistically. Zhang himself often reflected on the benefit of his good command of English in his later translations (Sun 2004). The connections between his Chinese literacy accomplishment and his success in translation are also noted by other translation researchers. As noted by Xiong (2005),

> Zhang Guruo had familiarized himself with classical Chinese poems and books when he was only a child, and had developed excellent writing ability with classical Chinese. Upon graduating from primary school, he had finished many Chinese classics and laid a solid literacy foundation of Chinese. His poems or writings in parallel style often appeared in the school paper while he was in middle school. Therefore, he can translate English parallel structures with facility and often in one sprint (p. 254).[7]

From analysis of Excerpt 2, it is clear that, blessed with literacy, Zhang exercised his global power to decide what aspects of the ST should be preserved, and what reading effect should be achieved in the TT; accordingly choosing appropriate words, structures, and rhetoric devices with his local power to accomplish his global design of the translation task.

Excerpt 3

Dialogue A

ST: "Do you love me now?"
"Who can say?"
"Tell me; I will know it!"
"I do, and I do not," said he mischievously. "That is, I have my times and my seasons. One moment you are too tall, another moment you are too do-nothing, another too melancholy, another too dark,

---

[7] Translation by the author. The source text is:
"打下了深，在高小就已博览古典著作，擅长写作，张谷若自幼熟读诗书
翻译排比结构可谓得，读初中时已常在校刊发表诗及骈体文。厚的汉语功底
。一蹴而就，心应手"

another I don't know what, except that you are not the whole world
to me, that you used to be, my dear. But you are a pleasant lady to
know, and nice to meet, and I dare say as sweet as ever-almost." (p.
96)

TT: "你现在还爱不爱我?"

"谁知道那。"

"你得告诉我; 我一定要弄个明白。"

"我也爱 也不爱"他故意逗着说 "换句话说 我有我的节气和时季。有的时
候你太高傲 有的时候你太娇懒 有的时候你太忧郁 有的时候你太凄楚
有的时候我也说不上来究竟你怎么样 我只知道你已经不是从前那种我惟一的
意中人了, 我的亲爱的, 不过和你认识起来 还是令人愉快 和你相会起来
还是令人舒服 而且把你整个看来 我敢说还是跟从前一样地甜美——
差不多一样的甜美。" (p. 115)

Dialogue B

ST: "Yes, yes—that's it. But, Timothy, hearken to me," said the
Grandfar earnestly, "Though known as such a joker, I be an
understanding man if you catch me serious, and I am serious now. I
can tell'ee lots about the married couple. Yes, this morning at six
o'clock they went up the country to do the job, and neither vell nor
mark have been seen of 'em since, though I reckon that this
afternoon has brought 'em home again, man and woman-wife, that
is. Isn't it spoke like a man, Timothy, and wasn't Mis'ess Yeobright
wrong about me?"

TT:

"是 是 正是。不过 提摩太 你听俺说 "阚特大爷恳切地说 "虽然都知道
俺开哈哈 可是俺只要一正经起来 俺就是一个很明向理事的人了。这阵儿俺
正经起来了。俺能告诉你们 他们 新成家的那两口子许多故事。今儿早起六点钟
他们一块去办这件事了。从那个时候以后, 他们 可就无影无踪了。不过俺想
他们 今儿过晌儿已经都回来了, 成了一男一女——
啊 不是 一夫一妻。边похож说话 不像个人儿似的吗?姚白太太不是冤枉俺了吗
?"(p. 25)

(As cited in Xiong 2005: 255)

In Hardy's *The Return of the Native*, accent was successfully used as a
linguistic marker to distinguish people of different social and educational
backgrounds. The author's use of "Wessex dialect" was lauded as a
distinctive stylistic feature of his novel. Comparison between the two
dialogues in Excerpt 3 reveals how this feature is reflected in the printed
form. In dialogue A, Standard English is used with no spelling or
pronunciation deformations. Also the relatively long sentence with
obvious parallel structures spoken in the last paragraph also indicates the

well-educated background of the male speaker. In dialogue B, however, there are a bundle of linguistic deformations, such as: "'ee" for thee, "'em" for them, "Mis'ess" for Mistress/Mrs, archaic expressions like "hearken", "thee", as well as ungrammatical expressions such as "I be an understanding man", "Isn't it spoke like a man". These non-standard expressions, known as dialect markers, were deliberated by Hardy to show the rustic background of the speaker in dialogue B.

This stylistic feature was clearly noticed and perceived by Zhang Guruo. When translating the rustic flavours of the dialogue of speaker B, Zhang employed local dialect expressions used in the countryside around his hometown (in Shandong province) to replace those dialect markers in the ST. The underlined expressions in the TT of dialogue B, such as "俺" "打哈哈" "明向晓事" "这阵儿" "不像个人儿似的"[8] etc., are highly vernacular local expressions that do not appear in standard mandarin Chinese. With their strong countryside flavour, they leave Chinese readers with a strong impression of the rural background of the speaker, who sounds rustic and vulgar, without much education—an impression exactly the same as that conveyed to the source text readers. Therefore, with the employment of his hometown dialect, Zhang successfully traversed the stylistic meanings of the source text across spaces. Though the move was doubted and challenged later by other translators or researchers over its appropriateness or legitimacy, and although the debate is on-going even to this day, the sample suffices to show how the global and local power of the translator's agency interact with each other during the translator's decision-making process concerning what aspect of the ST should be preserved and how to achieve it.

Divided opinions on Zhang's final version of dialogue B also indicate that the translator's agency power can be exercised locally, as demonstrated in his distancing of the translation from the ST to domesticate the source culture, or alternatively, preserving the ST culture in the translation to inform the target readers, but the final direction of the choice is shaped and determined by the global perspective of the translator's agency, or the meta-cognitive awareness of the translator. The debate over Zhang's practice also shows how vulnerable the source text can be when heading into a new culture. This, in a sense, further reveals the increase in the translator's power position and the decrease in the source text's supremacy upon the final stages of the translation process.

---

[8] All are typical expressions in the Shandong dialect. '俺' means 'I'; '打哈哈' means 'joking'; '晓事明向' means 'understanding or considerate'; '这阵儿' means 'at this moment'; '不像个人儿似的' means 'not like a man'.

5.2. From literacy to translation literacy

The above analysis indicates that language literacy indeed contributes as a driving force underpinning the translator's use of global power and local power during comprehension and meaning-restructuring. But language literacy alone is not enough to explain Zhang's awareness of the ends and the means of his translations; nor is it enough to justify his translation choices. Likewise, it is not enough for a person who possesses high literacy in two languages to become an expert translator naturally since "mastery of a foreign language does not suffice (to produce successful translations); it can only be a good base for translation" (Shiyab & Lynch 2006: 264).

However, understanding Zhang's literacy can be different if it is combined with a translator's local and global power and perceived under the larger social context of translation studies and literacy studies. Enlightened by the New Literacy Studies' recognition of "multiple literacies" (Street 2000: 1), Zhang's literacy and translation expertise, as demonstrated in the process, practice and protocol of his translation, explains his high "translation literacy", that is, his expertise in understanding the norms and nature of translation and the fulfillment of the task. It is the possession of both literacy and translation literacy that enables Zhang's acquiring of "translation competence" (Wilss 1982; Nurbert 2000).[9]

Therefore, the translation literacy proposed here includes "expertise", identified as one of the three basic categories[10] in the history of translation (Lefevere 1990: 15). It includes, at a global level, a translator's meta-cognitive awareness of translation, and at a local level, his exercise of

---

[9] Wilss's concept of translation competence subsumes "three partial competences: first-language competence (L1), second-language competence (L2), and a supercompetence that allow mediation between L1 and L2" (2001, first published 1982). Neubert and other scholars specify five parameters of translational competence, viz. "(1) language competence, (2) textual competence, (3) subject competence, (4) cultural competence and, last but not least, (5) transfer competence" (Neubert 2000; Schaffner 2000).

[10] Lefevere defines three basic categories in the history of translation. "These categories are: **authority** (the authority of the person or institution commissioning or, later, publishing the translation: the patron; the authority of the text to be translated, in this case a central text in the source culture; the authority of the writer of the original, in this case the most absolute authority one can imagine, and the authority of the culture that receives the translation); **expertise**, which is guaranteed and checked, trust, which survives bad translations; **and image**, the image a translation creates of an original, its author, its literature, its culture."

agency and proficiency. Translation literacy highlights the translator's social awareness and political engagement, and helps translators to

> [D]ecide on a foreign text and develop a discursive strategy, taking the target language on ... a 'line of escape' from the cultural and social hierarchies which that language supports, using translation to 'deteriorate' it. (Venuti 1992: 11)

The notion of translation literacy is especially illuminating for the development of professional translators. Literacy is only the first step to establishing trust. Translation literacy guarantees the successful execution of that trust. While literacy alone does not produce accomplished translators, translation literacy is the final step of translator development.

6. Conclusion

On the basis of scrutiny of Zhang's translation process and his agency power trajectory during translation, the following conclusions can be generated.

First, the trajectory of the translator's agency power can be best captured in the various steps of the translation process, in the translator's empowerment, and, above all, in the interactions of the translator's global and local agency power throughout the constructing of the translation enterprise. The translator's subjective agency is the source, means, and end of the translator's empowerment. It is, therefore, the very element that enables and guides the translator traversing the various levels of source text meanings across languages. With substantial reading and research, the translator starts as a meek and docile reader, but gradually emerges as a spokesman of the source text and its author. With interactions between his meta-cognitive knowledge towards the translation task, and the specific means and moves to be adopted, the translator exercises his subjective agency power globally and locally while re-writing the ST in the target culture. Therefore, the distinction of the global power and the local power of a translation is conducive to revealing the power trajectory of a translator's agency.

Second, the translating procedure is never innocent, or void of argument or contention. Instead, it is full of hesitations, recursions, compromises, and deliberations. It provides the very site where a translator exercises his local and global agency power to manipulate the ST and the TT, and to counterbalance with the original author through all the decisions he/she makes to achieve an adequate "re-writing" in the target culture. Therefore, the product of this procedure—translations—are never innocent

"… in the purest possible lexical chamber, untainted by power, time, or even the vagaries of culture. Rather, translations are made to respond to the demands of a culture, and of various groups within that culture" (Bassnett & Lefevere 1990: 7).

Third, language literacy is the force underpinning the translator's exercise of agency. It empowers the translator, equips him with the forceful and effective use of words and expressions in the target language. It also enables the translator to add personal aesthetic and ideological values into the translation. As revealed in the case of Zhang, literacy serves as an indispensable part of the translator's control and competition with the source text author, because "… writing is usually associated with power, and particularly with specifically modern forms of power" (Collins and Blot 2003: 5). However, literacy alone does not cover all the expertise that Zhang has demonstrated in his translations. Combined with his translation literacy, Zhang successfully traverses the distance in meanings between the source text and the target text.

References

Bassnett, Susan and Andre Lefevere, eds. 1990, *Translation, History and Culture*, London and New York: Pinter.

Bassnett, Susan 1996, "The meek or the mighty", in R. Alvarez and M. Carmen Africa, eds., *Translation, Power, Subversion,* Philadelphia PA: Multilingual Matters Ltd, 10-24.

——. 2002, *Translation Studies* 3rd ed., New York: Routledge.

Borgeaud, Emily 2011, "The agency of the printed page: Re-contextualizing the translated text", in Anthony Pym, ed., *Translation Research Projects 3,* Tarragona, Spain: Intercultural Studies Group, 31-42.

Catford, John Cunnison 1965, *A Linguistic Theory of Translation*, Oxford: Oxford University Press.

Chan, Leo Tak-Hung 2004, *Twentieth Century Chinese Translation Theory: Modes, Issues and Debates*, Amsterdam and Philadelphia: John Benjamins Publishing.

Collins, James and Richard Blot 2003, *Literacy and Literacies: Text, Power and Identity*, Cambridge: Cambridge University Press.

Fairclough, Norman 1989, *Language and Power*, London: Cambridge University Press.

——. 2001, *Language and Power*, 2nd ed., London: Pearson Education Limited.

Flavell, J. 1979, "Metacognition and cognitive monitoring: A new area of cognitive development enquiry", *American Psychologist*, 34, 906-911.

Flavell, J. H. 1987, "Speculations about the nature and development of metacognition", in F. E. Weinert, and R. H. Kluwe, eds., *Metacognition, Motivation and Understanding,* Hillsdale, NJ: Erlbaum, 21-29.

Graddol, David 1994, "Three models of Language Description", in David Graddol and Oliver Boyd-Barrett, eds., *Media Text: Authors and Readers*, Clevedon UK: Multilingual Matters, 1-27.

Haddadian-Moghaddam, Esmaeil 2011, "Agency in the translation and production of *The Adventures of Hajji Baba of Ispahan* into Persian", *Target*, Vol. 23, no. 2, 206-234.

Basil and Jeremy Munday 2004, *Translation: An Advanced Resource Book*, London and New York: Routledge.

Hermans, Theo 1996, "The Translator's Voice in Translated Narrative", *Target*, Vol. 8, no. 2, 23-48.

Krings, Hans P. 1987, "The Use of Introspective Data in Translation", in C. Færch and G. Kasper, eds., *Introspection in Second Language Research*, Clevedon UK: Multilingual Matters, 159-176.

Lefevere, André 1990, "Translation: Its Genealogy in the West", in Susan Bassnett and André Lefevere, eds., *Translation, History and Culture*, London: Pinter, 14-28.

Lefevere, André 1992, *Translation, Rewriting and the Manipulation of the Literary Fame*, London and New York: Routledge.

Li, Yingying 2004, "A tentative study of two Chinese versions of *David Copperfield"*, in Sun, Yingchun, ed., *Zhang Guruo Fanyi Yishu Yanjiu: On professor Zhang Guruo's Art of Translation,* Beijing: China Translation and Publishing Corporation, 248-282.

Lukits, Stefan 2007, "The power of translation", *Babel*, Vol. 53, no. 2, 147-166.

Merkle, Denise 2009, "Vizetelly & company as (ex)change agent: Towards the modernization of the British publishing industry", in John Milton and Bandia Paul, eds., *Agents of Translation.* Amsterdam/Philadelphia: Benjamins Publishing Company, 85-106.

Milton, John and Paul Bandia eds. 2009, *Agents of Translation,* Amsterdam/Philadelphia: Benjamins Publishing Company.

Munday, Jeremy 2001, *Introducing Translation Studies,* New York: Routledge.

Newmark, Peter 1981, *Approaches to Translation.* Oxford: Pergamon Press.

Neubert, A. 2000, "Competence in Language, in Languages and in Translation", in Christina Schaffner and Beverly Adab, eds., *Developing Translation Competence*, Amsterdam /Philadelphia: John Benjamins Publishing, 3-18.

Nida, Eugene A. 1964, *Toward a Science of Translating*, Leiden: E.J. Brill.

Nida, Eugene A. 1993, *Language, Culture and Translating*, Shanghai: Shanghai Foreign Language Education Press.

Nobrega, Thelma Medici and John Milton 2009, "The role of Haroldo and Augusto de Campos in bringing translation to the fore of literary activity in Brazil", in John Milton and Paul Bandia, eds., *Agents of Translation,* Amsterdam/Philadelphia: Benjamins Publishing, 257-278.

Nord, Christiane 2001, *Translating as a Purposeful Activity: Functionalist Approaches Explained*, Shanghai: Shanghai Foreign Language Education Press.

Paloposki, Outi 2009, "Limits of freedom: Agency, choice and constraints in the work of the translator", in John Milton and Paul Bandia, eds., *Agents of Translation,* Amsterdam/Philadelphia: Benjamins Publishing Company, 189-208.

Schaffner, Christina and Beverly Adab, eds. 2000, *Developing Translation Competence*, Amsterdam /Philadelphia: John Benjamins Publishing.

Shiyab, Said and Michael Stuart Lynch 2006, "Can literary style be translated?", *Babel*, Vol. 52, no. 3, 262-275.

Snell-Hornby, M. 1990, "Linguistic Transcoding or Cultural Transfer? A Critique of Translation Theory in Germany", in Susan Bassnett and Andre Lefevere, eds., *Translation, History and Culture*, London and New York: Pinter.

Street, Brian 2000, "The Limits of the Local-'Autonomous' or 'Disembedding'?", *International Journal of Learning*, 10, 2825-2830.

Sun, Yingchun 2004, *Zhang Guruo fanyi yshu yanjiu: On Professor Zhang Gu-ruo's Art of Translation,* Beijing: China Translation and Publishing Corporation.

Tang, Jun 2007, "The metalanguage of translation; A Chinese perspective", *Target*, Vol. 19, no. 2, 359-374.

Toury, Gideon 1995, *Descriptive Translation Studies—and Beyond,* Amsterdam and Philadelphia: John Benjamins.

Vandergrift, Larry 2004, "Listening to learn or learning to listen?", *Annual Review of Applied Linguistics*, 24, 3-25.

Venuti, Lawrence, ed., 1992, *Rethinking Translation: Discourse, Subjectivity, Ideology.* London and New York: Routledge.

Venuti, Lawrence 1995, *The Translator's Invisibility: A History of Translation*, London and New York: Routledge.

—. 1998, *Scandals of Translation: Towards an Ethics of Difference*, London: Routledge.

Volosinov, V. N. 1973, *Language and Ideology. Marxism and the Philosophy of Language*, Orlando FL: Academic Press.

Wenden, A. 1998, "Metacognitive knowledge and language learning", *Applied Linguistics* 19, 515-537.

Wilss, Wolfram 2001, *The Science of Translation: Problems and Methods*, Shanghai: Shanghai Foreign Language Education Press.

Xiong, Yin 2005, "Comparative analysis on the language characteristics of '*The Return of the Native*' and its Chinese Translation", in Guo, Zhuzhang et al., eds., *Fan Yi Ming Jia Yan Jiu: A Series of Translation Studies in China*, Hubei: Wu Han Education Press, 249-259.

Zhao, Junfeng 2005, "Zhang Guruo and English Literature Translation", in Guo, Zhuzhang et al., eds., *Fan Yi Ming Jia Yan Jiu: A Series of Translation Studies in China*, Hubei: Wu Han Education Press, 240-248.

Zhang, Guruo 1982, "Tan wode fanyi shengya [On my translation career]", in Wang, Shoulan ed., *Dangdai wenxue fanyi baijiatan* [A Collection of Thoughts on Translation by Contemporary Chinese Literary Translators], Beijing: Beijing University Press, 1989, 450-458.

Zhang, Ling 2003, "The translator father in my heart", in Sun, Yingchun ed., *Zhang Guruo Fanyi Yishu Yanjiu: On professor Zhang Guruo's Art of Translation,* Beijing: China Translation and Publishing Corporation, 2004, 18-28.

Zurbach, Christine 2009, "The theatre translator as a cultural agent: A case study", in John Milton and Paul Bandia, eds., *Agents of Translation.* Amsterdam/Philadelphia: Benjamins Publishing Company, 279-300.

MALAYSIA

VITAL ROLES OF A COMMISSIONER IN THE TRANSLATION OF AN ENGLISH NONFICTION TEXT INTO MALAY

NORHAZLINA HUSIN, ROKIAH AWANG AND HASLINA HAROON

1. Introduction

Translation is an activity that has undergone phenomenal growth in today's globalized world. The study of translation has also developed enormously over the years (Hatim & Munday 2004). In recent decades, the field of Translation Studies, particularly in the West, has undergone a shift, from a text-oriented approach focusing on the translation product to a sociological approach with the aim of exploring and investigating the various aspects of the translation process. While the micro-level approach which focuses on close comparative analysis of texts is still popular, it has now come to represent the traditional way of researching translation. Close textual analysis is no longer the sole or main method used to study translation. Translation Studies indeed has developed to include an analysis not only of the translation product but also the translation process.

In the context of Malaysia, where the academic study of translation is still relatively new, many researchers tend to resort to the investigation of translation as a product through the micro-analysis of texts. Many researchers have engaged in discussions on strategies and procedures in translating, covering a wide range of language pairs and genres. This is reflected in the titles of many academic dissertations by scholars in the various institutions of higher education in Malaysia that offer postgraduate studies in languages and translation. Macro aspects of translation receive less attention, possibly due to the fact that it is a relatively new area of research in Malaysia, and also perhaps because text analysis is considered a comparatively easier form of research because of the easy availability of pairs of texts for analysis.

This contribution attempts to demonstrate an alternative method of researching translation, taking as its starting point the view of translation as a process that involves a number of players. While translators are normally the focus in a translation endeavour, they rarely start working without being commissioned to do so. In other words, they often start working on a translation because they are called to do so by clients (Nord 1997). In this sense then, translation is a process involving many stages and continuous interaction among the people assigned to complete the task of bringing the translation to fruition. The people or agents involved in the interaction have certain functions or roles to play to ensure that the target text (TT) that is produced is of good quality. One of the parties involved in this complex operation is the commissioner. While it cannot be denied that the translator is crucial in rendering the source text into the target language, the commissioner plays an equally if not more important role, especially as he/she may influence the production of the TT.

This chapter discusses the vital role of a commissioner in the translation into Malay of a non-fiction text entitled *The World is Flat: A Brief History of the Globalized World in the Twenty-First Century.* Written by Thomas L. Friedman, an American journalist, this book was first published in New York in 2005, while the second and third editions were published in 2006 and 2007 respectively. The first edition of this book is considered as the source text (ST), having been used as the ST during the process of its translation. It was translated into Malay as *Dunia Sama Rata: Sejarah Ringkas Dunia Global Abad ke-21* by a freelance translator assigned by Institut Terjemahan dan Buku Malaysia (ITBM) or The Malaysian Institute of Translation & Books (formerly known as the Malaysian National Institute of Translation). The Malay translation was published in 2010.

2. The Role of a Commissioner

The commissioner is the person who initiates the translation project and requests the translator to produce a TT for a particular purpose and audience (Holz Manttari 1984 and Vermeer 1986 in Nord 1997). The commissioner is also the individual who manages and monitors the overall process of a translation project. The commissioner also decides whether a translation can be published after it has been submitted by the translator. In this paper, the commissioner refers to the institution which starts off the translation project and which offers the work of translating the selected text to the potential translator. Here, the commissioner also includes staff working at the institution.

The translation task is a complex one, involving a number of skills and expertise. It is an activity which requires constant thoughtful deliberation and careful decision-making in order to achieve the best results possible. To ensure the success of a translation task, meticulous planning is needed, a huge task that falls on the commissioner, who must first decide on the text to translate and on the direction and feasibility of the planned translation project.

3. Commissioning a Translation Project

A particular translation project and all the aspects involved in this huge undertaking must be made clear to all the people involved before it gets under way. The commissioning of a translation does not merely mean choosing a text to be translated. In practice it involves structuring the translation task, preparing the book specifications, preparing the work schedule, identifying, choosing and assessing translators and editors, providing the ST to translators, obtaining the translated material from the translators, editing and proofreading the translation, publishing the edited manuscript and distributing the translation to potential readers.

The process may continue if several other steps are included, such as critical reviews of the TT or possibly the translation of the TT into a third language. The translation process only ends when the TT is no longer read, rewritten or republished. This may take weeks, months or even years (Zabalbeascoa 1998). It can be said that the commissioner's role will only come to an end upon the completion of the whole process.

Before any translation work begins, the project must be defined. Commissioning a translation task should ideally start with a feasibility study, the main purpose of which is to gather information on all relevant details such as internal and external constraints which may affect the project, and to consider alternatives and options (Perez 2002). The feasibility of the project should be clear. As Larson (1984: 467) stresses,

> One of the greatest hindrances to producing a good idiomatic translation is the lack of adequate planning before the actual translation begins. Questions like: 'What text is to be translated? Who will translate it? Why has the particular text been chosen? Will it be read? By whom? What effect will it have on the audience? How long will it take to do the project? Is there money available?' should be asked and clearly defined at the beginning of the project.

During this stage, therefore, the commissioner is required to plan the whole process carefully and thoughtfully. Often, a commissioner does not work alone. Help from reviewers is sought when needed, and a good commissioner does not make decisions without asking the opinion of reviewers. The reviewers will normally suggest the suitability of the titles to be translated, which is important since the information given can assist the commissioner in deciding whether or not a particular title should be translated and published. Other pertinent matters, such as the importance and appeal of the text to be translated and its contents and potential readership, also need to be considered. This bird's eye view of the whole process can help the commissioner by ensuring that every step of the process is given due consideration and subsequently by undertaking the project as planned.

The translation activities of ITBM fall into two general categories. One involves the translation of documents such as birth certificates and other official documents, brochures, and manuals, and as such is short-term in nature. The other covers the translation of books and other publications, which will normally require more time. Since the translation of documents can be carried out once payment is received from the customer, the procedure is rather more straightforward. However, the translation of books and other publications involves a much more rigorous and meticulous process. The process of publishing a translated book by ITBM can generally be divided into the following stages: (i) planning the title, (ii) planning the publication, (iii) revising and editing, and (iv) publishing and distributing the final product. These four stages involve specific processes and procedures utilized by the people assigned.

3.1 Planning the Title

The translation of *The World is Flat: A Brief History of the Globalized World in the Twenty-First Century* started off with the planning of the title. This is a crucial initial stage in the translation project. However, it does not mean simply discussing and deciding on the titles to be translated, but also involves the processes of obtaining the copyright to translate and of setting up a project team which will be led by a project manager.

The process of choosing a title to be translated begins with a meeting which is held to discuss titles of books that are shortlisted for translation and which have been reviewed by reviewers appointed by the commissioner. At ITBM, books are chosen to be translated for various reasons. Some are based on a request from a particular institution or organization, others are chosen based on high demand for the ST; while for others, it is due to the importance of the content or because of the perceived literary value. If a particular title is requested for translation, the process of deciding whether or not to proceed can be significantly shortened if the title has already been reviewed and its target readers identified. Early review enables the commissioner to save time when determining the feasibility of the project.

In the case of *The World is Flat*, it was chosen for translation because of the high demand and popularity of the ST. According to ITBM, since the content of the ST was of great importance, it needed be flagged up to the Malay-speaking Malaysian public through a translation.

Once the text is chosen, the process continues, with the next step being to obtain copyright; this done, the copyright can provide the commissioner with facts about the book's specifications and work schedule. For every copyright, an agreed amount has to be paid, depending on the text chosen and its publisher. Some copyrights come with a number of conditions which have to be complied with. For example, some titles are translated through *e-file*. This means that the commissioner has to translate using a specific software package that has been agreed upon and that the cover of the TT cannot be changed. Some ST publishers require the TT to be finalized and published within a certain period of time. Failure to do so can oblige the commissioner, as the TT publisher, to pay an additional amount of money to renew the copyright.

The process of obtaining copyright also puts into motion the planning of the publication, which involves various other processes, for instance the design of the TT cover, the actual translation work, and subsequently the editing.

3.2 Planning the Publication

Planning the publication of the translation involves various processes, namely designing the TT cover, preparing the work and the book specifications, assigning the translator and editor, and translating and editing. Even though this stage of the process mostly involves translating and editing, and as such would mainly occupy the translator and the editor, the commissioner still has a role to play in ensuring that the process proceeds smoothly.

Designing a TT cover is a significant aspect in the process of publishing a translation, since the illustration used on the cover of a book must and should reflect its content and be made relevant and appealing to potential readers in the target culture. This aspect must be taken into consideration when publishing a TT as the illustration used on an ST cover sometimes fails to conform to the target readers' expectations. This element should be analysed in order to understand its function in relation to the book as well as to the source culture (Nord 1997). The design of the cover can sometimes carry negative connotations or invoke negative perceptions from the target readers. Therefore, the commissioner needs to ensure that the ST cover is also "translated" into the culture of the target readers. As for ITBM, the cover of every translated book is also "translated" by taking into account the culture of the target readers, except in the case of *e-file* translation. It is a norm that for an illustration to be used on the TT, it must not have any implicit meaning. This can be clearly seen from the cover of the text analysed.

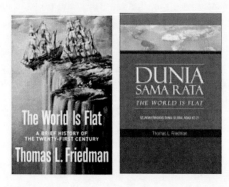

Figure 1: Covers of *The World is Flat* (Original First Edition Cover) and its translation (*Dunia Sama Rata*)

Sometimes, if a new title is translated and is regarded as a continuation of a previously published translation, a similar illustration is used on the subsequent TT published, as can be seen in the following illustration which features the cover of *Panas, Rata dan Sesak,* the Malay translation of Friedman's *Hot, Flat and Crowded*. In this book, Friedman proposes what he believes are the best solutions to global warming, and the best method that the United States should adopt to regain its economic and political stature and to embrace clean energy and green technology. The word *flat* used in this book refers to the term "flatism" which he explained in *The World is Flat.*

Figure 2: Covers of *Hot, Flat and Crowded* and its translation (*Panas, Rata dan Sesak*)

Designing the TT cover also means giving some consideration as to how visible the translator is going to be on the cover. With some publishers, translators will not be given due recognition and their names will not appear on the front cover. In the case of ITBM, the translator's name was previously not printed on the cover but this policy has since been revised, and every translation published will now have the translator's name on its imprint. Putting the translator's name on the cover can be seen as a form of recognition for the translator's hard work, so this initiative by ITBM recognises not only the work carried out by a translator but also the profession and professionalism of translators in Malaysia.

While the design of the TT cover is in progress, other technical tasks are also carried out before the next steps are taken. The preparation of book specifications should include arranging the issuing of the ISBN, and calculating the price of the book based on the publishing costs and the number of copies to be printed. All this might seem rather technical, but it is crucial that these tasks are dealt with before the committee proceeds to the next stage, which is translating.

The commissioner now has to ensure that the translation brief and work specifications are prepared prior to the appointment of a translator, by making certain that before the translator starts translating, he/she receives all the necessary information pertaining to the project which can assist him/her in the translating task, including its objectives, deadlines, the frequency of feedback and the function of the translation. This is the translation brief, which does not tell the translator what to do in detail but provides general guidelines on how to approach the target text. According to Nord (1997: 60), the translation brief should contain the following details:

i)   the intended text function(s),
ii) the target-text audience(s),
iii) the (prospective) time and place of text reception,
iv) the medium over which the text will be transmitted, and
v)   the motive (reason) for the production or the reception of the text.

This should give the translator all the necessary information to enable him/her to undertake the translation. It may be difficult for a translator to proceed without a translation brief, as he/she will need not only to analyze the text but also to identify the potential target readers and the purpose of translating the text. Understandably this is time-consuming, which is why it is much easier for the translator if the client is able to provide him/her with the information needed.

With reference to the translation project, in practice, the information in points (iii) to (v) is usually not stated clearly by the commissioner. Instead the responsibility of conveying this information falls on the in-house staff appointed by the commissioner because they are the actual people who are involved in the process of producing the TT. According to ITBM, the function of the translation of *The World is Flat: A Brief History of the Globalized World in the Twenty-First Century* was to explain and discuss hotly-debated world issues, and was targeted at Malaysians who were interested in knowing and understanding current global concerns. In addition to the obvious sales factor, the motive of ITBM in translating and publishing this work was to help target readers understand the relevant issues and to eliminate unnecessary fear among nations, companies, communities and individuals as they prepared for a globalized future.

Once the translation brief is ready, a translator will be appointed. This process does not merely involve identifying a translator or an editor based on his/her background or qualifications, or sending an appointment letter with the necessary details. As a common procedure, a commissioner will assess the ability of the potential translator by asking the person identified to translate a few pages of the ST within a certain period of time. The commissioner does not normally appoint a translator who does not fulfill the job specification and who does not adhere to the work schedule that he has been given. Although this appears trivial, this specific role of the commissioner will ensure that the translation works proceeds according to the criteria decided. This way, the commissioner will be able to ensure that the project runs smoothly, that the work schedule can be monitored at all times, and subsequently that good translation work can be produced.

The same procedure is applied in appointing an editor. ITBM will normally assign an external editor to do the editing and at the same time to assist the commissioner in reviewing the translation. This review does not mean that the editor will decide on the quality of a translation. It simply provides a snapshot for the commissioner of the translation to be produced. In this way, the commissioner can anticipate the understanding of target readers. After a review has been given by the external editor, the commissioner will proceed with updating the work schedule.

When all instructions, translation information and the work schedule have been clearly understood by the translator, the translation process can proceed. Translating, which is the core part of a translation task, involves the mental operation and/or the linguistic ability of the translator who is given the task of translating, and the process begins when the translator starts to analyse the ST and continues up to the point when he/she has succeeded in transferring or translating the whole text into the target language (TL) (Zabalbescoa 1998).

It is obvious that although translating does not involve the commissioner as the main actor, he/she has a role to play in ensuring that the translation produced is accurate. Before translating a text, a translator is required to hand in a checklist of terms or words that he/she believes will be difficult to translate or that may prove problematic. The project manager will then inform the translator whether the publisher, as the commissioner, has its own equivalent terms for the words given. The project manager must ensure that glossaries and possibly translation memories are up-to-date.

However, instructions alone are insufficient for a translator to complete his task. He must also take the expectations of the clients into consideration (Nord 1991), and must also comprehend fully the aims of the commissioner and the purpose of the TT. In other words, he needs a translation brief. This is the point at which the commissioner's role is played, since the translation brief, as noted, may help the translator in his/her task.

During the translating process, the translator will be closely monitored by the project manager assigned by the commissioner. The commissioner, through the project manager, will occasionally contact the translator in order to anticipate any potential problems. The translator's progress will also be observed according to the timeframe given, and if the commissioner has reason to think that there will be a delay, the translator will be called upon to discuss the matter. The commissioner can therefore decide whether the translation produced actually fulfils the criteria that have been decided. This process is also carried out to minimize errors on the translator's part, which in turn may cause delay in publication if a longer period of time is needed to edit or correct the translated text.

Where the method or strategy of translation is concerned, there is normally no requirement on the part of the commissioner for the translation to be carried out using a certain method or strategy. The translator thus can use any strategy and procedure which he/she believes will be able to fulfill the requirements of the translation and convey the message of the ST. Occasionally, the translation produced may not be agreed upon by the commissioner because certain requirements in the translation brief are not fulfilled. If the translation produced does not meet the requirements, the translator may have to correct it, but if the translation is acceptable, editing will follow. However, if errors are minimal, the translated text will be reviewed by the project manager before being sent to the editor.

3.3 Revising and Editing

Revising and editing are needed in a translation for several reasons. At times the translator, while writing, may briefly forget about his future readers, therefore possibly producing sentences that are not suitable for them. On occasions, a text produced during translation does not adhere to grammatical rules, translation principles, or the writing style of the TL. Revising and editing can also help produce a good translation that has the same effect as the ST, as well as achieving the translation brief. These stages are as important as the rest of the process, and no translation project is finished until sufficient time has been allocated for revision work relating to grammar, spelling, correctness and other technical aspects. The commissioner must ensure that the translator has reviewed his/her work before confirming completion of the work.

According to ITBM and based on the analysis that was undertaken, it was found that the translated text of *The World is Flat* was re-edited to ensure that it fulfilled the predetermined criteria. It might be assumed that the commissioner had no role or influence during the editing and revising stages. However the commissioner's position is significant here, since even though the TT produced by the translator has been edited by an externally appointed editor, the commissioner will still do some editing of his/her own before the typesetting is carried out.

During the revising and editing processes, several types of editing are normally carried out on the text translated by the translator (the TT1). One of them is copyediting. Copyediting is common in the publication of any book, including translations. Copyediting may be defined as checking and correcting a document to bring it into conformity with preset rules. Copyediting involves editing based on correct spelling, sentences, idioms, punctuation, the use of proper grammar and the house style of writing. Copyediting is micro-level work that focuses on the small details of the text. It is therefore done after the translator and editor have completed changes to the content and structure of the text at the macro-level. There is very little point in copyediting a paragraph which the author will later delete (Mossop 2001).

(1)   ST[1]   : ... running the back rooms of major American and European-based multinationals ...

         TT1   : ... sedang menguruskan kerja-kerja sokongan bagi syarikat-syarikat **multinasioanl** Amerika dan Eropah ...

         ETT   : ... sedang menguruskan kerja sokongan bagi syarikat **multinasional** Amerika dan Eropah ...

         TT2   : ... sedang menguruskan kerja sokongan bagi syarikat **multinasional** Amerika dan Eropah ...

The editing of spelling errors (1) is an example of copyediting. The word **multinasional** has been incorrectly spelled as **multinasioanl** and is edited by the initial editor in ETT and retained in TT2.

Besides slowing down the reading and understanding as well as giving an unfavourable impression of the translator, there are times when spelling errors (2) will also cause misunderstanding and confusion on the part of the readers (Mossop 2001).

(2)   ST   : ... on what he presumed to be an open <u>sea</u> route to the **East Indies** – rather than going south and east around Africa ...

         TT1   : ... yang beliau sangkakan sebagai laluan **luat** terbuka timur **India** – berbanding dengan melalui arah selatan dan timur ...

---

[1] ST: Source Text
TT1: Translated Text by Translator
ETT: Editing by Initial Editor
TT2: Published Translated Text

*BT[2]   : ... on what he presumed to be an open **despise** route to **East India** – rather than going south and east around Africa ...

ETT   : ... yang <u>disangka</u> laluan **luat** terbuka <u>ke</u> timur **Hindia** – <u>tidak menuju ke</u> arah selatan dan timur ...

TT2   : ... yang disangka laluan **laut** terbuka ke **Hindia Timur**. Beliau tidak menuju ke arah selatan dan timur ...

There are two spellings that were edited by ITBM (2). The spelling of the word itself is not totally incorrect but the word, if retained, conveys a meaning that is different from the intended meaning. The word **luat** is used in the translation and edited by the initial editor. It can be assumed that the word **luat** is a typing error on the translator's part. Hence, the word **luat** is edited into **laut** to suit its equivalent term, **sea,** in the ST.

Another word edited is **Indies**. This word is translated as **India** by the translator. It is then edited as **Hindia** in ETT by the external editor. However, the phrase **timur Hindia** in ETT is edited by ITBM and changed into **Hindia Timur** in TT2. **Hindia Timur** and **timur Hindia** are two different phrases with two different meanings. **Timur Hindia** is a phrase that refers to the eastern part of India, while **Hindia Timur** is a proper name that refers to the geographical area covering South and Southeast Asia. It is obvious that if the phrase is not edited, it will produce a different meaning from the ST.

The initial editor may sometimes overlook errors in the TT1. This commonly happens if it involves words that are in frequent use. Spelling errors create a bad impression; they suggest that the author and editor are sloppy thinkers, and that the publisher tolerates carelessness. In view of this, and to ensure that the TT is error-free in spelling, the commissioner re-edits the text to rectify the mistakes made.

During the revising process, content editing is also carried out on the translated text. One reason why a text needs to be content-edited is that others may not recognize factual errors. It will not always be obvious that there is an error, especially if there is no spelling error in the phrase or sentence (3).

---

[2] BT: Back translation of TT1

(3)   ST   : *The Bible tells us that God created the world in six days and on the seventh day he rested.*

TT1   : Kitab **Injil** *menceritakan* kepada kita bahawa Tuhan menjadikan dunia dalam masa enam hari dan pada hari ketujuh Dia berehat.

ETT   : Kitab **Injil** *menceritakan* kepada kita bahawa Tuhan menjadikan dunia dalam masa enam hari dan pada hari ketujuh, Dia berehat.

TT2   : *Kitab **Bible** menyatakan bahawa Tuhan menjadikan dunia dalam masa enam hari dan pada hari ketujuh, Dia berehat.*

In this sentence, the word **Bible** is translated as **Injil** by the translator. **Injil** is not a suitable translation for the word **Bible** because these two words carry different meanings with different concepts and teachings. It is undeniable that sometimes translators mistranslate the word **Bible** into **Injil**. To avoid any misunderstanding and confusion, the commissioner has edited it into **Bible**. This means that eventually, the word **Bible** in the ST is transferred directly into the TL.

The commissioner also carries out stylistic editing on every translation produced and submitted. Stylistic editing involves the editing of the use of vocabulary and sentence structure (4) so as to enable it to be easily understood by readers. Stylistic editing is more challenging as it involves the target audience. In this sense, the editor should consider using words that are familiar to the target readers by identifying the target audience, their background and proficiency level because each group has different needs (Mossop 2001).

(4)   ST   : Needless to say, I had only the vaguest appreciation of all this as I left Nandan's office that day in Bangalore.

TT1   : **Tidak perlu untuk dikatakan, saya hanya menerima penghargaan paling kabur** terhadap semua ini **sebaik** saya meninggalkan pejabat Nandan tempoh hari di Bangalore.

ETT   : **Saya sebenarnya masih kurang jelas** terhadap semua ini tatkala saya meninggalkan pejabat Nandan di Bangalore tempoh hari.

TT2   : **Saya sebenarnya masih kurang jelas dengan** semua ini tatkala saya meninggalkan pejabat Nandan di Bangalore tempoh hari.

The phrase **Tidak perlu untuk dikatakan, saya hanya menerima penghargaan paling kabur (BT:** *needless to say, I only received the vaguest appreciation*) has been edited and changed to **Saya sebenarnya masih kurang jelas (BT:** *I am actually still unclear*) by the initial editor so that it will be easier for the target readers to understand. The phrase **Tidak perlu untuk dikatakan, saya hanya menerima penghargaan paling kabur** is considered to be long and too literal and may prove difficult to understand. Simple Malay language should have been used considering that the general public is the target readers. The commissioner will accept the editing done by the initial editor if favourable.

Nevertheless, if the final editing causes confusion, despite the correct spelling, the commissioner will edit it again to ensure that it reflects the content (5).

(5)   ST   : "<u>Honey</u>," **I** confided, "I think the world is flat."

TT1   : "Sayang," **saya** berbisik, "saya rasa bumi ini rata."

ETT   : "Sayang, **abang** rasa bumi ini rata," saya berbisik.

TT2   : "Sayang, **saya** rasa bumi ini rata," saya memberitahunya dengan nada berbisik.

The word **I** in the ST is translated as **saya** by the translator as a pronoun in reference to the writer when he is speaking to his wife. This word was then edited by the external editor to **abang** in ETT. The word **abang** is commonly used by Malays in reference to a husband. Nevertheless, this word is deemed improper to be used among Malaysians in general due to the country's multi-ethnic composition. This word is then edited by the commissioner to **saya**. The first meaning of *abang* is *brother.* To avoid misunderstanding, the commissioner has edited the word with the one that is thought to be more appropriate. This example shows that the commissioner sometimes does agree with what has been translated by the translator.

Before any editing is done, and to ensure that the editing conforms to the required style, the editor is usually provided with a manual or guidelines on the house style of writing (Mossop 2001). This is due to the fact that each publishing house has its own style of writing. The initial editor may overlook this matter since he/she does not work at the institution and is still not familiar with the house style (6).

(6)   ST :   Flattener #2
                  8/9/95
                  When Netscape Went Public

         TT1 :   Perata #2
                  8/9/95
                  Apabila Netscape dibuka kepada orang ramai

         ETT   **PERATA # 2**   :
                         8/9/95

                  Apabila Netscape dibuka kepada orang ramai
         TT2:
                  9 Ogos 1995
                  Apabila Netscape Dibuka kepada Orang Ramai

Based on the writing style decided on by ITBM for the text, every topic is written in bold capital letters. Evidently the translation done by the translator was not favoured by the editor at ITBM. This translation was also accepted by the initial editor. The translation brief indicates that the translation is targeted at Malaysians who use the Malay language. In Malay, the symbol # is not used to indicate numbers. The writer may use the word **Nombor** followed by the numerical figure or just the numerical figure by itself. As for the translation, **Flattener #2** is translated as **PERATA 2** without the # symbol.

This example also demonstrates the different styles of quoting dates between the original writer and the acceptable norm of the TL. The original writer uses numbers and '/' to show dates. In the ST, the number 8 that represents the month of August is followed by day (9) and year (95). This style of writing is common in the West. The convention, however, is different in Malay. According to the Malay convention, the date is mentioned first, followed by month and year. Originally, the date **8/9/95** was translated through borrowing and was not edited by the first editor. If it is retained, most target readers will read it as **8 September 1995**. It was, therefore, edited by the ITBM editor into **9 Ogos 1995** and retained in the final publication. The changes were made in order to conform to a writing style with which the target audience in Malaysia is familiar and to avoid any confusion. In this sentence, the initial editor suggested correcting the initial letter of the words **dibuka, orang** and **ramai** to capital letters and it seems that the commissioner agreed with the suggestions.

In editing a translation, copyeditors are widely expected to make texts conform to something variously called 'correct usage' or 'good grammar' (refer to (7) and (8)).

(7)   ST   : The *fall* 2003 class had 297 Chinese graduate and undergraduate students and 23 Russians.

          TT1   : Kelas pada musim *panas* tahun 2003 mempunyai 297 siswazah yang berasal **daripada** China dan 23 siswazah daripada Rusia.

          ETT   : Kelas pada musim *luruh* tahun 2003 mempunyai 297 <u>orang</u> siswazah yang berasal **daripada** China dan 23 <u>orang</u> siswazah daripada Rusia.

          TT2   : Kelas pada musim *luruh* tahun 2003 mempunyai 297 orang siswazah yang berasal **dari** China dan 23 orang siswazah dari Rusia.

The word **daripada** is edited and changed to **dari** because in Malay, the preposition **daripada** is used to describe a source that is derived from humans, animals, abstracts, the origin of a certain object and difference or comparison. **Dari** is used to describe direction, place or time. In this sentence, the students who attend class during **fall** come from Russia, a country which denotes that the source is a place. It is obvious that the word *panas* in TT1 is edited as *luruh* in ETT. The word *luruh* is the translation of *fall*. The first editor has edited the word with the word that has the correct meaning of *fall* (i.e. autumn).

(8)   ST   : ... left [the Dell factory] to head to the Penang, Malaysia, airport."

TT1   : ... meninggalkan [kilang Dell tersebut] menghala ke **lapangan terbang *Penang*,** Malaysia."

ETT   : ... meninggalkan [kilang Dell tersebut] menghala ke **lapangan terbang *Pulau Pinang*,** Malaysia."

TT2   : ... meninggalkan [kilang Dell tersebut] menghala ke ***Lapangan Terbang Pulau Pinang*,** Malaysia."

The word *airport* in the ST is translated as *lapangan terbang* in TT1 (8). The spelling of the word of *lapangan terbang* is retained in the ETT. It is then re-edited as *Lapangan Terbang* because *Lapangan Terbang Pulau Pinang, Malaysia* is a proper name in Malay and the first letter of every word should be capitalized. The word *Penang* is also edited in ETT and it is retained in TT2. It should be noted that *Penang* is not a word in the Malay language. The name *Pulau Pinang* is normally used in reference to an island state in the north of Malaysia.

During the editing process, it is obvious that when the commissioner does not agree with the translation produced, a correction is made. In some cases, he/she will also change the translation procedures used. This is obvious, as shown in (3) and (6).

As in (3), *The Bible* is translated to *Kitab Injil* through cultural equivalence. It is then edited as a borrowing (*Kitab Bible*) in TT2. The borrowing in Example 6 (*8/9/95*) is edited as a cultural equivalent in TT2. This editing by the commissioner is a good example of the vital role played by the commissioner in the translation of selected text.

Evidently, editing by the initial editor in (3), (5) and (6) was not acceptable to the commissioner's editor. However, this does not mean that the commissioner does not agree with the editing at all. There are times when the commissioner's editor agrees with the editing done by the initial editor (9).

(9)   ST   : Many of the pioneer investors in China *lost their shirts and pants and underwear* – and with China's Wild West legal system there was not much recourse.

TT   : Ramai pelabur pelopor di China *kehilangan baju dan seluar dan pakaian dalam mereka* dan dengan bersandarkan peraturan China's Wild West, tidak terdapat banyak pilihan jalan yang lain.

ETT :   Ramai pelabur awal di China *hilang segala-galanya* dan berdasarkan sistem China yang menindas itu, tidak ada apa yang boleh dilakukan lagi.

TT2 :   Ramai pelabur awal di China *hilang segala-galanya* dan berdasarkan sistem China yang menindas itu, tidak ada apa yang boleh dilakukan lagi.

From the examples given, it can be said that even though the translator has his/her own procedures and strategies for translating, the commissioner may make changes in order to ensure that the translation produced is correct. The commissioner may decide that if the first editing is retained, the translation brief may not be entirely fulfilled. As a commissioner, the publisher has the right to improve a translated text before it reaches the target readers. The commissioner may make some corrections or improvements to the translation during the editing process to ensure that the translation can be accepted and understood. As such, it can be said that the commissioner still has a say in the editing process.

4. Publishing and Distributing the Final Product

Publishing and distributing the final product is the last stage in publishing a translated text, and can only be carried out when the translated text has been revised and edited. This is the point at which the translated text is sent to the Publication Unit, where the process of preparing the mock-up of the translated book is carried out. Here, the design and layout of the book takes place before being sent to the Printing Division for printing. The number of copies printed usually depends on the decision that was made during the initial stage of the process. In the case of ITBM, translated books are usually taken to international conferences or book fairs to be launched, since aside from promoting the books on their own website, this is another way of promoting books that are translated and published by ITBM.

5. Conclusion

Translation is a complex operation which not only involves many different parties but also requires coordination between them. While this process undoubtedly involves many different stages, the commissioner is a central figure in each of the steps involved. From the initial identification and selection of the titles to be translated to the actual publication of the translation, the vital role played by the commissioner is undeniable. While the translator and the assigned editor are also important figures in the process, they act only as mediators who facilitate the processes of translating and editing. It is the commissioner who shoulders most of the responsibility in making sure that the title chosen to be translated is produced as planned and reaches the readers for whom it is intended.

References

Friedman, Thomas. 2005, *The World is Flat: A Brief History of the Globalized World in the Twenty-First Century*. New York: Farrar, Straus and Giroux.

Friedman, Thomas. 2010, *Dunia Sama Rata: Sejarah Ringkas Dunia Global Abad Ke-21*. (mohd. Dayd Mat Din, translator). Kuala Lumpur: Institut Terjemahan Negara Malaysia.

Friedman, Thomas. 2008, *Hot, Flat and Crowded*. New York: Farrar, Straus and Giroux.

Friedman, Thomas. 2011, *Panas, Rata dan Sesak. (Mohd. Mustamam Abd. Karim & Nurulhuda Abdul Rahman, translators).* Kuala Lumpur: Institut Terjemahan Negara Malaysia.

Hatim, Basil and Jeremy Munday 2004, *Translation: An Advanced Resource*. London: Routledge.

Larson, Mildred 1984, *Meaning-Based Translation: A Guide to Cross Language Equivalence*, Lantham: University Press of America.

Mohd Daud Mat Din (translator) 2010, *Dunia Sama Rata: Sejarah Ringkas Dunia Global Abad ke-21*, Kuala Lumpur: Institut Terjemahan Negara Malaysia.

Mossop, Brian 2001, *Revising and Editing for Translators*, Manchester: St. Jerome Publishing.

Nord, Christiane 1991, *Text Analysis in Translation: Theory, Methodology, and Didactic Application of a Model for Translation-Oriented Text Analysis*, Amsterdam and Atlanta GA: Rodopi.

Nord, Christiane 1997, *Translating as a Purposeful Activity: Functionalist Approaches Explained*, Manchester: St. Jerome Publishing.

Perez, Celia Rico 2002, "Translation and Project Management", *The Translation Journal*, Vol. 6, no. 4, http://translationjournal.net/journal/22project.htm *from the 4th International Congress on Translation* (Benjamins Translation Library No. 32), 117-128. Amsterdam/Philadelphia: Benjamins Publishing Company.

Zabalbeascoa, Patrick 1998, "From Techniques to Types of Solutions", in A. Beeby, D. Ensinger, and M. Presas, eds., *Investigating Translation: Papers Century*, New York: Vintage Books.

INDIA

"NAMES ARE FOR OTHER PEOPLE'S LANGUAGE": REVISITING LANGUAGE AND TRANSLATION IN INDIA

RITA KOTHARI

1. Unanswered Questions about India's Multilingualism

In what I consider to be *déjà vu* moment, a panel on translation held at a Goa Arts and Literary Festival (15 December 2012) began with the moderator underlining the need for translation in a multilingual society. The understanding of multilingualism in this context is the co-existence of multiple languages in the vast space called "India". Each language in such an imagination is unique and discrete, occupying space (culturally, but also physically). Sheldon Pollock stresses how the "universe of literary cultures in the history of South Asia is plural, multi-faceted and richly diverse" (Pollock 2003: 17). As a result, the same region, text, or person has multiple languages without thinking of them as "different" languages, always requiring an act of translation. Throughout history there has been no lack of writers and thinkers who have known several languages; indeed, these forms of multilingualism have sometimes inhabited the same work. The historian Sisir Kumar Das (1991: 5-6) points out the verses of the fourteenth century Sufi poet Amir Khusrau, written in a mixture of Persian and Braj, and a vast body of Buddhist and Jain literatures which are preserved in Pali, Ardh Magadhi and Sanskrit. Earlier, Ashokan inscriptions were recorded in various dialects. The famous tale of Shakuntala, in one of the first literary works to have fired imaginations in Europe, was composed in Sanskrit, Saurasheni, Maharasthri and Magadhi, and yet maintained a unity (ibid). Who can tell whether Meera, the famous Bhakti singer composed in Gujarati or Marwari? Vidypathi wrote in three languages—Sanskrit, Avahatta and Maithili. How are we to divide Premchand's work in Urdu and Hindi? How do we understand traders, shopkeepers, salesmen who (without any formal training in translation) constantly straddle what would appear to linguists to be different languages?

This means that languages in India are not spatially arranged isomorphs but sites constituted through diversity and pluralism. However, when "nations are made by turning languages into distinctive national markers" (Pollock 2003: 17), translation in particular acquires a humanist and nationalist colouring. It is allegedly the only "bridge" by which different linguistic nations would understand each other. This rhetoric about the importance of translation in a multilingual society is a historical construction. It needs to be seen in the context of the way India, following philological classification in colonial scholarship, began thinking about languages; the rise of nationalism and its attendant sentiments in the twentieth century as well the linguistic reorganisation of India in the 1950s. Historical developments from the nineteenth century onwards have created in contemporary India what David Washbrooke provocatively refers to as a "society of language jatis" (quoted in Sarangi 2009b: 6).

A question that now haunts my engagement with translation is: what happens when languages in a given society are not clearly marked off from each other as village and city boundaries are in a geographically demarcated landscape, but instead shade off into each other? (Kaviraj 2010: 142). Are the speakers then aware of a "carrying over", an onerous self-conscious act by which meaning is assumed to move from one discrete entity to another? Would those speakers simply be making adjustments in their repertoire of speech-acts, depending upon the interlocutors with whom they speak, or are they unselfconsciously involved in translation practice? How do we understand translation when what appears as "Hindi" to some also gets labeled as "Urdu" elsewhere? Is that the same "thing" with different labels and therefore not in need of translation? On the other hand, Urdu and Hindi are polarized along political ideologies and seek mediation that emphasizes their common roots, an act made possible by both translation and interpretation. Similarly, in the far corner of Western India where the Indo-Pak boundary divides India from Pakistan, one language is "Kutchi" and another "Sindhi", with both seeking to claim a common syntax and vocabulary, but becoming different by choosing to be so (Kothari 2013). These form the questions for an ongoing study on multilingualism in India and its relation with translation. The first and foremost step in this direction is the Linguistic Survey of India that "situates" and enumerates Indian languages.

2. Grierson's Linguistic Survey of India: Introduction and Context

The first and largest documentation of language in India, undertaken by G. A. Grierson in his Linguistic Survey of India (1903-1928), would appear to have an unlikely relationship with translation. It is after all a document of India's multilingualism that reinforces the apparently unarguable need for translation to "bridge" different languages. However, Grierson deployed translation to merge and separate languages into philological families, and along the way also set up hierarchies between "standard" and "non-standard" languages, classifying them into languages and dialects. This was a multi-stage endeavour, involving translation of the English Bible (a "source" text constituted through translation) into several Indian languages. Specimens of the English and non-English translations of the Parable of the Prodigal Son were provided to speakers to "identify" their home language, effecting yet another stage of linguistic and cultural translation. An overarching translation was also one by which Grierson brought to Indian soil an imagination of languages as discrete entities, causing Sarangi to remark that "Grierson's appreciation for people's languages and tongue was Herderian in spirit, which looked for an isomorphic relationship between languages and cultures" (2009a: 22). I argue that the authenticity of language experience in India was achieved in Grierson's survey through translation, and the survey also became one of the foundational documents in invoking linguistic sentiments in India.

As I write this piece, a new linguistic survey of India awaits publication. However, Grierson's survey, in the hundred years since its publication, has served as a handbook for understanding languages in India. It has set the context for what the political scientist Asha Sarangi calls "linguistic ethnology" (2009a: 25), that is to say the shaping of linguistic community as a socio-ethnic collectivity. This, as Sarangi shows, has had serious ramifications on the communal politics of North India, as Hindi and Urdu—hitherto indistinguishable from each other—came to acquire mutually exclusive functions of serving the "Hindus" and "Muslims" respectively (Sarangi 2009a). Not unlike a range of discursive practices associated with colonial measurements and maps, language was constructed at the turn of the twentieth century and our understanding of its relationship with translation requires some revisiting. When translations from Hindi into Urdu or vice versa are carried out today, few realize that prior to the colonial classification, these were not experienced as distinctly different languages.

Grierson's study is yet to be scrutinized for constructing the linguistic landscape of India in ways that have deep implications for translation. I argue that translation was central to his classification and that Grierson's classification has implications for the way we understand translation. That being said, Grierson is but one part of a much larger inquiry I am making into translation in a multi-lingual nation such as India. By using the survey as a primary document for discussion, I show how notions of pure and corrupt, normative and deviating, language and dialect, standard and dialectic, reify people's experience of language, making it sedentary, distinct, and divorced from self-referentiality. Translation is mobilized to achieve this stultified view; but the discussion also helps question a stultified view on translation in India, as a "bridge" between languages that are otherwise incomprehensible to each other.

Grierson was both a linguist and an administrator, a member of the Indian Civil Service. He undertook "a deliberate systematic survey of languages of India" (Grierson 2005: 17) in 1894 and continued for thirty years, surveying and compiling his monumental *Linguistic Survey of India*. He noted in his Introduction that although "the languages of India have from the earliest times been an object of interest to those that spoke them, their serious study by foreigners is not more than three hundred years old" (ibid: 1). Citing an impressive list of narratives of histories, travel accounts, memoirs and specific studies carried out by European philologists, he provided an overview of language scholarship from Albiruni in the eleventh century to the late nineteenth century, claiming that "so late as the year 1878 no one had as yet made even a catalogue of all the languages spoken in India, and the estimates of their number varied between 50 or 60 and 250" (ibid: 16-17). Grierson's survey documented 179 languages and 544 dialects in India under British rule. Although he did not have the opportunity to include the states of Burma, Hyderabad and Mysore or the Presidency of Madras, his documenting of West, North, East and Central India led to eleven volumes in nineteen parts, that were published between 1903 and 1928. According to his own estimates, the survey covered 224 million out of a total population of nearly 300 million in India at the start of the twentieth century; to date, it remains the most ambitious as well as the core document on languages in India.

In his introductory volume, Grierson also mentioned that the existing scholarship on languages in India had neglected the vernaculars, and in most cases was restricted to Sanskrit, as if only the refined and cultivated language of the priestly class deserved attention. The discovery of languages other than Sanskrit, and an acknowledgement that they were distinct "languages" with their own grammar marked a beginning in

European scholarship in the latter half of the nineteenth century. Grierson himself represented a point of departure when he turned to the study and comparison of Indian languages other than Sanskrit, both building upon and departing from existing scholarship. For instance, he drew from William Jones, who pioneered comparative philology, and whose interest and focus lay almost entirely with Sanskrit and its relation to the Indo-European family of languages in 1786.[1] Grierson also turned to the Serampore missionaries (who had translated the Bible into many Indian languages in an exercise that had created an appetite for studying India's linguistic landscape), rather than to conventional colonial scholarship that was confined to the writings or sayings of the Brahmins. The missionaries' report prepared by W. Carey, J. Marshman and W. Ward in 1816 provided 34 specimens of 33 Indian languages, each accommodated within a version of the Lord's Prayer.

Grierson's survey, as conceptualized, was primarily a collection of three specimens. A standard passage was to be selected for purposes of comparison, and this was to be translated into every known dialect and sub-dialect spoken in the area covered by the operations. Thus the first and most crucial specimen chosen by Grierson was a translation, specifically a translation of the parable of the Prodigal Son. It was decided that Grierson's team would provide the passage in English (again a translation) if the speaker knew the language. Considering how even today English-speaking people form a miniscule number, it is highly unlikely that most of his respondents would ever have used the English passage. Perhaps in those situations, they were provided with a translation of a language that served as standard or benchmark. Thus in the region that today is West Bengal, Bengali would have been the language of the passage, and when speakers translated this into their own languages, those would have been classified on the basis of their relation with Bengali. A collection compiled with the help of the British and Foreign Bible society that contained 65 versions of "Specimen Translations in various Indian Languages" was used to carry out the scheme: "For the survey, it was anticipated that whoever might have to prepare a specimen, even if he did not know English, would find in this book at least one version from which he could

---

[1] I have discussed Jones's famous words on Sanskrit elsewhere in the context of translations from Sanskrit into English, but the following words form a cornerstone in indological studies, whereby Sanskrit came to be seen as the fount of the Indian knowledge system and Sanskrit texts a key to explaining India: "The Sanskrit language, whatever be its antiquity, is of a wonderful structure; more perfect than the Greek, more copious than the Latin and more exquisitely refined than either; yet bearing to both of them a stronger affinity" (Kothari 2013).

make a translation ..." (ibid: 17). Grierson explained his choice of an alien subject as wishing to avoid "Indian prejudices" (p. 18), requiring in addition a cultural translation from his respondents.

The second specimen was in Grierson's words, "not translation but a piece of folklore or some other passage in narrative prose or verse, selected on the spot and taken down from the mouth of the speaker." However, he also went on to mention that the specimen had to be written (a) in the vernacular character (if there was one) and (b) in the Roman character with a word for word interlinear translation, followed by free translation into good English (ibid: 20).

Subsequently, a third specimen was added to the scheme, involving a standard list of words and test sentences originally drawn up for the Bengal Asiatic Society in 1866 by Sir George Campbell and already widely used in India. Forms were sent out to each district officer and political agent with a request that he would fill in the name of every language spoken in his charge, together with the estimated number of speakers. On the basis of the documents that Grierson received from his team, he identified the grammatical and other peculiarities of the language or dialect. He also provided a brief introduction for each of the languages, distinguishing its various dialects, noting the number of speakers, the habitat of the language, as well as its literature, and concluding with a sketch of the grammar. "In a crucial sense, this monumental and authentic digest of Indian languages was a project of recurring translation by bilingual Indians" (Amin n.d.).

3. Difficulties Faced by Grierson

Grierson claimed in his introductory volume to have used stringent philological tests, and to have drawn careful conclusions based on a collection of facts. He had appointed officers working in different parts of India to document every language spoken in their district, which required both the officers and the speakers to be bilingual. He also mentioned that "there were scores of languages for which no one could be found who knew any one of them and at the same time English" (Grierson 2005: 21). This does not lead to a reflection on the assumptions of the project, which however valuable, was in Grierson's case pitted against enormous difficulties of translation. Grierson mentioned that,

> Each officer knew about the main language of his district, and if he had been there some time, probably had a working acquaintance with it. But over and over again no one with any education knew anything about the

little hole-in-the-corner forms of speech which were discovered as soon as a search was instituted (ibid: 21).

The fact that "hole-in-the-corner" also constituted the natural expression of a people and contributed to the multilingualism of the regions in which the officers were posted is not discussed by Grierson.[2] For instance, he describes how:

> In one of the Himalayan districts, the main language was Aryan. A small colony was discovered which originally hailed from Tibet, and which retained its own language. No official knew it, and intercourse with them was conducted through the medium of a lingua franca. The district officer entered the name of this language on his return. The name was not one word, or two words. It was a solemn procession of weird monosyllables wandering right across a page. It was 'I don't understand what you are driving at'.

What, in this case, was the *lingua franca*, and what made it so? The fact that languages are partly social constructions and that this made their "reality" only partially available to Grierson was not part of a survey discussion.

The survey operations were also based on an assumption that each speaker knew he had a distinct language. A view that most Indian speakers do not know whether they speak a language or dialect, or what the name of their speech is, is constantly reinforced. At the time Grierson undertook the linguistic survey of India, not all languages were aware of their own existence and therefore their difference from others. Since then, linguistic differentiation and sentiments in India have been on the rise, and recent scholarship shows the relation with colonial technologies (see Grierson 1927/2005).[3] Grierson mentions the "difficulty" of finding the local name of a dialect. His comparison is telling:

---

[2] Niranjana draws attention to the fact that "Marathi" and "Kannada" entered into a native/foreign battle in the nineteenth century, because "The determination of the British officials to create vernacular monolingual identities and map them onto geographical regions historically marked by considerable polylingualism, had far-reaching consequences in many regions of the country including the southern Maratha area." (2013: 43)

[3] For reasons of scope and focus, the discussion on Grierson's employment of translation in this chapter have excluded forms of selection, resistance, and intervention that it may have received in various linguistic communities in India. It is not meant to suggest here that the influence of Grierson was not uni-directional despite being profound.

Just as M. Jourdain did not know that he had been speaking prose all his life, so the average Indian villager does not know that he has been speaking anything with a name attached to it. He can always put a name to the dialect spoken by somebody fifty miles off, but, as for his own dialect, 'O, that has no name. It is simply correct language' (19).

In fact, many Indian languages use the same word for 'dialect' and 'language,' such as Sindhi-speaking people who refer to their "language" as "boli" (a term only used for a "dialect" in Gujarati).

Grierson's exercise remained oblivious to competing philosophies of language and communication. He isolated "standardness" out of a mass of speech-acts, infusing into an indigenous system a hierarchical differentiation that had not hitherto existed. That being said, the speakers' terms for self-description are important because in India, they do not point to a uniformly hierarchical view of language. It is true that languages are sites of hegemony, but these are also formed in India through extra-linguistic features such as caste. In Grierson's survey, language was wrenched out of its sociological contexts, and he made it clear that his task was enumeration and not ethnology. All the same, heavy prejudices against the colonial subjects imbued Grierson's perceptions of the kind evident in his comment, "… one illiterate Persun shepherd who was found after a long search, and who knew no language but his own" (ibid).

However, Grierson's linguistic operations deserve some attention, as they reveal the difficulties of representing the realities of one society in the terms of another, thereby providing interesting insights into translational equivalence. The philosophical differences between Grierson's experience of languages in Europe and India and his attempt to iron out questions furnish interesting examples of a smooth translation. This is most evident in the "difficulties" cited by Grierson, which throw into relief the different ways in which he and his team "identified" languages, and the way his respondents would have done. We get to know of the respondents only through Grierson; they serve as examples not of his inadequate methodology, but rather of his frustration at not finding neat equations between expectations and results.

There are also colonial and unrealistic expectations of a kind evident here:

Again in the case of one of the Kafir languages of the Hindukush, no one who spoke it could at first be got hold of. At length after a long search, a shepherd of the desired nationality was enticed from his native fastness to Chitral. He was exceptionally stupid, probably very much frightened and knew only his native language (ibid: 21).

The gulf between his project and people's participation was wide, so that "many of the specimens would come from the mouths of uneducated people hardly able to grasp the idea of what was required." All the same, Grierson's self-reflection on the accuracy of his project was unwavering, despite instances such as the following:

> One of the witnesses in the Chittagong Hill tracts knew only the Khami language. This was translated into Mru, which was then translated into Arakanese, which was again translated into the local dialect of Bengali, from which version the Magistrate recorded the quadruply refracted evidence in English (ibid).

In this instance the mediation, as on similar occasions, remains unacknowledged, and the translation of both language and society, despite forming an essential part of Grierson's survey, has remained an unnoticed dimension in its hundred year old history.

4. Fixing Languages, Defining Nations, Translating Differences

As part of the colonial production of knowledge and power, as Sarangi notes, the survey,

> [...] worked through an ideology of identifying languages with civilizations. He [Grierson] emphasized that the understanding of a language was equal to an understanding of a civilization and its constituents. In the course of 'differentiating' a language from dialect, one language family from another, Grierson notes that there is another factor which exercises influence in this differentiation. 'It is nationality. It is said that some English peasants would in Holland find little difficulty in making themselves understood, or in understanding what people say. Yet no one would deny that Dutch and English are distinct languages; and this factor is all the stronger when each nationality has developed an independent literature' (2009a: 24).

Grierson was imposing the European experience of language-as-nation on ground that did not see languages as discrete entities of territories, of the kind that can be observed in post-colonial India when language became a rallying point for sub-nationalism (cf. for example Sarangi and Pai, 2011). Grierson follows the case of Dutch and English by stating that,

> [...] there is an excellent illustration of this in Assamese. This form of speech is now admitted to be an independent language, yet if merely its

grammatical form and its vocabulary are considered, it would not be denied that it is a dialect of Bengali. Yet its claim to be considered as an independent language is incontestable. Not only is it the speech of an independent nation, with a history of its own, but it has a fine literature differing from that of Bengal both in its standard of speech, and in its nature and content. Here, therefore, we have an example of a language differentiated from its neighbours not by mutual unintelligibility but by nationality and literature (Grierson cited in Sarangi 2009b: 24).

Did Assamese and Bengali represent different nations at a time when the nation-state had barely formed as an idea? On the other hand, if as Grierson remarks, the languages were not separated by mutual unintelligibility, how did he arrive at fixing the boundaries of the two as separate entities? Grierson is uncritical of his own contradictions so that on one hand he refers to "parts of India which seem to have had each a special Tower of Babel of its own" (Grierson 21), while also admitting that "the differentiation of a language does not necessarily depend on non-intercommunicability with another form of speech" but rather on "nationality" (ibid: 24). If translation between languages rests upon "difference" and mutual unintelligibility, Grierson's discussion unwittingly interrogates India's need for linguistic translation within specific clusters, while also revealing his own interpretation as an act of translation. Grieson admits that,

> The identification of the boundaries of a language, or even of a language itself, is not always an easy matter. As a rule, unless they are separated by great ethnic differences, or by some natural obstacle, such as a range of mountains or a large river, Indian languages gradually merge into each other and are not separated by hard and fast boundary lines (30-31).

A brief discussion on the following verse serves as an illustration of how colonial technologies make us regard languages as discrete entities today, but the cartography of narratives interrogates such a notion.

Sorath gada sun utri
Janjhar re jankaar
Dhrooje gadaan ra kangra
Haan re hame dhrooje to gad girnaar re ...
    (Kothari 1973: 53)

As Sorath stepped out of the fort
Not only the hill in the neighbourhood
But the walls of Girnar fort trembled
By the sweet twinkle of her toe-bells

The verse quoted is just one from the vast repertoire of a musician community called Langhas, found in Western Rajasthan, Western Gujarat in India and also in Sindh in Pakistan. The version above came to me from a book about "native traditions in Rajasthan". It is composed in Thari, considered to be one of the dialects of Rajasthani.

However, the story with which the verse assumes familiarity also draws from states and nations beyond Rajasthan. It is enshrined in the Sufi verses of Sindh's well-known sixteenth century poet Shah Abdul Latif, and circulates in Pakistan as one of the folk stories that is familiar to singers and musicians. Since Kutch in Gujarat and Southern Sindh were inseparable in linguistic, cultural and also geographic terms prior to 1965 (when an international boundary parted them), the story is also sung, heard and transmitted in Kutch. The reference to Girnar locates it in present-day Gujarat, and more specifically in the district of Saurahtra, since Sorath, referring to a beautiful woman in the verse, is also another name for Saurashtra, perhaps taken after the story narrated below:

King Diyach who ruled over Junagadh (present-day Gujarat) was married to a beautiful woman named Sorath. The neighbouring king Anirai was jealous of King Diyach's reputation as a powerful ruler, as well as of his beautiful wife. King Anirai commanded his *charan* (bard) Bijal to ensnare Raja Diyach and have him killed. Bijal was a mesmerizing singer who played a musical instrument called the *chang* and held his audiences captive. As a bard, it was his tradition to seek generous gifts from the king, and to displease the seeker, especially if from the bardic/*charan* caste, was considered inauspicious. Bijal acted on Anirai's command and headed off to Junagadh where King Diyach lived with his wife Sorath. A sensitive and kind man, Bijal undertook a mission filled with cruelty to save his own life. His voice made life in Junagadh come to a standstill; it filled the air with pain and longing. The king begged him to name his reward, whilst his queen Sorath watched him with misgivings. She offered him riches in the hope that he would not seek anything more serious. But Bijal stood his ground and sought the king's head as his reward. True to his word, the king cut off his head and gave it to Bijal for him to carry to Anirai. Meanwhile, Sorath followed her husband and jumped into the fire. The story becomes a glorious documentation of Sorath's love, and the king's generosity.

There are many smaller stories attached to this; for instance, ones that report Bijal's identity as the King's nephew, or Sorath as also belonging to Anirai's family, or the Sufi version in which the ultimate surrender of the body is celebrated. However, the emphasis in the discussion is on the mobility of the story, its various versions notwithstanding. The cartography of the song includes two districts (Kutch and Saurashtra from Gujarat), parts of Rajasthan, and Sindh (in Pakistan). In the postcolonial imagination, these are considered to be distinct and different regions, each with its own language. However, the story and its various versions and recitations have elements from Sindhi, Thari, Kutchi, Sorathi, Gujarati and dialectical inflections. This points to an embedded multilingualism in the story, and also its mobility in Western India, comprising regions that, with varying intensities, show many threads of continuity. If the story has travelled, so have the communities associated with it, thereby dislodging the fixity of source, language, and society. This dislodging imagination runs counter to the linguistic and territorial boundaries within and beyond nation-states. The two states of Rajasthan and Gujarat with whose languages and memories the story is imbued, are divided in India along linguistic lines, whereas the region of Sindh in Pakistan is perceived in the popular imagination as the "other". Meanwhile, the verse does not "belong" to either Rajasthani, or Marwari, or Sindhi in particular, but is formed through the mobility of all three.

The mobility and indistinctness of the kind we see above is what Grierson refers to as the "composite nature" or "multiple nomenclatures" in Indian languages; a bewildering phenomenon that he encountered, as in the example of Bengali and Assamese. Governed by the experiences of a monolingual world, Grierson interpreted languages as either one or the other. His survey showed that languages were created, assimilated, written off, subsumed and differentiated. For instance, Thari spoken in Rajasthan (a territorial name invented by Colonel Tod) became part of "Rajasthani", a language "invented for the purposes" of the survey. In Grierson's own words, "Natives do not employ any general name for the language, but content themselves with referring to various dialects, Marwari, Jaipuri, Malvi, and so forth." So "Rajasthani" had to be invented to distinguish it from Western Hindi on the one hand, and from Gujarati on the other (Grierson ibid: 170-15). After creating an institution (that a priori did not exist), Grierson suggested that Marwari was Rajasthani's most important dialect. He even admitted that the natives employed the term Marwari for a large spread of variations. Rajasthani, an invented label created by Grierson, now evokes a nationalism (associated with the state of Rajasthan) and its advocates deploy an array of strategies to assert its identity; in other words, "the political battles being waged over the recognition of the Rajasthani language" are in "stark, life and death terms" (Merill, 2009: 44).

5. Conclusion

In the process of laying out a background to Grierson, the historian Shahid Amin notes that,

> [...] after the Great Uprising of 1857, the reestablishment and deeper penetration of the colonial state in India resulted in the systematic collection and codification of knowledge about things and people Indian. This period witnessed the planning and execution of several big surveys: the Archaeological Survey, the Geological Survey, the ethnographic survey (subsequently divided into smaller, provincial series), and perhaps most ambitiously, a linguistic mapping of the Indian Empire (Amin n.d.).

I have discussed elsewhere how colonial knowledge production in the nineteenth and twentieth centuries was an act of translation, motivated by a desire to know and to administer the colony (Kothari, 2003). Sarangi also draws attention to the fact that, in nineteenth century colonial India, a number of enumerative practices and discourses were instrumental in defining the politics of linguistic codification, quantification and gradually the shaping of the linguistic identity formation of various communities and groups. Her study, based on North India (and more specifically on the way "Hindi" and "Urdu" came to be separated and positioned as two mutually exclusive languages) shows the role that the "logic of numbers" played "through regular census operations, gazetteers writings, linguistic survey reports and records of various kinds to standardize and construct new modes of 'disciplining' the linguistic diversity and its communicative rationale" (Sarangi, 2009a: 30).

The "creation" of Rajasthani to separate it from Gujarati, or declaring Oriya as a dialect of Bengali is but one instance of the disruptions of a linguistic balance that may or may not have existed in the nineteenth century. However, it is such documentation that formed, at least in some cases, the basis for a distinct "language" experience and fuelled the reverence for the "mother-tongue".[4] In some parts of the country, a complex network of contexts enabled the creation of language as a marker of regional cultural nationalism. Self-referentiality, hierarchy, notions of pure and corrupt languages, and awareness of similarities as well as differences reconfigured the way India thought about languages. This also

---

[4] In this regard, see Yildiz (2012) as an excellent discussion on "mother-tongue as a construction". For specific studies on how languages came to be imagined as mothers and territories, evoking strong sentiments, see Ramaswamy for the Tamil language (1993) and Mitchell for Telugu (2009).

paved the way for language as a means of mobilizing territories, resources and representation.

What is significant for our argument is that such knowledge was arrived at through translation, and its process was also a form of translation. Grierson's survey was an attempt to make reality legible, to make sense of fluidity, and to organize it into straitjacketed definitions. As a translator, Grierson "tamed" the fundamental differences that lay between himself and the interlocutors. The "difficulties" encountered by Grierson unwittingly reveal a tendency to see the "problem" outside; and not in the representation of another society and culture.

References

Amin, Shahid n.d., "Introduction, Linguistic Survey of India", Digital South Asia Library http://southasia.uchicago.edu/highlights/2010-2011/111710-lsi.shtml (accessed 21 February 2013).

Das, Sisir Kumar 1991, *A History of Indian Literature: 1800-1910: Western Impact, Indian Response,* New Delhi: Sahitya Akademi.

Grierson, G. A. 1927; reprint 2005, *Linguistic Survey of India,* Vol. 1 (Part 1), Delhi: Low Price Publications.

Kaviraj, Sudipto 2010, *The Imaginary Institution of India*, New Delhi: Permanent Black.

Kothari, Komal 1973 *Monograph on Langas: A Folk Musician caste of Rajasthan*, Jodhpur, Rupayan Sansthan

Kothari, Rita 2003, *Translating India*, Manchester, UK: St. Jerome Publishing.

Kothari, Rita 2013, *Memories and Movements: Borders and Communities in Banni, Kutch*, New Delhi: Orient Blackswan.

Merrill, Christi 2009, *Riddles of Belonging: India in Translation and Other Tales of Possession,* New York: Fordham University Press.

Pollock, Sheldon 2003, *Literary Cultures in History: Reconstructions from South Asia*, Berkeley CA: University of California Press.

Mitchell, Lisa 2009, *Language, Emotion and Politics in South India: The Making of a Mother Tongue*, Bloomington IN: Indiana University Press.

Niranjana, Tejaswini 2013, "Music in the Balance: Language, Modernity and Hindustani Sangeet in Dharwad", *Economic and Political Weekly*, Vol. 48, No. 2, 41-48.

Ramaswamy, Sumathi 1993, "En/gendering Language: The Poetics of Tamil Identity", *Comparative Studies in Society and History*, Vol. 35, No. 4, 683-725.

Sarangi, Asha 2009a, "Enumeration and the linguistic identity formation in colonial North India", *Studies in History*, Vol. 25, No. 2, 197-227.

—. 2009b, *Language and politics in India*, New Delhi: Oxford University Press.

Sarangi, Asha and Pai, Sudha (eds.) 2011, *Interrogating Reorganisation of States: Culture, Identity and Politics in India*. New Delhi: Routledge India.

Yildiz, Yasemin 2012, *Beyond the Mother Tongue: The Postmonolingual Condition*, New York: Fordham University Press.

MAKE IT TELUGU:
LEGITIMIZING PATRON, AUTHOR AND TEXT[1]

SRINIVAS REDDY

1. Legitimization via the Past

If we believe, as the poet W. H. Auden states, that "there is only one thing that all poetry must do; it must praise all it can for being and for happening",[2] then we may ask, "Why does one feel the need to praise?" In my view, it is to proclaim the value and legitimacy of a person, an object, or an idea. In South Asia, such legitimacy was established through the embodied representation of a particular tradition or lineage—a complex set of inherited norms and practices that defined a unique way of being and knowing. Regardless of discipline, all South Asian knowledge systems certify their authority by connecting to a canon of past masters and celebrated works. In the classical literature of medieval South India, a poem functioned as an artifact of such legitimization—a consciously-crafted composition that concretized and promulgated specific cultural tropes that bound and informed the author, the patron and the text itself. Each of these elements had a specific tradition that defined its normativity, and collectively, all three interactively constituted a symbiotic relationship that generated a cultural nexus uniting language and literature with politics and poets.

Although this paper focuses on what may be deemed the dominant brahmanic traditions of classical Telugu literature, the formulation of legitimacy as an act of recourse to an authoritative literary past is equally applicable to the so-called anti-brahmanic counter-movements. Whereas a

---

[1] A rough outline of the content in this paper was first presented at the Fifth Asian Translation Traditions Conference held in Sharjah, UAE, 27-29 November 2012. I am indebted to the participants of the conference for helping me refine and give more definite shape to these ideas.
[2] From W. H. Auden's inaugural lecture upon accepting the post of Oxford Professor of Poetry, 11 June 1956.

high-class court poet such as Nannaya paid due homage to the sanctity of
the Vedas, a reformist Vīraśaiva poet like Pālkuriki Somanātha claimed
that his compositions were tantamount in status to the sacred scriptures.
For example, with regard to his *Basava Purāṇam*,[3] the latter clearly states:
"Let it not be said that these words are nothing but Telugu. Rather, look at
them as equal to the Vedas" (Narayana Rao 1990: 5-6). In each case,
regardless of impulse or effect, the Vedic corpus is never left
unacknowledged, nor is it dismissed outright. Rather, both poets reify (in
whole, or at least in part) the prevailing notion of Vedic prestige. Thus,
while Nannaya borrowed themes from the pan-Indic *itihāsas* (epics) and
legitimized himself through the exalted stature of the Sanskrit tradition,
Somanātha drew from oral sources and claimed authority by connecting to
a lineage of local Śaiva masters. Both poets were compelled to merge with
the flow of an established tradition, follow in the stream of past poets, and
bring new bends to a widening river of literary production.

In classical South Asian literature, the hegemonic influence of the
Sanskrit tradition is evident in every region and every epoch. Along with
well-prescribed criteria for genre-specific conventions, compositional style
and aesthetic appreciation, this pervasive impact also carried with it the
socio-political framework that defined and structured the patron-poet
relationship. In particular, the classical Sanskrit model of kingship
presented a mutually beneficial relationship between the mighty *kṣatriya*
king and his wise *brahman* poet. In this paradigm, the poet praised (often
fabricated) the king's noble lineage, extolled his patron's virtues, and
proclaimed his sovereignty through song. In return, the king supported the
poet, lavishing upon him the most valued gifts, lands, and honours. It was
a symbiotic pairing that cemented the bond between the two upper castes
(*varṇas*) and also concretized the literary themes and tropes that would
define each of their roles. As the seventeenth century Telugu grammarian
Appakavi succinctly stated: "Just as a gem enhances a bracelet, and the
bracelet enhance the gem, so a poet and his patron make each other
famous"[4] (Narayana Rao and Shulman 2002: 238).

Although this idealized model of the patron-poet relationship was
disrupted and reconceived in medieval times due to shifting political
scenarios and expanding modes of religiosity,[5] the inspirational source for

---

[3] This Vīraśaiva *dvipada* text tells the story of Basavanna, the tradition's founder.
The choice of calling the work a *purāṇa* is again another example of resistance
through reclamation of an established term and the redefinition of a genre's scope.
[4] From the seventeenth century *Appakavīyamu* of Appakavi.
[5] See the Afterword in Narayana Rao and Heiftz (1987) for a detailed analysis of
this evolution.

classical Telugu works remained the Sanskrit corpus. Literature in Telugu only existed with a dedication (*aṅkitamu*), either to an earthly sponsor or a heavenly deity—the patron might be a Chalukya king on the Godavari, or the great god Rāma, and the poet might be the king's poet laureate or a poor brahman farmer—but in all cases, the source text was always from Sanskrit. The South Asian vernacular revolution of the second millennium CE, of which classical Telugu is an important part, did little to refute the literary prestige of Sanskrit. On the contrary, it validated it—first through outright praise, then by conventionalized acknowledgement, and later by subtle critique and reformulation. More broadly, social, political and religious developments in medieval South India, including the birth of new literary vernaculars, did not subvert the preeminence of Sanskrit; in fact, it could well be argued that they fortified it.

The key to this trajectory is the way in which a dominant, pan-Indic cultural mythos embodied in Sanskrit literature framed and inspired new regional literatures. It is an issue of an inescapable past, so deeply ingrained in the Indian consciousness that it could never be overturned. A poem, its author, and its patron all found legitimacy in the power and cachet of that which came before. Poets drew thematic seeds from the two great epics (*itihāsas*) and the multiple old mythologies (*purāṇas*) by aligning themselves with the "authoritative structure of the literary past, indeed, a canon of great poets"[6] (Narayana Rao 2003: 390). Kings linked their genealogies with the *sūrya* (sun) or *candra* (moon) dynasties of the *Rāmāyaṇa* and *Mahābhārata* respectively, and modelled their behaviour on the celebrated monarchs of yore. The mythic hero kings and their exploits were known to most through osmosis[7] and not through military conquest or political submission. In short, Sanskrit cultural hegemony was won by myth—though the circulation of tales and legends—sung by travelling bards, recited by village elders, and whispered within shadows as bedtime stories.

2. Mahābhārata and Bhāgavata Purāṇa

In this paper, I reflect on two seminal works of Sanskrit literature, along with their celebrated retellings in Telugu. Composition of the Sanskrit *Mahābhārata* and the Sanskrit *Bhāgavata Purāṇa* are accredited to the mythic sage Veda Vyāsa, and both texts occupy a place of sanctity and

---

[6] From Rāmarājabhūṣaṇa's invocatory poem to the goddess of speech in his *Vasucaritramu*.

[7] I owe this metaphor to Professor Rajmohan Gandhi.

prestige in the greater Sanskrit literary canon. The Telugu poets Nannaya Bhaṭṭu and Bammĕra Potana rendered these works into classical Telugu in the eleventh and fifteenth centuries respectively. And although there were some striking differences that separated these authors (as explored later), both were brahman poets who drew inspiration from venerated Sanskrit sources.

Nannaya is considered the *adi-kavi* or first poet of Telugu and his decision to compose the *Āndhra-mahābhāratam* was a fully conscious choice, loaded with important socio-cultural and political ramifications for a newly-literarizing regional culture. His work set the standard for all later Telugu poets, not only in terms of his innovative *campu* style that mixed verse (*padya*) with prose (*gadya*), but also in regard to diction, prosody and aesthetics. It is said that the *Mahābhārata* contains some things that can be found elsewhere, but many things that can be found nowhere else, including in this case, the standards for proper grammar. And as its name suggests, it is the great story of the land ruled by the legendary King Bharata, the land known today as India.[8] To give it a vernacular voice would be to translate, absorb, and embody the entire linguistic/cultural complex of the classical Sanskrit worldview. Nannaya himself says that:

> Those who understand the order of things
> think it is a book about order.
> Metaphysicians call it Vedānta.
> Counselors read it as a book about conduct.
> Poets read it as a poem.
> Grammarians find here usage for every rule.
> Narrators of the past see it as ancient record.
> Mythologists know it to be a rich collection of myth.
> Vyāsa, the first sage, who knew the meaning of all the Vedas,
> Parāśara's son, equal to Lord Viṣṇu, made the *Mahābharata*
> a universal text." (Narayana Rao and Shulman 2002: 61)

The poet's vision does not explicitly justify the creation of a new text, rather it highlights the multiple readings that a single text of such multi-layered richness provides. When Nannaya's patron Rājarājendra asks him to clarify the "proven meaning bound to the *Mahābhārata* text,"[9] (Narayana Rao and Shulman 2002: 59) there is an implication that the eternal

---

[8] The geo-spatial imagination of the *Mahābharata* extended well beyond the boundaries of the modern Indian nation. *Bhārata-varśa* or *bhārata-deśam* included areas in today's Pakistan, Afghanistan, Nepal and other countries.

[9] Translation of Nannaya's *Āndhra-mahābhāratamu* I.1.16 by Narayana Rao and Shulman. I give another translation of the same passage later in the paper.

message of the beloved epic requires commentary, interpretation, and explication. The garb that this exposition takes is a new language, thereby clothing the principal text[10] in a diction and register that would speak to a new readership in an enlightening new way. And although Narayana Rao observes that "Nannaya's own intention was only to compose a Telugu work—not to begin anything, let alone a tradition" (2003: 393), it is well accepted that the poet had no literary predecessors in Telugu. Unlike subsequent Telugu poets, he pays no homage to any previous Telugu author, only to the great Sanskrit poet-sages: Vālmiki, the *adi-kavi* and progenitor of all *kāvya* (poetry), and the prolific wise guru Vyāsa.

At the core of the *Mahābhārata* is a story of warring princes. From this kernel, it expands into a *magnum opus* of unwieldy proportions, including a veritable mishmash of moral, scientific and narrative discourses. Its essence, however, is the delineation of *dharma*—the righteous conduct of man in the world—and more specifically, a model for Indian kingship and sovereignty. As such, Nannaya's decision to retell this text in Telugu was critical not only to the emerging literary tradition, but also to freshly articulated (and localized) patterns of South Indian governance.

The *Bhāgavata Purāṇa* is the most influential and widely read Sanskrit *purāṇa*. And like all *purāṇas*, it includes an account of the world's creation, its dissolution, and a narration of the ten *avatāras* of the preserver god Viṣṇu. This particular work chronicles the amorous/epic adventures of the boy/god Kṛṣṇa, and soon became the foundational text for many rapidly proliferating sects of Kṛṣṇa devotion. The spread of these *bhakti* movements had a profound influence on the religious and literary landscape of medieval Andhra. Poets once employed at royal courts in imperial centers now found succor at large temple complexes dotted across the South India geography. One poet who typified this transition from court to countryside was the mid-fifteenth century Telugu brahman Bammĕra Potana. Early in his career, he was court poet to a local potentate named Sarvajña Siṅgabhūpāla, but a transformative mystical experience seems to have inspired him to abandon court life and settle down as a simple farmer.

This self-styled *sahaja kavi*, or natural poet, refused to dedicate his *Mahābhāgavatam* to his erstwhile employer. According to legend, Lord Rāma appeared to Potana and commanded him to compose a Telugu *Bhāgavatam*. As the poet explains in his preface: "The *Bhāgavatam* is

---

[10] We may question if there is such a thing as a principal text, an Ur-document that functions as an original and constant referent for all other tellings. The idea requires theorizing, but in regard to Nannaya, he clearly refers to the Sanskrit *Mahābhārata*, and is ever-conscious of Vyāsa's originality.

what I speak, and Rāma makes me speak it. Speaking it relieves suffering, so why speak any other story."[11] In this new relationship, the patron is god himself, and the poet but a humble devotee in the service of his lord. Potana is a fascinating case example because his life embodies the shift from court poetry to bhakti poetry. Unlike Somanātha who was conspicuously positioned outside the cosmopolis, Potana occupied both spaces during his career—he belonged to the high brahmanic tradition, lived as a respected court poet, wrote secular works, but also, we are told, relinquished his possessions, shunned state patronage, and composed devotional poems. This dialectic plays out in the linguistic terms as well, and the poet declares that: "Some like Telugu, others like Sanskrit, and some like both. So I'll please everyone in different contexts."[12] The critical point is that even the divinely inspired Potana could not break free of Sanskrit literary models or texts of authority. His true innovation came through his earthy language, genuine devotional spirit and resistance to court sponsorship.

3. Commissioned by Kings and Gods

The poets of premodern South Asia functioned as media outlets for their patrons—they had agendas that were inherently political and their poems spread a message to readers and listeners well beyond their local domains. In this sense, poets could reinvent their patrons—they could wipe away blemishes and accentuate achievements, devise glorious genealogies and mythic histories, and effectively, or at least ostensibly, elevate a patron's status. Whether they were supported by kings or inspired by gods,[13] their works legitimized their patrons in powerfully eloquent and affective ways.

---

[11] Potana's *Āndhra-bhāgavatamu* I.18.

[12] Potana's *Āndhra-bhāgavatamu* I.20. Note the highly interpretive translation of Potana's simple diction given by Narayana Rao (1995: 33): "Seeing its erudition, some say it's tough as Sanskrit. Hearing the idiom, other says it's nothing but simple Telugu. Let them say whatever they want. I couldn't care less. My poetry is the true language of this land."

[13] There is a deep connection between the evolution of both gods and kings in South Asia. Local folk deities were constantly brought into the larger Sanskrit pantheon through their identification with the classical *purāṇic* gods and goddesses, particularly as forms of Viṣṇu, Śiva and Śakti. Poets composed *sthala-purāṇas* and *māhātmyams*, most often in Sanskrit, to formulize a local deity's genealogy within a *purāṇic* mythological framework, and to graft grand geo-histories onto localized cults. In this way, kings and gods were both, for lack of a better word, Sanskritized through the medium of poetry.

For royal patrons, the choice of commissioning a work in a vernacular like Telugu often had a political rationale with concomitant implications for state governance. For example, it has been suggested that Nannaya's patron Rājarājanarendra, an Eastern Chāḷukya sovereign of Tamil stock who ruled from Rājamahendravaram (modern day Rajahmundry) in the heart of Andhra country, purposefully patronized a Telugu work in an attempt "to make himself more popular among his Telugu-speaking subjects" (Narayana Rao and Shulman 2002: 55). Half a millennium later, Kṛṣṇadevarāya, the iconic god-king of the Vijayanagara empire made a similar choice based on his predominantly Telugu constituency and court of warrior elites. In the king's own *Āmuktamālyada*, the god Āndhra Mahāviṣṇu asks him in no uncertain terms: "Having spoken to all your lords gathered at court, didn't you realize that Telugu is the best among the regional languages?"[14]

These sponsored works, though written in a new vernacular, still carried with them the age-old formula of describing a sponsor's celebrated pedigree. These *vaṁśa-stutis* or celebrations of lineages precede the main text and constitute an important part of a work's meta-narrative. A king's legitimacy was constituted in large part by proclaiming his descent from the stock of exemplary 'Sanskrit' sovereigns, like the Six Universal Monarchs (*ṣaṭ-cakravartis*) and the Sixteen Great Kings (*ṣodaśa-mahārājas*).[15] In Nannaya's prologue, Rājarājanarendra proclaims:

> Generations of my ancestors, originating from the Moon and descending through the illustrious monarchs Puru, King Bharata and Lord Pāṇḍu, ruled the earth and brought fame to my lineage. So whenever I hear the stories of the virtuous Pāṇḍava heroes, I want even more![16]

The king's commissioning of the *Mahābharata* is thus framed, not as a retelling of a great epic, far removed by time and space, but as an endearing account of his own beloved forefathers.

Potana on the other hand offers a stark contrast when he praises his celestial patron King Rāma and offers us a passionate critique of poets who wrote for human kings and lived off their worldly rewards:

> Rather than giving my work to those vile lords of men,
> and accepting towns, chariots and measly money,
> I'll leave this tired body without Death's hammer blows!

---

[14] Kṛṣṇadevarāya's *Āmuktamālyada* I.15.
[15] cf. *Āmuktamālyada* II.80 which explicitly mentions all 22 monarchs.
[16] Nannaya's *Āndhra-mahābhāratamu* I.1.14.

> For only I, Bammĕra Potarāju, happily give my *Bhāgavatam*
> to Śrī Hari, for the benefit of the world.[17]

In addition to praising their noble patrons, poets were also deeply concerned with validating their own personal genealogies and connecting themselves to a venerated literary lineage. Nannaya describes himself as "versed in the Veda corpus, having command over a vast vocabulary, and fascinated with various *purāṇas* ... famous for composing poetry in both languages ... a worthy brahman son of the Āpastamba line and the Mudgala family ..."[18] He makes clear his brahman pedigree and implies that his thorough knowledge of the high Sanskrit tradition will be brought to bear in his new Telugu work. As mentioned earlier, he also goes on to honour the mythic Sanskrit writers Vālmiki and Vyāsa, and establishes himself as a worthy inheritor of their venerated tradition.

In the introduction to his *Bhāgavatam*, Potana also claims descent from the Āpastamba line but focuses on his ancestors' unswerving religious devotion to Lord Śiva rather than their brahmanic erudition. In terms of his literary lineage, Potana makes no mention of the great Sanskrit poets; rather, he is fully rooted in the flourishing vernacular tradition and pays due respect to earlier Telugu poets, specifically mentioning Nannaya and Tikkana who he says Teluguized the Sanskrit *purāṇas* (*purāṇāvaḷur tĕnugun ceyucu*).[19] Therefore, by the fifteenth century, the Telugu tradition had matured enough that Potana did not have to trace his literary heritage back to Vālmiki or Vyāsa—his acknowledgement of the celebrated Telugu poets of the past was enough to confer the legitimacy he sought to project.

Later, a full-fledged *bhakta* like Annamayya, whose *padams* are often not even classified as poetry, found no need to legitimize himself or his compositions:

> Without a patron who sought social and political status from the act of sponsoring poetry, Annamayya was his own grammarian, his own literary theorist, and his own master. His legitimacy as a poet did not depend upon the mention of a great poet, grammarian, or guru of the past (Narayana Rao 2003: 409).

This is what Narayana Rao calls "temple poetry", an area that has "yet to be seriously studied" (2003: 413).

---

[17] Potana's *Āndhra-bhāgavatamu* I.13.
[18] Nannaya's *Āndhra-mahābhāratamu* I.1.9.
[19] Potana's *Āndhra-bhāgavatamu* I.21.

In this regard, Potana is an important transitional figure who bridges the highly refined poetry of courts with the unpretentious songs of temples—he provokes us to question and problematize the traditional bifurcations of classical/folk, cosmopolitan/vernacular, court/temple, aesthetic/devotional, and also, original/translation.

4. Translating into Telugu

It is now well established and accepted that translation as we conventionally understand it today—that is, the direct transfer of inaccessible content from a source language to a disparate target language—was unknown in premodern South Asia. In this context, we must explore the dynamics involved when a known narrative or theme is rendered in a new language. Is the new work a translation or a (re)telling? How do these categories intersect, overlap and/or subsume each other on a potential spectrum of literary composition? Or more generally, are all translations types of retellings, and all retellings forms of translation?

The term *anuvādam* (Telugu) / *anuvād* (Hindi) is a neologism of modern Indian parlance that reflects a distinct historical shift in the conceptualization of Indian authorship, translinguistic comprehensibility and compositional originality. This transformation, largely a product of the colonial encounter, has been discussed by some scholars but still requires further exploration and theorization.[20] From a historical perspective, premodern Telugu poets never used the term or anything like it. They preferred to speak of themselves as "remaking" Sanskrit works in Telugu. A few textual examples will make the point clear. Nannaya is asked to "compose in Telugu to enlighten the inherent value of the *Mahābhārata*" (*mahābhārata baddha nirūpitārtharm erpaḍa tĕnuguna raciyimpu*),[21] while Kṛṣṇadevarāya is persuaded to "craft a work in the language of Āndhra" (*āndhra-bhāṣan ... andun ŏkka kṛtin vinirmimpumu*).[22] Lord Rāma commands Potana to "make the *Śrī Mahābhāgavatam* Telugu" (*śrī-mahā-bhāgavatambu tĕnuṅgu seyumu*),[23] and, in a fascinating turn of phrase that verbalizes the nominal designation of the language, to "Teluguize this *Bhāgavatam*" (*bhāgavatamun dīnin tĕniṅgiñci*).[24] Clearly

---

[20] See, for example, Harish Trivedi's "*In Our Own Time, On Our Own Terms*: 'Translation' in India", in Hermans (2006: Vol. I, 102-119).

[21] Nannaya's *Āndhra-mahābhāratamu* I.1.16.

[22] Kṛṣṇadevarāya's *Āmuktamālyada* I.13.

[23] Potana's *Āndhra-bhāgavatamu* I.17.

[24] Potana's *Āndhra-bhāgavatamu* I.21. *tĕniṅgiñci* is glossed with the neologism *āndhrīkariñcu* = "to make Āndhra".

these poets were working under a paradigm of translation that differs from our modern notion. The reasons for this phenomenon, especially in the context of South Asian heteroglossia, are profound and complex, and require a separate and more focused analysis.

In the case of Nannaya's *Mahābhārata* and Potana's *Bhāgavatam*, their translations were strictly what we would now consider retellings—new vernacular versions of Veda Vyāsa's Sanskrit works that consciously sought to align themselves with the high tradition of Sanskrit learning and literature by drawing on thematic and narrative material from the "originals". In this process, they edited out huge portions of the text, condensed and reworked others, added regional variations and sub-stories, but never, by any stretch of the imagination, did they produce slavish literal translations. In essence, they were creating true original works with powerfully inventive and significant meanings for new audiences.

As Narayana Rao rightly observes:

> Veda by definition cannot be translated or even retold, while *kāvya*, too, is completely resistant to translation. Only *śāstra*, *itihāsa*, and *purāṇa* are available for translation; indeed, since their meaning can be constituted in different ways, they may be thought of as requiring repeated telling and reinterpretation (2003: 422).

Court patronage, in particular, actively supported the translation of Sanskrit works as a means of elevating the cultural capital of the state, thereby promulgating hegemonic forms and registers while relegating original, localized productions. In this context, a translation inherently privileged the source language even as it sought to enrich the target language. The veneration and sanctity of the source text is reaffirmed, propagated and further legitimized, while the target text gains a position of legitimacy and validity by aligning itself with the well-established canon of the high tradition. In doing so, a translation confers upon the target language a proprietary respectability which had hitherto been unavailable to it, if not inconceivable.

Citation and reference were certainly legitimizing actions for the translating poet, but they also had implications for altering the perception and reception of the root text. Just like today when authors refer to how many citations their paper has received, the work of a translator glorifies and validates the original as much, and sometimes even more, than the translation. Interestingly, premodern translations from South Asia seem to have reduced the readership of the original text, for "before the twentieth century, no literary critic compared the translation with the original in order to comment on the quality of the translation. Faithfulness to the original was never an issue. Sanskrit originals apparently provided legitimacy, while Telugu renderings were actually read" (Narayana Rao 2003: 427).

5. Translation as Preservation

Today, hardly anyone actually reads the *Mahābhārata* or *Bhāgavatam* in Sanskrit, and contrary to the medieval period, even less so in Telugu. As India modernizes, interest in classical studies has waned in favour of the immediate relevance of contemporary literature. As the classical genres of South Asia ceased to be living traditions, the only corpus to survive the rupture to any significant extent was that of Sanskrit. This speaks strongly to the powerful influence and level of prestige that the language of the gods commanded in the colonial period, and continues even to this day to exert in the subcontinent. When I tell people in Andhra that I study Telugu literature, they often look at me with a puzzled sense of wonder, but when I add that I read Sanskrit as well, they appreciate my efforts to preserve our heritage. Sadly, the value of India's rich vernacular literary traditions seems to be lost among the present generation.

The Sanskrit literary tradition has received considerably more philological attention from scholars than any of the many regional vernaculars. Critical editions of several seminal Telugu texts are left to be compiled and thousands of precious palm-leaf manuscripts are quickly disintegrating under the dead weight of neglect. Even the available printed materials of/on classical Telugu literature, mostly produced in the late eighteenth and early twentieth centuries, lie in dusty, dilapidated libraries—untouched, uncared for, and unread. In my own work as a translator of classical Telugu, I often see translation as an act of preservation—a way to connect an inaccessible past to a dynamic present and bring new life to a fading tradition. I can relate to Hugh Kenner when he writes that Ezra Pound "came to think of translation as a model for the poetic act: blood brought to ghosts" (Kenner 1973: 150). Translations revitalize and rejuvenate that which is deemed valuable from the past. They also prompt translators to determine which texts (from a vast constellation of works in the case of classical Telugu) are worthy of being surveyed, studied and translated. In this sense, even the modern translator joins in the continuous act of legitimization.

Translating the rarefied world of classical Telugu into modern English allows this rich literary tradition to speak to an international readership. Unlike the retellings of the past that we explored, these translations are most often precise and in direct, parallel correspondence with their source texts. For modern writers, this is what makes a translation scholarly, and ultimately authentic. In order to make them literary however, they must not become overly literal or restrictively scholastic. Finding that balance is what I see as the core philosophy of translating premodern South Asian literature into modern, living languages. Vamsee Juluri recently wrote a piece which poignantly describes the Telugu-speaking world's need to engage with English as well as other languages. He says:

> Writing in English, I believe, can help us be vernacular without becoming provincial. Without English, or some sort of engagement with the world outside one's own, the vernacular can turn into an artifice, a state-supported pickle-jar exhibit, and worse, a language without a voice in the world to speak for itself ... Most of all, we need to write, in English, and in other languages, and write our Teluguness into it (Juluri 2012).

That being said, both the *Mahābhārata* and *Bhāgavatam* are still very much alive in Andhra and other parts of modern South and Southeast Asia, not as texts to be read but mythological metaphors to be experienced in new ways, and crucially, in languages other than Sanskrit. To put it another way, the textual lives of these seminal works live on in new media translations, from films and plays to cartoons and video games. What is central here is the power of myth and its remarkable ability to penetrate, endure and thrive. Translation, in its broader non-textual sense, provides the key to this robustness. The layers of meanings embedded within these cultural matrices of text and myth allow for them to be reformulated in a dazzling variety of forms and permutations. These translations thus enrich the lives of new generations of listeners, both in India and abroad. Or as Nannaya would say:

> With words steeped in wisdom and glowing with multiple meanings I became absorbed in composing the Telugu *Mahābhārata* for the good of the world.[25]

References

Bronner, Yigal and David Shulman 2006, "A Cloud Turned Goose: Sanskrit in the Vernacular Millennium", *The Indian Economic and Social History Review*, Vol. 43, no. 1.

---

[25] This a loose translation from *Āndhra-mahābhāratamu* I.1.26, reformulated in the first person.

Brown, C. P. 2004, *Telugu-English Dictionary*, Vijayawada: Victory Publishers.

Hermans, Theo, ed., 2006 *Translating Others*, Manchester: St. Jerome Publishing.

Juluri, Vamsee 2012, "Being Telugu in English", *The Indian Express* 29 December 2012, http://www.indianexpress.com/news/being-telugu-in-english/1051530/0

Kenner, Hugh 1973, *The Pound Era*. Berkeley CA: University of California Press.

Mitchell, Lisa 2009, *Language, Emotion and Politics in South India: The Making of a Mother Tongue*, Bloomington IN: Indiana University Press.

Nannaya 1968, *Āndhra-mahābhāratamu*, Hyderabad: Osmania University Press.

Narayana Rao, Velcheru 1995, "Coconut and Honey: Sanskrit and Telugu in Medieval Andhra", *Social Scientist,* Vol. 23, No. 10/12, 22-40.

—. 2003, "Multiple Literary Cultures in Telugu: Court, Temple, and Public" in Sheldon Pollock ed., *Literary Cultures in History: Reconstructions from South Asia*, Berkeley CA: University of California Press, 383-436.

Narayan Rao, Velcheru and Hank Heifetz 1987, *For the Lord of the animals; poems from the Telugu: The Kālahastīśvara-śatakamu of Dhūrjaṭi*. Berkeley CA: University of California Press.

Narayana Rao, Velcheru and David Shulman 2002, *Classical Telugu Poetry: An Anthology.* Berkeley CA: University of California Press.

Potana, Bammĕra 2004, *Śrīmadāndhra-bhāgavatamu.* Rajamhundry: Rohini Publications.

Pollock, Sheldon, ed. 2003, *Literary Cultures in History: Reconstructions from South Asia.* Berkeley CA: University of California Press.

Pollock, Sheldon 2006, *The Language of the Gods in the World of Men*, Berkeley CA: University of California Press.

Pound, Ezra 1934, *Make it New: Essays by Ezra Pound*, London: Faber and Faber.

Rao, T. Koteswara 2001, *Āmuktamālyada Saundaryalaharī Vyākhyānam.* Hyderabad: T. Koteswara Rao.

Venkatarayasastri, Vedamu 1964, *Āmuktamālyada Āndhra-vyākhyāna sahitamu,* Madras: Vedamu Venkatarayasastri and Brothers.

IRAN

Agency in Literary Translation: The Case of Women Translators in Iran

Esmaeil Haddadian-Moghaddam[*]

1. Introduction

Until recently, studies of Iranian translation practices by scholars based in Iran have been far from numerous. This is especially true as far as research into the period from the early twentieth century to the present is concerned (for early translation in Iran as far back as the sixth century, see Zakeri 2007). Articles written by Iranian scholars during this period have mainly discussed linguistic aspects, while cultural and ideological aspects have largely been overlooked. One of the reasons for this unfortunate situation has been censorship, especially when research has dealt with what have been regarded as ideologically sensitive issues.[1]

Hardly surprisingly, with the increase in the number of graduate programmes in Translation Studies (TS hereafter) in the post-Revolution era, interest has been sparked in issues that were previously seen as taboo or risky to explore. One such area has been research into the role women translators have played in modernisation projects in Iran.

This paper is a study of three literary women translators who have translated from English in the post-Revolution era. Methodologically, the research is based on archival materials and on in-depth interviews conducted by the author with the translators. Theoretically, the research draws on Pierre Bourdieu's concepts of field, capital and *habitus*, which have been incorporated into a three-tier model of agency (see below). The research has two goals. First, it discusses the following three questions: 1)

---

[1] There is no official state censorship in Iran. There is, however, pre-publication control of books and all other cultural products. The Ministry of Islamic Culture and Guidance (hereafter the Ministry) runs a Book Bureau which is responsible for the censorship of books and for issuing publication permits, and no publisher in Iran is allowed to publish materials, even re-prints, without the Bureau's permission. The only study containing statistics on censorship in the post-Revolution era is that by Rajabzadeh (1380/2001).

who—the translator or the publisher—decides what to translate; 2) what motivates the translators; and 3) what influences their agency? The second goal is to explore some of the theoretical and methodological challenges facing sociologically-informed translation research when translation practices of Iran are studied.

2. General Overview

Following the Persian translation and publication of *The Adventures of Hajji Baba of Ispahan* (1905), a Constitutional Revolution occurred in Iran (before 1935, Iran was called Persia). The Revolution sounded a call for reform and modernisation. The religious and intellectual segments of Iranian society opposed the despotic kings of Qajar. The intellectuals had benefited from "differentiated patronage" (Lefevere 1992: 17) in their quest for modern sciences as followed in the West; at some periods they had been supported by the court, but at other periods they sought political refuge in exile and engaged in various practices, one of which was translation and/or language instruction. The case of Mirza Habib Esfahani and his exilic agency is now known to us. His adventures as a translator and political activist in exile provide evidence for revisiting our understanding of the possibilities and impossibilities bestowed upon individual agencies in exile (see Haddadian-Moghaddam 2011).

In nineteenth century Persia, a call for modernity was raised to oppose the ruling system, which was at odds with the increasing awareness of what lay behind the borders of Persia. To the curious mind, the Qajars' conscious opposition to modernity was hard to digest, given their fervent desire for everything labelled as *farangi*, i.e., of the Western world. For one thing, some of the late Qajar kings made frequent visits to the West. Nasir al-Din Shah (1831–1896), for example, made three trips to Europe in 1873, 1878 and 1889. The Qajars' fascination with photography and cinematography also contributed greatly to illustrating the modern history of Iran,[2] while Nasir al-Din Shah's personal library shows that his Western reading list, compiled in 1881, included works by such writers as Rousseau, Montesquieu and Voltaire, among many others (Behzadi 1390/2011). In fact, the late Qajar kings liked modernity as long as it did not topple them. Therefore they punished those who crossed this line,

---

[2] The moving image was introduced into Persia just five years after its introduction in France in 1855. During his trip to Belgium in 1900, Mozaffar-al-Din Shah ordered the first Gaumont camera, which was used by Mirza Ebrahim ʿAkkas-bāshii to film a flower festival in Ostend, Belgium (Gaffary 1991).

whether ministers or translators, and the case of Amir Kabir, the chief minister to the king, and his murder in the bathroom was a sensational episode in Iran's modern history. Of the translators, the case of Mirza Yousef Mostashar-al Doleh, Iran's *chargé d'affaires* in Paris who was the translator of a summary of the first French Constitution in 1869, is exemplary. Although the translation, "One Word Treatise", was softened in its tone by some Islamic verses and narratives, the translator was arrested and tortured. The King's intolerance was because he did not want to think of a constitution "as having the same value for the King, the beggar, the serfs and the war lords; otherwise he favoured the idea of reconciling Western civilizations with that of Islam" (Hashemi 1391/2012).[3]

One way or another, modernity through translation found its way to Persia.[4] A significant proportion of translations were literary translations, and translation flows from 1920 to 1975 show that, of the 6,375 books translated from foreign languages into Persian, 3,449 (54.19%) of them were "literature", i.e., novels, short stories, poems and plays. One would expect to see a higher score for scientific books; however, there were only 345 titles (4.41%) translated in "applied sciences", and 236 titles (3.7%) in "pure sciences" (*Farhang va zendegi*, 1355/1976). Here, modernity did not move much through science. Rather it moved through fiction, opposition to otherwise non-modern courtiers, and above all through a network of agents of translation. The importance of these agents has not diminished in post-Revolution Iran and this will remain true for many years to come.

3. Agents of translation and their agency

The term "agents of translation" is suggested by the editors of *Agents of Translation* (Milton and Bandia 2009), a definition that is built upon an earlier definition of an "agent in translation" presented by Shuttleworth and Cowie; that is, a person who "is in [an] intermediary position between a translator and [an] end user of a translation" (1997: 321). The newer

---

[3] All translations from Persian sources are my translation into English. In quoting from Persian resources, I refer to the original date of publication using the Iranian Solar Hejri calendar, followed by its equivalent Christian date.

[4] Modernity and its arrival in Persia were not only through translation. There were other, perhaps more adventurous carriers, such as Western travellers, dignitaries, and businessmen. The considerable volume of writings they have left behind, mainly in the form of diaries and travelogues, illustrates the ways in which modernity was exchanged, traded and desired.

definition covers a broad range of individuals and even cultural or political bodies as being agents of translation (cf. Buzelin 2010). In terms of the effects of the agents of translation, the above editors distinguish between (1) translation agents whose translations bring about "stylistic innovations", and (2) those who play cultural and political roles in their immediate environments.

In employing the term "agents of translation", we should not use it loosely. If we do, everything that fills the gap between the producer (here the translator) and the end user may simply be called an agent of translation. For example, is the postman who delivers a translated book purchased online to our door, an agent of translation? And what about certain individuals or institutions who act as gatekeepers or censors, whose positive/negative impact on translation is by no means welcoming towards other agents of translation or conducive to the free exchange of ideas? It appears, then, that as much as we would like to have desirable agents of translation, we also have the opposite scenario. In addition, one often finds agents of translation who combine "stylistic innovations" with broader cultural, social and political roles in their environments. The example of Esfahani noted above is such a case, and because of this, I have suggested elsewhere the use of concepts of pro-risk translation agents as opposed to risk-averse ones (Haddadian-Moghaddam 2011).

The volume *Agents of Translation* provides insights into fascinating, sometimes adventurous, and often risky ways through which agents of translation have practised their agency, while also offering some methods for conducting research on the issue. The latter needs more work, in particular when some subscribe to the notion that attempting historical biographies of individual agents of translation is not valuable or worthwhile (see for example Demircioğlu 2009), and that it should therefore be avoided. While this may be partly true elsewhere, a critical survey of the practice of agents of translation in a context like Iran needs such biographies more than anything else. In other words, the critique of a sociological study on translation in a developing context should show awareness of the methodological problems facing researchers (see below).

For the author, agents of translation in this chapter are translators, various text editors, and publishers, with the Iranian state as the authority that regulates the publication of books and translations. That said, we do not aim to analyse each of them in turn, but to try to draw inferences from available data.

Although the word "agency" appears in *Agents of Translation*, it is in *Translators' Agency* (Kinnunen and Koskinen 2010) that a clear definition and a rather thorough study of agency within TS is presented. These authors define agency as "willingness and ability to act" (2010: 6). Clearly, definition alone cannot explore the complicated issue of agency, which has its roots in philosophy, sociology and political sciences; nonetheless, it is a good starting point. Pym (2011: 76) finds the solution in the agents themselves, i.e., in "the contradictory social determinations of the translatorial subject".

One possible model (she does not call it as such) for the study of agency within the field of TS was proposed by Paloposki (2009: 191); this was built upon a three-level distinction of visibility proposed by Koskinen (2000: 99). Agency in this model is of three kinds: textual, paratextual, and extratextual. Although this model can explore agency in texts, it says little about agents' decisions in selecting texts for translation, their motivations, and the context that, for better or for worse, affects their agency.

With the help of Bourdieu's concepts such as capital, field and *habitus*, I have developed a model for the study of agency in the translation and production of novels from English into modern Iran (Haddadian-Moghaddam 2012). These concepts have been well-outlined, explored and criticized within the field of TS (starting with the special issue of *The Translator* in 2005; Wolf 2006; Pym *et al.* 2006; Wolf and Fukari 2007; Wolf 2010; and the special issue of the *MonTI* in 2010; as well as Wolf 2011, among others). They helped me to stay focused and to explore possible similarities and differences between the French and the Iranian contexts. For example, my study showed that Bourdieu's classification of publishers as literary or commercial is inadequate when trying to accommodate certain publishers in Iran, which do not fit into either category (see Haddadian-Moghaddam 2014). Likewise, my study of the publishing field demonstrated that, more than competition and position-taking, key components of Bourdieu's logic of the field are at work in the poetics of publishing, translation, and working with state constraints in a society-in-transition like modern Iran.

A recent trend has been to move beyond Bourdieu's sociology and to use other sociological theories and concepts as found in the actor-network theory of Callon and Latour (Buzelin 2005), and Luhman's systems theories (Hermans 2007; Tyulenev 2011). A clear critique of Bourdieu's sociology, understandable for those not versed in sociology, states that "it says little about interculturality or cooperation, and it remains the sociology of a nation [France] comprising antagonistic groups" (Pym 2011: 86–87). Nevertheless, if the research shows areas of cooperation between agents in the context under study, unravels the capacity of agents to work in the intercultures (physical or virtual), and explores agents' *habitus* in coping with various constraints of agency, concepts borrowed from Bourdieu, or any other sociologist for that matter, will be useful as long as something interesting can be found.

In my study of agency, I was looking for a model that could account for the particularities of translation in the context of Iran. I was not only concerned with an under-researched subject, but was trying to obtain data from those agents of translation who were understandably reluctant to communicate for various reasons. They were living in the field, had learned how to deal with historical ups and downs, and were partly dependent on the sale of their translations. In addition, the larger cultural policies of the post-Revolution era, reflected in the practice of the Ministry, were and remain, an "agent of translation". This agent was omnipresent and could be felt strongly in the course of research and the collection of data; nonetheless, it was not directly available for close inspection.

The three-tier model of agency (as developed and presented in Haddadian-Moghaddam 2014) compromises three levels: decision, motivation, and context. Originally, the agents of translation were both the translators and publishers, but could just as easily be other agents if clearly defined. The level of decision determines who decides what to translate and publish. The level of motivation accounts for the various motivations of agents of translation in their specific practice. The level of context explores the context in which agency is exercised, constrained or enhanced. The level of decision is important here because evidence shows that, contrary to the Western tradition, Iranian translators have often acted as the selectors of titles for translation, though there has been a growing trend among some publishers to play a greater role in the selection process.

Levels 1 and 3 of the model each have sub-levels because decisions can extend beyond the selection of titles and the impact of context can affect both the text under translation and the agents working with the texts, be they translators or publishers. Therefore, two sub-levels of title and meta-title are distinguished for the level of decision, and two sub-levels of textual and extra-textual are distinguished for the level of context. A simplified illustration of the original model is given in Table 1 (for the full model, see ibid):

Table 1: The simplified three-tier model of agency

LEVELS sub-levels	1. Decision title meta-title	2. Motivation	3. Context textual extra-textual
AGENTS			
Translator			
Publisher			
Others			

This model does not solve the problem of agency per se; nonetheless, it has the potential to explain certain key aspects of power relations between agents of translation. It might help us to find out who has more agency over others in the field of translation and publishing. However, depending on the determinants under each level that the research examines, it also helps us break agency down into more manageable variables, which in turn may lead to a better understanding of agency in literary translation.

4. Agents of translation in Iran:
insights on women translators

According to some estimates, when the Persian translation of *The Adventures of Hajji Baba of Ispahan* was published in 1905, the population of Persia barely exceeded 10 million.[5] Possibly 130 translators were active during the Qajar dynasty (1795–1921) and in total 500 titles were translated (Afshar 1381/2002). Iran's population rose from 33,708,744 million in 1976 to 78,868,711 million in 2012 (Statistical Centre of Iran 1390/2011; World Fact Book 2012). According to some estimates, the number of Iranian publishers rose from around 200 in 1979 to 8,900 authorised publishers in 2008, of which 4,000 were classified as

---

[5] Because the first national census of Iran was held in 1956, all previous statistics are only estimates, based on the works of historians, travellers and the like. Bharier (1968), from whom this estimate is quoted, presents an overview of the issue.

"semi-active", i.e., publishing only four titles a year to retain their authorisation. Only 600 publishers were classified as "active" (*Hamshahri* 1387/2008).

Although evidence shows that literary translation has attracted a considerable number of translators and publishers, there are no statistics on the number of translators, the number of full-time translators, and particularly the number of literary translators in Iran. First, they do not have any professional association to represent them.[6] Second, professionalisation of translation in Iran has never been clearly defined, and it remains largely unexplored.[7] My recent study revealed that few translators call themselves full-time translators, i.e., that translation is their main source of income. The professionalisation of translation in Iran is at best transitory, and translators have to combine translation with other professions to make a living. Above all, it depends on the cultural policies of the state and the potential of the publishing field. For example, the reformist policies of President Khatami, in office from 1997 to 2005, partly contributed to the professionalisation of literary translators in the limited sense of more translators working full-time, new translators (women included) entering the field, new titles being translated, and all of these contributing to the development of the publishing field.

The reverse trend, however, can be partly explained as the result of the harsher cultural policies of President Ahmadinejad. First, his policy of cutting out subsidies for paper received a mixed response from Iranian translators, publishers and readers. Initially, some showed concern that books would be too expensive to produce and sell, while some translators expected to earn higher royalties.[8] For example, Reza Rezaei, the translator of Jane Austen, remarked in a personal interview that the

---

[6] The reason Iranian literary translators have not formed any professional association needs research. Furthermore, such a formation of translators or writers has hardly been successful because the state has not tolerated them, mainly for political reasons. Although Iran is now represented by a group of technical translators as a regular member in the International Federation of Translators (FIT), it is not yet represented by literary translators.

[7] Under current regulations of the Ministry, Iranian translators can receive some basic forms of social security. Although basically nominal, it is the first official step towards the professionalization of translators in Iran.

[8] Generally, Iranian translators receive a certain percentage of the cover price of each print run, if they have not transferred the rights to the publisher. For example, the translator's royalty for a translated novel of 2,000 copies, with a back cover price of 50,000 rials, at 15 percent for a celebrated translator, will be 15,000,000 rials. For the next print runs, it is usually kept at the same percentage or at a lower rate.

publishing field was just starting to re-define itself, getting rid of fake publishers, i.e., those who were receiving state-subsidised paper and selling it at a higher price on the black market. For a professional translator like Rezaei, professionalisation is defined by the happy deletion of non-professional translators from the field, as he most recently declared (personal communication, 25 January 2012). Professionalisation here can also be partly explained by the quality of translations, which is probably more apparent in the translations of professional translators than those of non-professionals.[9] Nonetheless, starting from 2011, the growing political and economic complications and the general policy of subsidy cuts in Iran, have forced the publishers to publish less, often with a print-run of 1,000 copies and at higher prices. The outright contradiction here is to find out how these expensive books reach a frustrated readership that struggles hard to make ends meet in a country with rampant inflation.

Apart from small-scale studies, mainly within linguistic approaches in Iran (e.g. "do women translators translate more accurately than men?"), there is an urgent need for more critical studies on the social and larger cultural effect of women translators in the development of modern Iran. Furthermore, there are as yet no reliable studies and statistics on the number of women translators vs. male translators. Nonetheless, general trends among women translators in modern Iran can be shown in the context of literary translation. These trends were observed in my own personal engagement with the translation and publishing field in Iran, in various conversations with women translators, and while exploring the discourse of translation in Iran (see Haddadian-Moghaddam, 2014, esp. ch. 2). For example, a study of the agency of Shamsol Molouk Mossaheb, the translator of Austen's *Pride and Prejudice* in pre-Revolution Iran, showed how her practice as an educator, politician, and poet formed her translation approach in the early modernisation of Iran. The translator thus worked as an agent of translation from within the system towards broader social and cultural reforms for Iranians, with women being the main focus (cf. ibid).

As to the publishing field in Iran, it has attracted as many women as men, and a considerable number of literary works has been translated by women translators. In addition, women publishers, whom we do not address here and which deserve further research, have performed key roles in the field and have expressed their concerns about various issues,

---

[9] I am fully aware of the fuzziness of the term "quality". Here in the context of literary translation into Persian, it refers to a translation that has undergone various revisions by the translator, possibly an editor, or even a pre-print reader, in order to maximize its accuracy and fluency.

including publishing fields and censorship (e.g. see Lahiji 1387/2008). Similar to male translators, women translators have tried to make symbolic capital out of translations. For example, a translator like Farzaneh Taheri, wife of the late author Hushang Golshiri (1938–2000), has produced works of no lower quality and in even greater number than her late husband and has been engaged in various practices. For instance, she was the only Iranian woman translator invited to give a talk on human rights in Iran at the Waltic Congress in 2008 in Stockholm (see Taheri 1387/2008).

Another example is Taheri's recent retranslation of Virginia Woolf's *Mrs. Dalloway*, published in 1388/2009, which is an exemplary instance of a rather distinctive approach in literary translation in Iran (Figure 1). This approach has three features: first, it is practised by those who prioritise their cultural role over their translatorial one. Second, in terms of translation product, they write long introductions, annotate the translation heavily, and produce a translation that is not inaccurate but often very literal. Finally, working from the dialectic of responsibility and/or accuracy, their translation is done in an often self-professed cooperation with various agents dispersed across time and space. By way of illustration, Taheri's retranslation runs to 435 pages, while a similar full-length translation by Keyhan (see below) has only 240 pages. It starts with a Persian translation of Woolf's introduction to her first American edition published in 1928 (the scanned copy of the original was sent by "a young friend" who in turn obtained it from the British Library), and includes Woolf's full biography and timeline in Persian; a map of Mrs. Dalloway's London; 43 pages of translator's endnotes after the translation; the Persian translation of David Bradshaw's "introduction" to the new Oxford edition (2000), and of Merry M. Pawlowski's introduction to the Wordsworth edition (1996); and a selected English bibliography, among others. The Persian readership is likely to associate Taheri's extra work to a certain approach in translation according to which accuracy and thoroughness define the translator. The readership then reads the translation not for entertainment but probably for its added symbolic value; in one respect, for the translator with high symbolic capital, and in another, for the translation itself (for more on the translation, see Zahed 1389/2010).

5. Profiles of the translators

The three translators chosen for the present case study had taken part in a survey that I had carried out in 2008 during the initial stages of my doctoral research on agency,[10] and had agreed to sit for in-depth interviews. At the time of the interviews in spring 2010, these three translators lived in Tehran, and the interviews were conducted in Persian. I should add that I also knew the first translator because of my reading of her translations and as I had also previously held a brief interview with her while I was working for the Persian translation journal *Motarjem*. I had also read some of the translations of the two other translators. That said, I note here that the first two translators are typical of women translators who translate in post-Revolution Iran because, as I show later, the path they have taken in their practice of translation is not very different from that of a younger generation of women translators, which is not covered in this chapter. However, reference will be made to them where necessary. The third translator may be somehow atypical in that she has kept a very low profile and has not translated as much as the first two. I must also mention that I am not concerned here with women translators who work as non-literary translators, although they deserve equal enquiry elsewhere.

Mozhdeh Daqiqi

The first translator in this case study, Mozhdeh Daqiqi, was born in 1956, and has an undergraduate degree in Political Science. She started translating from English for the Persian press and gradually found herself working as an editor for publishers. Editing soon became her main source of income. Years later, having established contact with influential individuals—for example, famous translators, publishers, critics and so on—working for one major publisher, and completing various courses in editing, she started to translate short stories from English.

The translation of short stories from foreign languages, mainly from English, has historically provided material for the Persian press. In addition to the general readership, which often finds these stories entertaining and informative, avid readers in particular look for possible models in their attempts at writing short stories in Persian. The exact impact of these translations on the development of Persian short stories, and equally Persian novels and their position in the Persian literary polysystem, needs further investigation. The findings could then be compared with a recent study that found the Persian novel to be in a peripheral position, suffering from the critical discourse and faulty

---

[10] Out of 50 translators chosen for the 2008 survey, 17 were women, and the rest were men.

networks applied to its distribution in world literatures (see Azadibougar 2014).

After translating three Sherlock Holmes stories at the request of a publisher who planned to publish the whole series in Persian, Daqiqi translated a collection of six short stories, which had all appeared originally in various American literary magazines. The selections were made by the translator, and what seemed to be the preliminary norm (Toury 1995) was the fact that they were all prize-winning short stories, and as such would be of good quality. For example, the story that gave the collection its title in Persian was Lorrie Moor's *People Like That Are the Only People Here,* which had first appeared in *The New Yorker* on 27 January 1997. The operational norm for the translator was to make sure that the stories would not face censorship and the publisher would not risk publishing a book with no sales potential. The translation of these stories has been reprinted four times, and the total print-run in all the editions is 7,150 copies. Except for Stephen King, whose works are known to the Persian readership, the rest of the authors were translated for the first time. Because of this, the translator was concerned about their reception in Iran, given the fact that many were full length stories that would not fit the few pages available for them in the Persian literary magazines.

The translator's agency here was at the level of decision, operative insofar as it observed the "red lines" (i.e., unwritten guidelines) of the Ministry that are generally known by Iranian agents of translation. The translator's concerns about the possible sale of the translation were also at work. However, the assurance given to the translator by some consecrated member of the publishing field, including the publisher's realistic estimate, seemed to increase her agency. Of course, as elsewhere, the trade-off of various capitals were and are at work in translation and publishing in Iran; however, in the latter area, some agents of translation often tend to mask their practice (i.e., motivations for translation and the amount of economic capital gained) with altruistic if not sweet talk, the unravelling of which is ethically and professionally challenging, if not impossible.

The motivation of the translator, as stated in her introduction to the translation, was said to be "sharing the pleasure of reading good stories with the [Persian] readership" (Daqiqi 1379/2000: 9). Nevertheless, it seems plausible to say that the translator was moving herself away from the obscurity of working as a non-literary translator and editor (often with slightly higher rates of pay) to the more visible level of literary translation (with an average lower pay rate at the outset, but higher prestige and pay along the way). Although the translator here opted for an alternative position, there was hardly any cast-iron guarantee that she would remain unchallenged, or would not trade part of her symbolic capital for an economic one. For example, in a recent communication, the translator informed me that because of the strict policies of the Ministry, the high prices of the books, and the lower print-runs, she was translating more for the Persian press, preferring to keep her translations for future publication (personal communication, 21 October 2012). A similar strategy was shared in my interview with a woman Iranian translator who lives in exile.

Daqiqi has published seven more short story collections including the works of Isaac Bashevis Singer and Alice Munro, all of which she selected herself using a similar approach, i.e., finding original stories in various literary magazines, literary collections, anthologies and so on. Beyond the operational norms at work mentioned earlier, the translator had difficulty in finding stories that were not too far from Persian social and cultural norms: "often the cultural terms and the atmosphere of the stories are too unfamiliar for the Iranian readership to translate properly" (Daqiqi 1387/2008: 113). Daqiqi's translations are not limited to short stories. She has translated such novels as Kazuo Ishiguro's *When We were Orphans*, in 1381/2002, and Aravind Adiga's *White Tiger* in 1389/2010.

A look at Daqiqi's works shows that she has worked as a translator and journalist for the Persian monthly *Zanan* (Women), a magazine that garnered some fame as a reformative platform for modern Iranian women to express their concerns on wide-ranging issues, especially those affecting their status in the post-Revolution era. Daqiqi herself interviewed a number of women translators. However, the magazine was banned by the Ministry on various charges, one of which was "presenting a disappointing and negative image of Iranian women" (BBC Persian 1386/2008).

Daqiqi has an interesting account of her encounter with censorship. In her translation of eleven short stories by Isaac Bashevis Singer, the Ministry asked for strict censorship, which made the publisher ask her to give up the translation. They made some changes to certain words and expressions; however, the censor was still not satisfied. She says she asked for a personal meeting, and after three requests she secured an appointment with the head of the Bureau of the Ministry. The censor working for the Bureau was asked to attend the meeting. The Head asked the censor what was wrong with the work and whether or not the author's religious affiliation was an issue. The translator, assuring the censor that the author was "religious", finally managed to reach an agreement with the Bureau and was given permission for the translation. As the translators did not provide examples of the things the censor asked to be changed, there is no way to determine the level of agency of each agent involved.[11] What can be inferred is that the translator's agency at the level of context was extra-textual, bargaining with the censor over words, expressions, sentences and possibly full paragraphs. In contrast, the censor's agency at the level of context extended beyond the translator's preliminary and operational norms. The translator's and also the publisher's agency in this instance were subordinate to the agency of the state, although the former employed their various strategies such as astute selection, adaptation, networking and direct negotiating in order to maintain their agency. Experience and adaptive expectation have taught these agents of translation how to deal with state constraints, though they have not always been successful, and future prospects are hard to predict.

Within the framework of Bourdieu's sociology, competition with other agents in securing higher positions in the field is essential. In a country like Iran, in which the professionalisation of translation has yet to be defined, what kind of competition is at work? Many of the agents of translation in Iran tend to undermine competition in their work for several reasons. For one, if competition concerns the quality of translations (see footnote 9), they hardly read other translations to begin with. Those who read do not talk about these translations openly; however, they often become sharply critical of those translations in their small circles. Those who read other translations quite often become nostalgic, and in their attempt to explore those translations critically, praise the dead translators highly. It is because of this that in theory a good translator in Iran is often, unfortunately, a dead one.

Perhaps one can explain retranslations (i.e. in the strict sense of two translations of the same title) in Iran in the light of competition. Until very recently, translators were working in a vacuum, i.e., they did not know whether other translators, say competitors, were translating the same titles. To avoid competition/retranslations and in order not to lose a place in the highly unstructured publishing field in Iran, they would continue translating, hoping to be the first to bring the translation to the market. This strategy was not always successful, and quite often, retranslations appeared within a short time of the first translation. Such was the case of Daqiqi's translation of Jhumpa Lahiri's short story collection, *The*

---

[11] I have asked various Iranian translators several times to provide samples of the censors' comments; however, to date, none has been willing to do so, which is quite logical given the risks involved. What is clear is the fact that the above Book Bureau has a certain method in imposing censorship. It simply passes an unofficial paper to the publisher, asking the latter what should be changed or deleted. An example of this can be found in Haddadian-Moghaddam (2008).

Interpreter of Maladies (2005), which saw two retranslations within a month. According to the translator, "some journalists and publishers created side issues about the quality of translations". In this case, two translators and a representative of the third translator, a university lecturer, attended the meeting. Apparently some kind of micro-level, comparative analysis was carried out, and one translation received a low score. With very few exceptions, a similar kind of analysis has been predominant in translation reviews in Iran, generally by certain journalists who often borrow heavily from others, the deader the better, to display their erudition, leaving no stone unturned, except the translation, the social, cultural and historical facts surrounding the translation under study, and its production and reception.

That said, few translators, including Daqiqi, see competition working at the level of selection, towards bringing new voices to the otherwise classically-dominated field of translation and publishing. Many of the brighter days of the translation and publishing fields in the post-Revolution era can be seen from this perspective. It is here that the younger generation of literary translators and publishers challenge not only the older generation (i.e., the consecrated members), but also the Ministry, thus moving the whole field of cultural production ahead. Faced with a sudden flow of cultural productions (literary translations included), all in need of permissions of some kind, the Ministry becomes a tortoise lagging behind and adopting a more conservative stance. Translators and publishers are then affected by this, and as a result, a new form of competition arises, employing multiple strategies for pressing the Ministry to obtain the requested permission faster than others. As to other applicants in other fields, some go underground, some go to warm Dubai, and some find a solution in joining the growing community of Iranians living in exile.[12]

---

[12] Over the last decade, some of the best Iranian artwork, incuding paintings, calligraphy and sculptures have been sold at the Christie's auctions in Dubai, mainly to rich Arabs. Persian singers, including the Tehrangeles and other pop singers who left Iran for the US in the aftermath of the 1979 Revolution, as well as increasing numbers of young singers who find the Ministry regulations too strict, have also produced and/or staged many of their concerts in Dubai, either for the increasing number of Iranians who combine business with pleasure, or as alternatives to production inside Iran. As for publishers in exile, they have either become too political or so limited in their distribution that their role remains unexplored. Some translators living in exile continue to publish their works in Iran, and some have followed the Ministry regulations better than their counterparts at home. The late translator Bahman Farzaneh is a good example, whereas others

Khojasteh Keyhan

The second translator, Khojasteh Keyhan, who translates from French and English, was born in Iran in 1948 and has a combined education in sociology, urban development, and a Master's degree in English Literature from L'université Sorbonne, Nouvelle-Paris 3. Apart from some occasional translations, she embarked on literary translation only after her return to Iran, the first project being Paul Auster's *City of Glass* (1985), published in 1380/2001 in Tehran. Upon her return, she also established contact with the editor of a Persian journal, *Bukhara*, for whom she translated several articles. At the editor's suggestion, she turned to Woolf's works because the editor told her that this was what one could do "to make a name for oneself in the field of translation and publishing in Iran". The translator was financially dependent on translation for two years; however, she has since secured other sources of income in addition to translation.

As stated earlier, Woolf's writing appeals to a group of intellectuals in Iran, and her works represent a complicated narrative and style that are often copied by Iranian authors and critics. With some exceptions, the reason that authors like Woolf, William Faulkner and a martyr-like poet such as Sylvia Plath, appeal to certain translators, intellectuals, and the advocates of women's rights, lies not so much in the quality of their works per se, but rather and partly in their capacity to be resurrected from their graves, butchered to pieces, and consumed as magical potions to seek fame. The hazier the image of the original authors, the better the chances of success.[13]

Competition in translation and publishing came to a new phase when an Iranian publisher published the Persian translation of Auster's *Invisible* (2009) just three weeks after its first appearance in English in 2009. Although Iran is not a signatory to any international copyright conventions, the publisher obtained the copyright for the Persian translation and its simultaneous appearance from the publisher of the original. According to the translator, she was given a photocopy of the

---

express harsh criticism (e.g. Nikfarjam 2010). There is then a new form of competition between exiled translators in securing sales for their books back home.

[13] Without complicating the issue, historical evidence demonstrates how certain Iranian intellectuals have favoured authors who are disliked in their own countries, but liked in Iran. In my examination of the Tehran office of the Franklin Book Programs, available at the Harry Ransom Center, I came across various items of correspondence between the Tehran office and the head office in New York. While the Iranian side was persistent, for example, about publishing Faulkner and Jack London, the latter opposed it in the strongest terms (see Haddadian-Moghaddam 2013).

novel, and an agreement was made with the Iranian publisher to complete the translation as soon as possible (Puramini 1388/2009: 10). In an exceptionally rare instance the Ministry gave permission in time, and the translation was published as planned.

Apart from three works by Woolf (see below), and a book by the title of *Deux heures de lucidité: entretiens avec Noam Chomsky* (1387/2008), the translations of which were commissioned by different publishers, the rest are the translator's selections. Up to now, they include eight novels from Paul Auster's oeuvres, as well as *In the Country of the Last Things* (1987), *The New York Trilogy* (1987) (a co-translation), *Leviathan* (1992) ("Monster" in Persian), *Oracle Night* (2003) ("The Night of Foretelling" in Persian), *Man in the Dark* (2003), *The Brooklyn Follies* (2005), *The Music of Chance* (1990), and *Invisible* (2009). Apart from these novels, Keyhan has also translated Auster's non-fictional works including a retranslation of *Hand to Mouth: A Chronicle of Early Failure* (1997), and *Winter Journal* (2012), which for one critic was enough to see Auster unable to "gin up the old magic" (Lennon, 2012), though for the Iranian publisher, it was motivating to have the Persian translation shortly after the appearance of the book in English. When an author such as Auster sells in Iran—to whom it remains to be explored—and has an aura of popularity, it is not the quality that matters, it is the name.

Keyhan has also joined the nation's experts on Woolf. In modern Iran, Woolf was, and remains, one of the golden keys to symbolic capital for the men of letters and business, and a faithful mascot who might lead the former to the depths of cold waters and sink them. However, once they whisper Woolf, they are saved. For Keyhan, translating Woolf was such a challenging job that it drove her "mad". She tells us that "Woolf is not my favourite author, and I was badly affected by translating her". Despite this, Keyhan has translated *A Writer's Diary* (1383/2004), *Mrs. Dalloway* (1386/2007), and *To the Lighthouse* (1386/2007). In a context in which having prestige is more important than one's bread and butter, some agents of translation undergo mental, if not physical trauma, and their agency is affected by the levels of decision and context, each of which in turn affects the translation: one translation becomes "Woolf for Dummies", accessible and marketable, the other "Woolf for Non-Dummies", inaccessible yet marketable, and all good items for fancy bookshelves.[14]

---

[14] Keyhan tells us that her translation of *Mrs. Dalloway* was reprinted twice in just three months. The data from the Ketab.ir database shows that the total print-run of the translation (1386/1387/1389) has been 6,000 copies.

Figure 1. Woolf's *Mrs Dalloway* in Persian, by Taheri (left), and Keyhan (right)

Keyhan's motivation in translating novels extends, however, beyond the works of Woolf and Auster. Partly influenced by the success of Robert Harris's historical novel *Pompeii* (2003), and because of her interest in ancient Rome and the Roman's "epicurean way of life", she translated the novel. Contrary to her expectations, the translation, 420 pages in length, was not successful. According to the translator, "the translation of this historical book did not appeal to the dominant intellectual readership in Iran". She is also equally interested in translating the so-called *eau de rose* books to encourage people to read more books. She says she is aware of the fact that this particular genre faces censorship; however, what constrains her in her selection here is the fact that publishing these novels "has no prestige for the publisher". She is also interested in translating D. H. Lawrence's *Lady Chatterley's Lover* (1928), not so much for its erotic qualities (an attractive variable for the readership yet an easy prey for censorship), as for its "being a literary masterpiece". For a translator like Keyhan, the level of context is important since it also provides a model of success. For example, she is hoping to be "as successful as Zabiholla Mansuri in attracting readership". Mansuri was a prolific Iranian pseudotranslator whose works have been widely read in Iran, while his practice has remained an open topic for discussion (see e.g., Haddadian-Moghaddam 1387/2008).

As an agent of translation working in the post-Revolution era, Keyhan has had various experiences with censorship. Many of her translations were exposed to censorship, at the level of words, expressions or paragraphs. Her translations of Marguerite Duras's *Dix heures et demie du soir en été* (1960) has not yet received publishing permission from the Ministry, and the translator believes former translations by R. Seyyded Hoseini are available in the bookshops, though I could not verify this. Her strategy of coping with censorship, for example, differs from one book to another. In translating Mario Vargas Llosa's *Tours et détours de la vilaine fille* (2008), she had to "accept censorship because the book had many erotic scenes, which were impossible to reproduce in translation".[15] At the time of interview, the translator told me that she did all in her power to increase the chances of obtaining permission. One of the things she had to be very careful about was to delete all the sections describing women's clothes: "We took all the precautions and yet they delete page by page, and I am waiting, worried about the permission." The translation was finally published in 352 pages (the French version has 417 pages). Given the different technical formats such as the length, it is possible to some extent to imagine the degree, or the agency, of censorship.

One might then wonder how Iranian agents of translation, i.e., translators in particular, live with such constraints and the highly consecrated, yet unstructured publishing field. On the one hand, they have to struggle to survive, and yet on the other hand, it is hard for them to meet the expectations of the field. One possible explanation might be in the position of translators in Iran. According to Keyhan, Iranian translators "enjoy a high level of social prestige, higher than elsewhere, and this leaves no room for complaining. Of course, financially, there is room for improvement." That said, the translator adds that she is well-respected whenever she comes to identify herself as a translator, and it is even better when she meets readers who know her translations. Similarly, one can perhaps look at translation prizes in Iran. Apart from the Iran Annual Book Prize for translations, some private institutions have awarded prizes to translators, either for the quality of their translations, or the selections and/or translations. The opinions of Iranian agents of translation about the impact of these prizes in increasing or decreasing their agencies differ.

---

[15] The original Spanish title reads *Travesuras de la niña mala* (2006). Interestingly enough, the title in French is probably more explicit than the Spanish in terms of the possible content. However, the back translation of the Persian title, 'A girl from Peru', is clearly an example of how cultural and political norms affect titles.

Although some see no noticeable effect on their economic or symbolic capital and therefore their agency at the level of context, some argue that the selections are biased (see Haddadian-Moghaddam 2014: 133).

Shirin Ta'avoni

The last translator in this case study, Shirin Ta'avoni, was born in 1945 and has a Master's degree in English and Library Sciences. This translator was chosen as an atypical translator: she has adopted a very personal approach in the selection and motivation for translation. This provides a counter to the previous translators, and hopefully, will help us to arrive at tenable conclusions.

Ta'avoni is a full-time employee of Iran's National Library and Archives, and because of this and her field of study, she has written and translated books and articles in the field, as well as translating some works in the field of theatre and cinema. Her literary translations include one collection of short stories by Katherine Mansfield and four books, by E. M. Forster, J. D. Salinger, Aldous Huxley, and Sidinie-Gabrielle Collette.

Ta'avoni's first literary translation was Forster's *Where Angels Fear to Tread* (1905), published in 1368/1989. The selection was random; as the translator explained: "I was visiting a friend and he had many books. I chose Forster's, read it and enjoyed it. I then decided to translate it into Persian". The same pattern was repeated in her selective translation from two of Mansfield's collections of short stories: *The Garden Party and other Stories* (1922), and *Bliss and other Stories* (1923). The main motivation in translating these stories was the fact the she "liked" them.

Quite often, the accumulation of various kinds of capital explains the motivations of agents of translation. However, there are motivations that cannot be explained using Bourdieu's sociology; which is especially true when people do not reveal their motives, or their motivational statements are vague. For example, in addition to her personal taste, two more things were at work for Ta'avoni: "Sometimes I translate to see how it comes out in Persian. My other criterion is the length of works. Voluminous books make me bored and I wonder how some translators can translate such works". Given that she has translated short stories that are quite popular in Iran, I asked her why she had not translated more. She replied that she did not like short stories, but liked novellas, and that she had some incomplete translations to be published in the future. Although she was not a prolific literary translator, she accepted that she had a very specific taste in translation and that she had not been motivated to translate merely "to prove something". Nevertheless, she added that some of those who read her translations had encouraged her and asked for more translations, while some, she argued, might not have liked her translations: "perhaps they found them difficult".

I asked whether she saw any differences between translations done by women and translations done by men in Iran. She said that she had not "felt any difference", and that any professional translators had leeway in selecting novels. She nevertheless read the works of two women translators in particular, Leili Golestan and Goli Emami, two prolific literary translators who had also published in the pre-Revolution era and had been engaged in such professions as editing, publishing and running an art gallery.

As regards censorship, she had been asked to modify some words relating to sexual organs in Colette's *Cheri and the Last of Cheri* (1926). Permission was given ten years later and the translation was then published without further censorship.

6. Discussion

6.1. Selection

The three translators in this case study selected titles and also accepted the publishers' suggestions for translations. Those offered to them were not necessarily their favourites. For example, Sherlock Holmes's novels proved challenging for Daqiqi at the level of decision: the translator commented that "in addition to the specific mood required for translating them, they demand hard work and looking up words in old dictionaries and reference works alike". With her careful selections of quality short stories, and in the absence of new voices in the classically-dominated publishing field, she gradually established herself as a literary translator with worthy selections. Similarly, Keyhan showed her frustration in translating Woolf's works. Her works, she conceded, had helped her to establish her position in the intellectually-dominated publishing field in Iran; however, translating Auster apparently eased the tension. For the third translator, nothing similar was shared except for the fact that Ta'avoni translated what she particularly liked. Excluding her translation of Huxley, the rest of the short stories/novellas were from a group of authors who did not seem to have much in common in terms of style or literary schools but rather in their ways of life, which might have been of interest to the translator. Salinger's legacy as a solitary, outspoken and rebellious critic of American values has appealed to readerships all over the world, and both Mansfield and Forster, in addition to their literary values, occupy a particular place in queer studies. In sum, both translators and publishers in our case acted at the level of decision. However, evidence shows that the agency of the translators was greater than that of the publishers.

6.2. Motivation

Translation as a complementary way of making a living was a motivation for the first two translators, whereas for the third translator who had a full-time job, it was more a case of something done out of a personal desire to produce art for art's sake. The first two translators had also combined translating literary works with other sources of income, including editing and translating non-literary texts.

With regard to literary translation, however, motivations varied considerably. For Daqiqi, reasons of introducing new authors and voices (including North American authors and underrepresented authors such as Singer and Babel) to the literary polysystem had been at work. In terms of content, a close analysis of Daqiqi's selections, given her agency at the level of decision-making, showed that she had chosen stories with themes common to all people across the world: people coming to terms with loneliness, middle age crises, and love and rejection. Moreover, the profiles of both translators revealed how the translation and publishing fields constructed them at the outset (their *habitus*), but how they had resisted this pressure by exerting a higher level of agency at the level of decision-making and motivation, and as a result had affected the level of context. In other words, agents of translation could be constructed by the field; nevertheless, the doxical belief that translation was worth the trouble helped them to construct the field once they were sufficiently consecrated, i.e., they had accumulated some symbolic capital. In the case of Ta'avoni, she did not see motivation as a form of "achievement motivation", following David McClelland's term (1961). For her it was something more personal and rare, a motivation through self-interest that was at odds with the general market demands, though her translations might have drawn an equally rare audience with similar interest.

6.3. Context

The level of context in our three-tier model of agency was no less important than the levels of decision and motivation. In the context under study, it appeared that all social, cultural and political phenomena were shaped by the larger state policies; however, these three translators had not been voiceless. The most observable agents of translation in this study were the state policies pertaining to the translation and publication of books and enforced by the Book Bureau. When censorship is enforced strictly (e.g. Merkle 2002), translators and publishers are forced to conform as well. They often do, but they also try to challenge it. For example, they employ various strategies, such as careful selection, adaptation, deletion, and self-censorship, sometimes use punctuation marks to mark missing parts in the text, and often speak publicly about censorship in their interviews, as is the case in Iran. In this case study, we saw that patience and translating for future possible publications were also under-researched strategies in coping with the agency of the state at the level of context. Similarly, the state had at one time provided subsidised paper for publishers, thus contributing to the exponential establishment of publishing houses on the one hand, while increasing paper-related corruption, as noted earlier, on the other. With no empirical studies available on the issue, it is hard to determine exactly the effect of that policy on the agency in our context.

Context can also increase the agency of translators and publishers. Until two decades ago, there was an absence of new voices both in modern Persian literature and in translated short stories. However, because of translations and the increasing publication of Persian fiction, that gap has been filled. This phenomenon has clearly increased the agency of translators and publishers, and as I remarked earlier, has created a transitory professionalisation for a limited number of translators.

6.4. Bourdieu's concepts and their application to Iran

Does Bourdieu score well in the context of Iran? The answer is both yes and no. Although his early fieldwork was done in a non-Western context (Algeria), many of his "thinking tools" were in fact the product of a French environment. One might even question the relevance of his historical data (i.e., nineteenth century France, in the case of his study of the literary field) to that of contemporary Iran, which might have a different economic structure. In addition, Bourdieu's sociology might seem ill-matched, as has been noted recently, for example by Shariati 1390/2012, and cf. Mir'abedini 1390/2012: 99, who views the "discontinuity of modernity" in Iran as a major challenge in using Bourdieu). However, given the considerable cultural exchange between France and Iran in the last two centuries (such as the substantial number of works translated from French into Persian up to the 1950s), the considerable number of Iranians living in France, and the intellectual impact of French thinkers on Iranian intellectuals and vice versa (e.g. see Nanquette, 2013), it is by no means irrelevant to the case of Iran.

For instance, Bourdieu's concepts of "field" (without worrying too much about the role of the institutionalization thereof; see Wolf 2011), were helpful for locating the considerable flows of translations as part of the publishing field.[16] Equally, his concept of capital was powerful enough to delineate the motivations of agents into accumulations of various capitals and their trade-off. As regards the concept of *habitus*, it was clear from the cases above that each agent's *habitus* affected their gradual inclination towards literary translation. Not all of the agents had had any specific training or education in literary translation, as is the case with many other translators in Iran; however, they had all found a literary *habitus* "durably incorporated" in their mind and bodies (Bourdieu 1993: 86). The effects of *habitus* were manifested in the way the translators worked in various capacities in the field of publishing (as translator, editor, consultant, and so on).

Nevertheless, adopting a sociological approach to translation, particularly those inspired by Bourdieu, is for a number of reasons easy to advocate but difficult to carry out. For one thing, researchers may not be sufficiently versed in sociology. Those with such backgrounds and the rest of the critics often find theoretical and methodological faults with Bourdieu, and find the solution in similar sociologies that have their own faults (cf. e.g. Tyulenev 2011). In addition, researchers from the so-called developing countries often deal with societies-in-transition, in which many sociological concepts and methods are not indigenous, being instead adopted mainly from the West. Such is the case in Iran, where there is hardly any commonly agreed social theorization on its particularities (e.g. Abrahamian's 1974 "Oriental despotism" article, vs. Katouzian's theory of *Jame'eh-ye kolangi* or the short-term society, 2004).[17] Nevertheless, until such theories are available, Bourdieu's (or for that matter any other sociologist's) sociology is helpful in exploring translation and publishing in Iran. For example, it can show discrepancies between the particularities of Iranian society with that of the western world. The data collected from

---

[16] According to Wolf, there are two reasons why translation does not constitute a field: agents cannot create enduring positions in the field because their contacts are of a temporary nature, and translators have less-established instruments for their consecration compared to authors (2011: 14). There is no reason to single out translators from authors solely for the temporary nature of contacts which, by extension, should be equally applicable to authors. In addition, a field for Bourdieu was never meant to be a fixed space with enduring positions.

[17] For an informative analysis of this, see Mahdi (2003).

such studies (including the present study) can also serve as the empirical base and momentum for Iranian sociologists towards theorization on, say, the complexities of cultural productions in Iran.

In addition, certain ethical and methodological challenges face researchers working with such adopted theories in developing countries.[18] For example, mapping the structure of the publishing field similarly to the way Bourdieu did in France (Bourdieu 2008) is impossible in Iran because Iranian publishers have valid reasons, for example, for not revealing their market share. This might be because Iranians are still experimenting with democratic practices (cf. Gheisari and Nasr 2006) whereas similar practices have a considerably more established tradition in the French context in which Bourdieu lived and collected his data.

7. Conclusion

Bourdieu's concepts of field, capital and *habitus*, and adopting a three-tier model of agency was used with the aim of describing and examining the agency of three women translators in the area of translation in post-Revolution Iran. We wanted to find out who decided which novels to translate, what motivated them to translate, and finally what affected their agency. We drew on personal interviews and used archival materials to do so.

The case study revealed that the three agents of translation had exercised their agency at the three levels of decision, motivation and context to varying degrees. For the most part, they were selectors of titles for translation, and their motivations were not limited to the accumulation of various kinds of capital. Their motivational accounts shed light on

---

[18] The author refers here to a personal encounter with an atypical woman translator (in the sense of being socially and professionally atypical). This translator, who remains anonymous, participated in an in-depth interview, but having been shown the transcript of the interview, wished to change certain parts, possibly the names of some individuals or publishers whom she had mentioned earlier. This was despite the initial agreement we had made in advance to proceed with the interview and its dissemination. When I refused, she employed a lawyer in Iran (though I could not verify the lawyer) through whom further communications were made. The lawyer informed me that if I planned to use his client's interview, he would take the case to court, and apparently informed my University of this. To avoid any further complications, I decided not to use the interview. I should say that being an Iranian who has lived there for 30 years, I was fully aware of sensitive issues, not to mention that in the course my of research I have been ethically responsible about disseminating my research in such a way that the lives and practices of my informants would not be harmed in any way.

rather fascinating areas that call for further research in TS: translating for possible publication in the future, and translating with no personal "achievement motivation". Belonging to a consecrated and intellectual field, and given the various constraints at work, our agents of translation had nevertheless maintained some symbolic independence through their selections.

The topic of this paper calls for more empirical research in an attempt to better understand the role of agents of translation, especially that of women translators in modern Iran. Among the many areas for further research, one is to determine whether censorship is always constraining. In other words, can censorship, similar to sanctions, have a double nature? Few have asked this question. Some argue that censorship has made Iranian movies more appealing to Western eyes. Could a similar pattern be at work in the production of fiction in translation, and also in the increasing volume of Persian works of fiction?

Acknowledgement

* The author acknowledges the kind permission to repreoduce some material from his 2014 volume published by John Benjamins.

References

Abrahimian, Ervand 1974, "Oriental despotism: The case of Qajar Iran", *International Journal of Middle East Studies*, Vol. 5, no. 1, 3-31.

Afshar, Iraj 1381/2002, «آغازه ترجمه کتابهای فرنگی به فارسی» [The beginning of translation of Western books into Persian], *Iran-shenasi* Vol. 14 (53) , 79–110.

Azadibougar, Omid 2014, *The Persian Novel: Ideology, Fiction, and Form in the Periphery*, London and New York: Rodopi.

BBC Persian Service 1386/2008, «امتیاز ماهنامه زنان لغو شد» [The Zanan publication permission is revoked]. Available at http://www.bbc.co.uk/persian/arts/story/2008/01/080128_bd-zanan-close.shtml (accessed 5 February 2013).

Behzadi, Mohammad Reza 1390/2011, «صورت کتاب های فرنگی ناصرالدین شاه قاجار در کتابخانه سلطنتی کاخ گلستان» [The list of Nasir-al Din Shah Qajar's books in the royal library of the Golestan Palace], *Payam-e Baharestan* 4 (14), 496–531.

Bharier J. 1968, "A note on the population of Iran, 1900–1966", *Population Studies: A Journal of Demography*, Vol. 22, no. 2, 273–279.

Bourdieu, Pierre 1993, *The Field of Cultural Production: Essays on Art and literature*, Cambridge: Polity Press.

—. 2008, "A Conservative Revolution in Publishing", *Translation Studies*, Vol. 1, no. 2, 123–153.

Buzelin, Hélène 2005, "Unexpected allies: How Latour's Network theory could complement Bourdieusian analyses in Translation Studies", *The Translator*, Vol. 11, no. 2, 193–218.

—. 2010, "Agents of translation", in Yves Gambier and Luc Van Doorslaer, eds., *Handbook of Translation Studies*, Volume 2, Amsterdam & Philadelphia: Benjamins, 6–12.

Daqiqi, Mozhdeh (translator) 1379/2000, «اینجا همه آدمها اینجوری‌اند: ششداستان برگزیده دهه نود» [The Persian translation of Lorrie Moor's 'People Like That Are the Only People Here' and more]. Tehran: Nilufar.

—. 1387/2008, «تجربه یک ترجمه (5): انتخاب دشوار» [The experience of translation (5): A difficult choice], *Motarjem* 18 (48), 111–113.

—. 2012, Personal email contact, 21 October 2012.

Demircioğlu, Cemal 2009, "Translating Europe: The case of Ahmed Midhat as an Ottoman agent of translation", in John Milton and Paul Bandia, eds., *Agents of Translation*, Amsterdam and Philadelphia: Benjamins, 131–159.

Farhang va zendegi 1355/1976. A Persian Journal, no. 23, 48–71.

Gaffary, Farrokh 1991, "Cinema i. History of Cinema in Persia", *Encyclopædia Iranica*. Available at
www.iranicaonline.org/articles/cinema-i (accessed 5 February 2013).

Gheissari, Ali and Vali Nasr 2006, *Democracy in Iran: History and Quest for Liberty*, Oxford: Oxford University Press.

Haddadian-Moghaddam, Esmaeil 2008, "The Namesake in Persian: An online translation workshop", *Babel*, Vol. 54, no. 2, 125–144.

—. 1387/2008, «شبه ترجمه های ذبیح الله منصوری» [Zabihollah Mansuri's pseudotranslations], *Motarjem* 18 (47), 80–88.

—. 2011, "Agency in the translation and production of *The Adventures of Hajji Baba of Ispahan* into Persian", *Target*, Vol. 23, no. 2, 206–234.

—. 2012, "Agents and their network in a publishing house in Iran", in Anthony Pym and David Orrego-Carmona, eds., *Translation Research Projects 4*, Tarragona: Intercultural Studies Group, 37–50.

—. 2013. "Agent of translation or agent of 'America'? Homayun Sanati and the Franklin Book Program in Iran", paper presented at the 7th International Congress of the EST, Germersheim, 29 August to 1 September 2013.

—. 2014. *Literary Translation in Modern Iran: A Sociological Study*, Amsterdam and Philadelphia: John Benjamins.

Hamshahri 1387/2008, The Persian Daily, «تازه ترین آمار ناشران کشور اعلام شد» [The latest statistics of the publishers in Iran]. Available at http://new.hamshahrionline.ir/details/53997 [accessed February 2013].

Hashemi, Seyyed Ahmad 1391/2012, «ترجمه فارسی در دوره معاصر» [Persian Translation in the contemporary period], *Encyclopedia of World of Islam*. Available at http://www.encyclopaediaislamica.com (accessed December 2012).

Hermans, Theo 2007. *The Conference of the Tongues*. Manchester: St Jerome Publishing.

Iran, Statistical Centre 2013, at www.amar.org.ir/Default.aspx?tabid=133 (accessed 5 February 2012).

Katouzian, Homa 2004, "The short-term society: A study in the problems of long-term political and economic development in Iran", *Middle Eastern Studies*, Vol. 40, no. 1, 1-22.

Kinnunen, Tuija & Kaisa Koskinen, eds. 2010, *Translators' Agency*. Tampere: Tampere University Press.

Koskinen, Kaisa 2000. *Beyond Ambivalence: Postmodernity and the Ethics of Translation*. Tampere: University of Tampere

Lahiji, Shahla 1387/2008, «نامه سرگشاده مدیر انتشارات روشنگران و مطالعات زنان به معاون وزیر ارشاد» [Open letter from the manager of Roshangaran va Motaleate Zanan Publishing to the Deputy Minister at the Ministry]. *Kargozaran* 16 Mordad, 12.

Lefevere, André 1992, *Translation, Rewriting and the Manipulation of Literary Fame*, London and New York: Routledge.

Lennon, J. Robert 2012, "Winter Journal by Paul Auster – review". Available at www.guardian.co.uk/books/2012/aug/15/winter-journal-paul-auster-review (accessed February 2012)].

McClelland, David 1961, *The Achieving Society*, New York: Free Press.

Mahdi, Ali Akbar 2003, "Sociology in post-Revolutionary Iran", *Journal of Iranian Research and Analysis*, Vol. 19, no. 2, 31-48.

Merkle, Denise 2002, "Censorship and Translation in the Western World", *TTR Traduction, Terminologie, Rédaction*, Vol. 15, no. 2. Available at http://www.erudit.org/revue/ttr/2002/v15/n2/007476ar.html

Milton, John and Paul Bandia, eds. 2009, *Agents of Translation*, Amsterdam and Philadelphia: Benjamins.

Mir'abedini, Hasan 1392/2012, «سرگردان در میدان ادبی بوردیو». [Lost in Bourdieu's literary field], *Nāmeh-ye farhangestān*, 4 (48), 89-100.

MonTI, Monographs in Translation and Interpreting 2010, *Applied Sociology in Translation Studies*, Alicante, 2.

Nanquette, Laetitia 2013, *Orientalism Versus Occidentalism: Literary and Cultural Imaging Between France and Iran Since the Islamic Revolution*, London: I. B. Tauris.

Nikfarjam, Omid, 2010, "Books Stuck in Iran's Censorship Quagmire", IWPR (Institute for War and Peace Reporting), at: http://iwpr.net/report-news/books-stuck-irans-censorship-quagmire (accessed December 2012).

Paloposki, Outi, 2009, "Limits of freedom: Agency, choice and constraints in the work of the translator", in John Milton and Paul Bandia, eds., *Agents of Translation*, Amsterdam and Philadelphia: Benjamins, 189–208.

Puramini, Ahmad 1388/2009, «نویسنده پایتخت دنیا: گفت و گو با خجسته کیهان به بهانه انتشار رمان ناپیدا نوشته پل استر» [Author of the world capital: interview with K. Keyhan on the translation of Auster's *Invisible*], *Etemad* 19 Azar, 10–11.

Pym Anthony, Miriam Shlesinger and Zuzana Jettmarovà, eds., 2006, *Sociocultural Aspects of Translating and Interpreting*, Amsterdam and Philadelphia: Benjamins.

Pym, Anthony 2011, "Translation Research Terms: A Tentative Glossary for Moments of Perplexity and Dispute", in Anthony Pym ed., *Translation Research Projects 3*, Tarragona: Intercultural Studies Group, 75–99.

Rajabzadeh Ahmad 1380/2001, ممیزی کتاب: پژوهشی در 1400 سند ممیزی کتاب در سال 1375 [The censorship of books: A study of 1400 censor files in 1996], Tehran: Kavir.

Rezaei, Reza 2012, Personal email contact, 25 January 2013.

Shariati, Susan 1390/2012, «کاربرد جامعه شناسی بوردیو در ایران» [The application of Bourdieu's sociology in Iran]." *Shargh*, 16 Esfand, no. 1482: 14.

Shuttleworth, Mark and Moira Cowie 1997, *Dictionary of Translation Studies*, Manchester: St. Jerome.

Statistical Center of Iran 1390/2011. Available at http://www.amar.org.ir/Default.aspx?tabid=133 (accessed March 2013).

Taheri, Farzaneh 1387/2008, «دمکراسی از لوله‌ی تفنگ بیرون نمی‌آید» [Democracy does not emerge from the gun], *Baran* 19/20, 5–15.

The Translator 2005, Special Issue on "Bourdieu and the Sociology of Translation and Interpreting", Vol. 11, no. 2.

Toury, Gideon 1995, *Descriptive Translation Studies and Beyond*, Amsterdam and Philadelphia: Benjamins.

Tyulenev, Sergey 2011, *Applying Luhman to Translation Studies: Translation in Society*, London and New York: Routledge.

Zahed, M. 1389/2010, «خدا را شکر داستان نویس نیستم: گفت و گو با فرزانه طاهری»
[Thank God I am not a novelist: An interview with Farzaneh Taheri],
Shargh 5 (1018): 10.

Zakeri, Mohsen 2007, "Translation in the ancient Iranian world [and]
Translation from Middle Persian (Pahlavi) into Arabic to the early
Abbasid period", in Harald Kittel et al. eds., *An International
Encyclopaedia of Translation Studies,* Vol. 2, Berlin and New York:
Walter de Gruyter, 1194–1206.

Wolf, Michaela, ed. 2006, *Übersetzen–Translating–Traduire: Towards a
'Social Turn'?* Wien: Lit Verlag.

Wolf, Michaela and Alexandra Fukari, eds, 2007, *Constructing a
Sociology of Translating*, Amsterdam and Philadelphia: Benjamins.

Wolf, Michaela 2010, "Sociology of translation", in Y. Gambier and L.
Van Doorslaer, eds., *Handbook of Translation Studies*. Amsterdam
and Philadelphia: Benjamins, 337–343.

—. 2011, "Mapping the field: Sociological perspectives on translation",
International Journal of Sociology of Language, 207: 1–28.

World Fact Book (CIA) 2012, "Middle East: Iran". Available at
https://www.cia.gov/library/publications/the-world-
factbook/geos/ir.html (accessed 5 February 2012).

TURKEY

WHO IS THE BOSS?
QUESTIONING *POWER RELATIONS* BETWEEN THE TRANSLATOR AND EDITOR IN TURKISH LITERARY PUBLICATIONS

AYSE AYHAN

Umberto Eco's *The Open Work* was first published in a Turkish translation by Kabalcı Yayinevi in 1992. Eight years later, in 2000, *The Open Work* was translated again, this time by Nilüfer Uğur Dalay, and published by Can Yayınları. However, a few months after the date of publication, Can Yayınları withdrew copies of this translation from retail stores and published a new translation of the book in 2001. The reason why the copies of the translation were withdrawn was a critique that had appeared on a news website (ntvmsnbc.com) by Salih Polat, a Turkish journalist. Sample sentences show that Polat was critical of the translation of *The Open Work* and claimed that it had been translated using very problematic Turkish with countless errors. In his statement he notes "It is understood that the translator is competent in Italian; however when she is also lacking knowledge of Turkish grammar and vocabulary and to cap it all any editorial supervision, the translator might end up with some bizarre translations like this one".[1][2] His ends his criticism with a question: "Who or what reasons might have caused such irresponsibility?"[3]

A couple of weeks later, the same website reported that the chief editor at Can Yayınları had informed them that the publishing house had decided to act responsibly and was withdrawing the copies of the translation from the shops. According to the website, the chief editor had stated that,

> We wanted to rush the book into print since we aimed to display *Açık Yapıt* [The Open Work] at the International Book Fair in İstanbul; as a result we couldn't handle the translation and editing processes as we usually do. We

---

[1] All translations are mine except indicated otherwise.
[2] http://arsiv.ntvmsnbc.com/news/52329.asp
[3] http://arsiv.ntvmsnbc.com/news/ 52329.asp

were aware that there were problems with the translation, although at the same time it should be admitted that Eco's *The Open Work* is a quite challenging book to translate. We edited the book as much as we could in a short space of time, and finally put it on display at the book fair. However, we were not comfortable with the final product, knowing that because of the rush we had ended up with an unwanted translation. Therefore, we stopped printing at the end of the fair. Now we are in the process of a meticulous editing and we will publish a 'readable translation' as soon as possible.[4]

Two months on, a local popular newspaper reported that Can Yayınları had published a new translation of *The Open Work* by a different translator, Pınar Savaş, instead of the previous, unwanted translation being edited. It was also emphasized that, by stopping the print run and by withdrawing all the copies of that translation from the market, and finally publishing a new "readable" translation, Can Yayınları had demonstrated a great example of responsibility.[5] The publisher stated that it had indeed been their duty to withdraw the translation, and the book's critics supported the publisher's attitude and underlined the responsible actions that had been employed in the translation and publishing processes.

However, I believe that the extent of the publisher's responsibility could be questioned. What in fact is the extent of a publisher's responsibility? Withdrawing an "unwanted" and "unreadable" translation and retranslating the source text by commissioning a new translator who also works as an editor for the same publishing house might appear quite a responsible act on the publisher's part, and it is also significant that they paid paramount attention to the views and comments of the rewriters in the literary field. However, one cannot help asking the question; would it not have been more responsible on the part of the publishers if they had not skipped the editorial supervision and had had better editing and publishing processes in place? Even though Can Yayınları is considered one of the reputable institutions among publishing houses in the Turkish literary field, it does seem that they also have problems in defining the positions and functions of the translator and the editor, in establishing the link between the translator and the editor as the agents in the field of translation, and in employing collaborative translation and editing processes.

Literary translation as a profession is considered to encompass relations among a number of agents working in the field, including the translator,

---

[4] http://arsiv. ntvmsnbc.com/news/56256.asp
[5] http://hurarsiv.hurriyet.com.tr/goster/ haber.aspx?i=6923

the editor and the publisher. Translating and publishing a literary or a non-literary text can be finalized basically by depending on co-operative relations among the agents working in the publication field. The above example, I believe, presents ample evidence with regard to the gaps in relations between translator, editor and publisher. Secondly, the example highlights the power relations and questions the importance of co-operation among translators, editors and publishers; and thirdly emphasizes how a publisher's primary interest in profit can result in the sacrificing of the quality of a published translation. In the light of these points, the main concern in this study is to question and understand the nature of the relationship between the translator and the editor as the agents in the field of publication in terms of power relations. Some of the questions to ask when analyzing the nature of the relationship include: What is the work of an editor? What sort of a power structure is constituted in the field of publication? Do translators negotiate with the editors during and after the translation process? What kind of difficulties arise in the relationship between the translator and the editor?

In her book *Constructing a Sociology of Translation*, Michaela Wolf states that the "cultural turn" in translation studies had "shed new light on the notion of 'translation', and thus on the discipline's research object", and that accordingly, this new understanding and approach in translation theory "would not only consider the intersecting spaces within the translation process, but would also give voice to the translators and other agents of this process as subjects ensuing from particular cultural dynamics" (Wolf 2007: 3). Along with the "cultural turn", the "power turn", as suggested by Tymoczko and Gentzler (2002: xi-xviii), broadened the scope of research in translation studies, and with this perspective the focus shifted to power imbalances between the source culture/text–target culture/text, and the author–translator. In addition, research in the field of translation started to develop a sociological perspective concerning external constraints on the translation process, while unequal power relations among translators, revisers, editors and publishers were also examined.

Since the agents of the translation and publication processes seem to be of importance, it might be necessary at this point to look at the concept of agency. As Chris Barker (2005) defines it, agency in general is the capacity of individuals to act independently and to make their own free choices. From this point of view, translator agency might be defined as the extent to which translators make choices and decisions in the translation process concerning their translations. After cultural and sociological issues and power relations had gained greater importance in the discipline of translation studies, new understanding and approaches in translation theory began to emphasize translator agency and gave voice to translators. For instance, Lawrence Venuti described a translator's agency by focusing on the translator's visibility (1995); while Theo Hermans focused on the translator's voice (1996).

The agency of the French theorist Pierre Bourdieu, on the other hand, is more like the social in its individual form. Regarding agents, Bourdieu noted that "the individual existed not just as individual but as a social product" (1985). His agent functions in a "field", a network of relations among individuals whose social positions are located in that field, where different forms of "capital" are in question, and his concept of capital can basically be defined as financial, non-financial, social and cultural assets and values that promote the social interaction of the individual. Capital can be categorized as economic, cultural, social and symbolic. Cultural capital, or, in other words, legitimate knowledge, can be seen in embodied, objectified and institutionalized forms. While skills can be considered as embodied cultural capital, libraries are objectified, and diplomas and certificates may be regarded as institutionalized forms of cultural capital. Symbolic capital, on the other hand, refers to honour and prestige. For Bourdieu, symbolic capital is a crucial source of power (see Bourdieu 1991). His concept of capital may be useful in understanding the dynamics of the agents who function in the translation process and in the publishing field. Even though economic capital is an important determinant in finalizing the process of translation, questions concerning the nature of the relationship between the translator and editor in terms of power relations might be understood more in relation to the concept of symbolic capital, since it seems more likely to be symbolic capital that defines the positions of the agents—translator, editor, publisher—in a particular literary field (Bourdieu 1998).

In a survey published in the Turkish literary magazine, *Kitap-lık*, that focused on the nature of the relationship between translator and editor, a couple of translators and translator/editors were questioned about the conditions prevailing in their field, and their reflections and their views on the translator-editor relationship (Ece 2007). Two of these questions were significant for my discussion: (1) what kind of co-operation do you have with the editor after submitting your translation to the publishing house? (2) what is your perspective on the ideal editor-translator relationship? Since my aim is to question and understand the nature of the relationship between the translator and the editor as the agents in the field of publication, I will develop the discussion using the answers that were given to these questions by the translators and translator/editors. The translators whose perspectives I have used are Kemal Atakay, Aslı Biçen, Necmiye Alpay, and Tuncay Birkan, all of whom are considered notable translators in the Turkish publishing field and who have translated various works, ranging from poetry to books in the social sciences, by several prominent international authors. In addition, all four are members of Turkey's Society of Literary Translators,[6] an association founded in 2006 to protect translators' rights and provide advice and training facilities. Tuncay Birkan also works as an editor and is the Society's founding member. The responses of the translators are given below, from which I attempt an analysis and conclusion as a means of understanding the nature outof the relationship between the translator and the editor in the field of publication in Turkey.

The answers of translator Necmiye Alpay to both the questions reflect the idea that the translator is the decision-maker throughout the translation and editing processes. She also emphasizes the significance of negotiation between translator and editor:

> Before I start translating I make a deal, an agreement with the editor; I'm open to all sorts of suggestions but what I expect is just a suggestion. In other words I, as the translator, would like to take the final decision. My co-operation with the editor is fundamentally based on the condition that no changes would be made without my consideration. However, it should be admitted that in every translation, there appear some points which require a second opinion (Ece 2007: 81).

> In an ideal translator-editor relationship, the editor should be an eye from outside and s/he should employ his/her experiences in publishing. However, I believe the decision-maker in the process should be the translator in considering whether or not the editor's suggestions would be suitable for the wholeness of the text (ibid).

Kemal Atakay's answer gives us his perspective on the ideal translator-editor relationship and his preference as to the type of co-operation translators and editors should enjoy:

> Once a translator is commissioned and given a text, the 'translated text', which belongs to the translator, should not be interfered with in any way. One exception might be the intervention of the editor who reads the translated text (in comparison with the source text) in order to negotiate with the translator concerning possible 'errors' and careless omissions. Then, if the translator agrees with the editor she might consider the editor's perspective and make the necessary changes. An editor's comparative

---

[6] http://www.cevbir.org

reading, in other words, a second eye reading, is quite valuable for a translator (Ece 2007: 79)

Kemal Atakay stresses that the translated text belongs to the translator, and that the editor, above all, should accept this and then do what falls to him/her, which might be identifying possible errors and omissions, and then negotiating with the translator to understand the reasons that lie behind the translator's decisions.

In her statement on the ideal translator-editor relationship, translator Aslı Biçen too makes the point that the translated text belongs to the translator. She notes:

> An ideal translator-editor relationship is based on trust. Both parties should be open to learning from each other. Sometimes translators over-personalize their translations, but at the same time the editors tend to be very strict in co-operating and negotiating with translators. Both parties should be open to co-operation, and the editors need to understand that the translated text belongs to the translator, and that their work is to supervise. (Ece 2007: 81)

Translator/editor Tuncay Birkan gives his perspective on the translator and editor relationship from an editor's point of view:

> As an editor, I'd like to work with translators who are open to collaboration and open to learn. I suppose translators basically ask for the same criteria; to work with an editor who might be open to a translator's criticism and who admits that the translated text belongs to the translator. (Ece 2007: 77-78)

> As a result I think the relationship between the translator and the editor should be released from power relations and based on collaboration. I also would like to emphasize that in most cases, publishers do not appreciate the translators and undervalue their work and their rights. (ibid)

It can be stated that translators' answers concerning the ideal translator-editor relationship particularly emphasize negotiation and collaboration. The perspectives of translators and editors confirm the importance of co-operation, and show that both parties need to be open to each other's opinions, comments, and criticism. However, as the translators also mentioned, the editor should always remember that the translated text belongs to the translator. Therefore, it can be concluded that the decision-maker in the process should be the translator.

Their answers also demonstrate that the prevalent relationship between translators and editors is shaped by unequal power relations among the agents working in the field of publication. Kemal Atakay commented that, "since editorship in Turkey has recently been institutionalized, I believe most of the work of editing so far, with some exceptions of course, has ended up with manipulation"(Ece 2007: 79). Aslı Biçen also emphasizes the problem, stating:

> As far as I understand, <u>a translator cannot effectively co-operate with an editor</u>. I saw some cases in which the editors themselves needed supervision since with their editing, they produced a work which might have damaged the whole tone of the text (Ece 2007: 81).

In the case of *Açık Yapıt* [The Open Work]*,* the publisher stated that the translator Nilüfer Uğur Dalay was not suitable or competent enough to translate the book, and that she had worked hastily and carelessly; thus they were not comfortable with the final product. On the other hand, the translator noted in her statement that she had initially made a test translation for the publisher and had started to translate only after she had received confirmation from the chief editor. After finishing and submitting the translation to the publisher, she had insisted on a meticulous editing and suggested the publisher should obtain some advice/opinions from scholars in related fields. It can be inferred from this that the translator had emphasized both the importance and the necessity of editorial supervision. Sometime later, hearing that her translation of *The Open Work* would be put on display at the book fair, she immediately contacted the publisher and asked whether the editing was finished. On learning that the editing was in progress, she got in touch with the editor and told her that she would like to co-operate and to see the edited version. The translator noted that the editor was only able to send her the text for two days, and that after spending two days analysing the text, she had written the editor a letter mentioning her perspective and stating that she was not comfortable with the editing process, since two days of negotiation with the editor was not sufficient.[7]

It can be understood from Nilüfer Uğur Dalay's statement that as the translator, she was not properly included in the editing process. In addition, the chief editor at Can Yayınları admitted that they could not employ the editing process they usually did, yet at the same time they were easily able to put the blame on the translator while abdicating their responsibility for employing established commissioning, translating and editing processes. Sabri Gürses, a translator and a member of the Society of Literary Translators, mentions that commissioning the right translator

---

[7] http://hurarsiv.hurriyet. com.tr/goster/haber.aspx?id=8208

for a specific text should be one of an editor's significant tasks (Ece 2007: 82). Therefore, if there was some kind of failure in the final product, the editor would be just as responsible for that failure as the translator. In his book on Pierre Bourdieu, Richard Jenkins states that a field is a "system of forces which exist between these positions; a field is structured internally in terms of power relations" (Jenkins 1992: 53). From the remarks of the translators on the relationship between translator and editor in the field of publication in Turkey, it can be understood that there is a power structure in the field and that the editor possesses a ranking position. What seems to be meant is that the editor is the representative of the publisher; thus, s/he shares the publisher's power.

Tuncay Birkan also underlined the hierarchical position of an editor, observing that he himself was one of the lucky translators who had the privilege of choosing texts which he liked to translate. However, he noted the discomfort of privilege that was obviously an outcome of his also being an editor in the field of publication. Similarly, Sabri Gürses emphasized the hierarchical position of the editor/publisher, commenting that it was unfortunately not the translator who specified the scope of collaboration. As he remarked, "If the publisher behaves attentively to the translator and protects the translator's rights just as much as his/her own, then we can talk about a real collaboration" (Ece 2007: 83). In *Rules of Art*, Pierre Bourdieu defines how "the field of power is the space of relations of force between agents or between institutions having in common the possession of the capital necessary to occupy the dominant position in different fields … the site of struggles between holders of different power" (1996: 215). Consequently, it can be argued that in the field of Turkish literary publication, a translator acts in a field which is mainly defined by the publisher. In this context, power relations demonstrate themselves "in the policy choices of those who control the publication process" (Kang 2009: 138), and imbalances of power shape the conditions of the field where the translator and editor make contact. It might be also added that the translators can be as visible as the symbolic capital they possess permits them to be.

References

Barker, Chris 2005, *Cultural Studies: Theory and Practice*, London: Sage.
Bourdieu, Pierre 1998, *Practical Reason*, Stanford CA: Stanford University Press.
—. 1996, *Rules of Art: Genesis and Structure of the Literary Field*, Stanford CA: Stanford.

—. 1991, *Language and Symbolic Power* (ed. John B. Thompson; tr. Gino Raymond and Matthew Adamson), Cambridge: Polity.

—. 1985, "The Social Space and the Genesis of Groups", *Theory and Society*, Vol. 14, no. 6, 723-744.

Ece, Ayşe 2007, "Soruşturma: Çeviriyi Yaşayanlar: Çevirmenler ve Editörler" [Interview: Those who live through the translation: Translators and Editors], *Kitap-lık* 110, İstanbul: Yapı Kredi.

Eco, Umberto 2001, *Açık Yapıt*, (tr. Pınar Savaş), İstanbul: Can Yayınları.

—. 2000, *Açık Yapıt*, (tr. Nilüfer Uğur Dalay), İstanbul: Can Yayınları.

—. 1989, *The Open Work* (tr. Anna Cancogni), Cambridge MA: Harvard University Press.

—. 1962, *Opera Aperta*, Milano: Bompiani.

Hermans, Theo 1996, "The Translator's Voice in Translated Narrative", *Target*, Vol. 8, no. 1, 23-48.

Heilbron, Johan and Gisèle Sapiro 2007, "Outline for a Sociology of Translation: Current Issues and Future Prospects", in Michaela Wolf, and Alexandra Fukari, eds., *Constructing Sociology of Translation*, Amsterdam: John Benjamins, 93–107.

Jenkins, Richard 1992, *Pierre Bourdieu*, London and New York: Routledge.

Kang, Ji-Hae 2009, *Routledge Encyclopedia of Translation Studies*, (eds. Mona Baker and Gabriela Saldanha), London and New York: Routledge.

Tymoczko, Maria and Edwin Gentzler 2002, *Translation and Power*, Amherst and Boston MA: University of Massachusetts Press.

Venuti, Lawrence 1995, *The Translator's Invisibility*, London & New York: Routledge.

Wolf, Michaela 2007, "Introduction: The Emergence of a Sociology of Translation", in Michaela Wolf and Alexandra Fukari, eds., *Constructing a Sociology of Translation*, Amsterdam: John Benjamins, 1-38.

ARAB WORLD

TRANSLATION IN THE ARAB CULTURE

AHMED ANKIT AND SAID FAIQ

1. Introduction

The study of translation has made significant strides over the last four decades or so. The contributions of an increasing number of scholars from different parts of the world and from different theoretical backgrounds have enriched and cross-fertilized the discipline. The openness to other disciplines and the turns that translation studies has taken as a result are only natural given the very nature of translation. Far from being an act of linguistic transposition, it is an act of re-writing and representation that has far-reaching political and cultural ramifications. As Bassnett and Trivedi (199: 2) appropriately put it, translation is not an isolated act, but is part of an ongoing process of intercultural transfer. Moreover, translation is a highly manipulative activity that involves all kinds of stages in the process of transfer across linguistic and cultural boundaries. Translation is not an innocent, transparent activity but is highly charged with signification at every stage; it rarely, if ever, involves a relationship of equality between texts, authors or systems.

As a cultural act, translation has become the site for the examination of agency, patronage, and its role in nation-building. Since it brings culture and language (its obvious components) together, translation is by necessity a multi-faceted, multi-problematic process with different manifestations and realizations in various cultures/traditions.

Culture can be defined as shared knowledge, i.e., the experience and identity that the members of a particular community ought to know to react towards and interpret in distinctive ways, while language can be seen as the system that offers its users the tools to realize such distinctive ways. The relationship between culture and language is thus so intrinsic and intertwined that Bassnett maintains it would be impossible to "take language out of culture or culture out of language" (1998: 81). Extending this relationship to include translation, Emig (2001: 203–4) believes that:

Culture itself is shown to be the result of translations, and these translations are depicted not so much as inevitable forces of history, but as individual acts that rely on their interplay with social and political contexts. Inside these contexts they often fail, and the consequences of these failures can indeed be fatal. But equally fatal is the attempt to ignore or even abandon translation as a crucial prerequisite of the formation of identity, be it personal, national or indeed cultural.

An examination of the historiography of translation as a transformative cultural tool is important for a discipline that affects the contact between peoples interculturally and even intraculturally (Faiq 2010). Within this context, the purpose of this chapter is to assess the status of translation in Arab culture. It is concluded that the cultural framing of translation during the different phases of the history of Arab culture has directly affected the state and the status of the culture itself on both local and global levels. As a social project fuelled by patronage and a clear agency, translation has played a central role in the rise of the Arab/Islamic Empire (transformation of a culture) that globalized the world for centuries (through the appropriation of knowledge from other cultures). Unfortunately, this is not the case with modern and contemporary Arab culture.

2. Medieval Arabic Translation (MEAT)

An article commissioned by the newspaper *The National* about the Arabic translation tradition on the occasion of the 2009 Arabic Booker Prize has this to say:

> When the Muslim armies were on the move, defeating their enemies in battle and giving birth to a glorious and widespread empire, it was the translator who brought home the greatest prize. As warriors overran foreign cities, he entered the libraries of earlier civilisations and redrafted in Arabic the wisdom found there, allowing Islamic scholars to absorb the knowledge of thinkers who had gone before. His work laid the foundation for a golden age, strengthening the Islamic empire and making Arabic the global language of the time (Faiq 2009).

It is within this historical context that the significance of medieval Arabic translation (MEAT) lies. Shortly after the establishment of the Islamic polity in the seventh century, the Arabs (newly converted to the new religion of Islam) recognised the importance of translation for spreading their new faith and strengthening their new nation, the *Ummah*. As a result, they pioneered the establishment of translation as a government enterprise, and successive rulers allocated to this activity its own budget and institutions. MEAT started to gain momentum early in the eighth century AD when Arabs began to produce paper on a large scale, reaching its zenith in the ninth and tenth centuries. In its historical development, MEAT evolved from a necessity phase through a truly golden and glorious phase, to a phase of decline. In general terms, three main features characterized MEAT:

1) Diversity of sources: Arabs translated from any language with which they came in contact in the course of their conquests: Hindi, Persian, Syriac, and Sanskrit. Their main source language/culture, however, was Greek.

2) Extensiveness: MEAT, particularly in Baghdad in the east and Cordoba in the west, covered almost all areas of knowledge of the time, including mathematics, astronomy, philosophy, logic, medicine, chemistry, engineering, politics, and geography.

3) Organization: in the eighth century, translation was seen as a necessity with a special focus on medicine and warfare. In the ninth and tenth centuries, the rulers encouraged translators, and even enticed them to translate by giving them, so the anecdote goes, the equivalent weight of translations in gold. The Abbasid Caliph al-Ma'moun (r. 813-833) established the House of Wisdom (*bayt al-hikma*), which was the equivalent of a modern centre of scholarship. The main political and cultural concern of the rulers was to make Arabic the language of knowledge and learning. In this they succeeded, as Arabic remained the main international donor language for centuries.

The Caliph al-Ma'moun is historically seen as the champion of MEAT. He recruited translators, including non-Muslims, from different parts of the world as long as they met the strict criteria for functioning as translators, appointed translators as state employees with regular pay, and organised *bayt al-hikma* into departments for translation, editing, research, publication and general scholarship. According to Khouri (1988), al-Ma'moun demanded a whole library in Constantinople as reparation in one of his peace treaties with Byzantium. Nutting (1964: 125) sums up the cultural and intellectual aspects of al-Ma'moun's reign in the following terms:

With a deep love of the arts and sciences, he [al-Ma'moun] became the greatest of all caliphal patrons of poetry, theology, philosophy, astrology and astronomy. He encouraged and imported men of learning regardless of race or religion. Christians, Greeks, Jews, Zoroastrians – even heathen Sabians whose star-worshipping was thought to make them experts in astronomy – were patronized and pampered in order that they might enrich the caliphate with their knowledge and creative power. The stream of culture that had earlier flowed into Greece from its sources in Egypt, Babylonia, Phoenicia and Judaea now poured back to refertilize the areas of its origins.

With the state firmly established and its resources diversified, an ideological (cultural) decision was made to stipulate an agency for translation as a national project, since, for the state to remain strong it needed science and technology. This triggered the sustained and large-scale translation of major books in various fields of learning. But MEAT moved to a phase of chaos and decline, partly because of the loss of direction (agency) of/for translation, losing its national momentum along the way.

Like all translators through history, medieval Arab translators faced the usual problems of language (mostly terminology) and matters relating to the universe of discourse of source cultures. These translators adopted three main strategies: literal, semantic and gist. Each strategy was necessitated by the requirements of the national policies (agency) set for translation. There were also strict criteria for recruiting translators, particularly during the glorious phase of MEAT. As quoted in Khouri (1988: 54), al-Jahidh, a medieval Arab scholar and critic who stressed the relativity of translation, especially the translation of Arabic poetry, stipulated the following main criteria for translators (which are not so different from today's requirements):

- a full understanding of the subject matter,
- an awareness of current methods of translation and
- previous apprenticeship with an established translator,
- a sound command of the translator's working languages,
- a full knowledge of the author of the original work, including his style and idiosyncrasies, while
- translating poetry and other sensitive and culturally bound works was to be avoided unless the translators wrote such texts themselves.

MEAT involved a process of appropriation that both reflected and contributed to a process of transformation of the nation. In this context, while purely practical considerations triggered MEAT, it was ideological (patronage and agency) framings that pushed it to its zenith. The great achievements of this historically unique tradition reflected the cultural resolve of the Arab nation. By the same token, translation was a natural response to, and a reflection of, the demands posed by such a resolve. Much appreciated by all sectors of the *Ummah*, the work of medieval Arab translators became the catalyst for native scholarship and the production of essentially Arab/Islamic works, the foundations of an empire that globalized the world for centuries. As Delisle and Woodsworth (1995: 103) explain,

Nestorian Christians, expelled from the Byzantine Empire after their patriarch Nestorius was condemned for heresy by the Council of Ephesus (431), settled in what is now southwestern Iran; they were responsible for translating the great authors of ancient Greece, along with Indian, and even some Chinese, medical texts. Ancient Greece and Syriac manuscripts were housed in the Bayt-al-Hikma or "House of Wisdom" in Baghdad, where they were translated into Arabic in the ninth century. In the twelfth century, these Arabic translations, many of which had outlived their originals, were translated into Latin in Toledo. Many of these Latin translations, medical works particularly, were subsequently retranslated into vernacular languages throughout Europe during the Middle Ages and the Renaissance.

But how did MEAT succeed in transforming the medieval Arab into a global player? The answer lies in that "process" of appropriation that was championed by its patrons and the agency attached to translation as a national project. Like all other traditions, MEAT did not happen in a cultural vacuum or in isolation from the cultures and ideologies that surrounded Arab lands. At the same time, their decision to translate did not spring from a genuine interest in Greek or any other culture, but rather was prompted by their urgent need to satisfy the necessities of a young nation.

Culturally, MEAT was the tool for an interactive dialogue between the Arabs and other cultures, but most importantly, it was seen as the means for the transformation of a group into a nation through the appropriation of the intellectual heritage (goods) of other nations.

3. Modern Arabic Translation (MOAT)

The Arab World has changed and in the process, so have its educational, social, political and even psychological realities. In the field of translation, national or pan-Arab documentation is very hard to come by. Al-Khouri (1988), for example, reports that, between 1970 and 1980, sixteen Arab states translated a total of 2,840 books into Arabic, broken down as follows:

General	42
Philosophy	165
Religion	235
Social sciences	560
Languages	20
Sciences	408
Arts	93
Literature	1,002
History and geography	315

The figure of 2,840 translated books over a decade and for a total population of about 200 million was meagre indeed. The great majority of these books were (and still are) for university students and most, if not all, were translated by university teachers who never trained as translators, but translated because of their status as experts in their field.

This rate of translations is a far cry from what al-Ma'moun had managed alone. The following figures are mere examples of the number of books translated during al-Ma'moun's caliphate:

Philosophy	114 books
Mathematics	123 books
Medicine	149 books

This was a remarkable achievement given the kind of technology available then. If al-Ma'moun had managed to create a culture of translation that led to the translation of hundreds of books when the acquisition of these books and the production of the translations were laborious and time-consuming activities, one might wonder why, between them, sixteen modern Arab nations managed only 2,840 translations, despite all the modern technologies at their disposal. In the Arab world, a number of institutions have been set up since the 1960s with the aim of promoting and sustaining translation activities. But these institutions have been at the mercy of politicians, who have generally not given translation appropriate consideration. Rather, translation has, by and large, been left to academics in language departments.

The problems of translation and translator training cannot be effectively addressed unless the problems of education in general are addressed first. The steps that have been taken over the years to train translators are the results of the endeavours of people with good will and of *ad hoc* political decisions. But these decisions have no long term ramifications. There are, of course, exceptions. In Morocco, the King Fahad School of Translation, which opened in 1986, is a case in point. But although the school has endeavoured to create a translation culture within Morocco in particular, and the rest of the Arab World in general, its programmes remain largely directed at training would-be translators in their languages, lexicography and a number of areas such as the languages of economics, international relations, etc. The school and other recent projects such as the Abu Dhabi-based Kalima project represent promising developments but the ultimate goal should be a pan-Arab initiative which will better serve the needs of the Arab nation as a whole.

One isolated project or institution cannot fulfil the needs of a world made up of some 400 million inhabitants with diverse social, political, economic and linguistic characteristics. The official language of all Arab countries is of course Arabic, but there are almost as many spoken varieties of Arabic as there are Arab states. Furthermore, the area is divided between the colonial languages (English and French, with Spanish and Italian having restricted uses as well).

As Hatim (1997) notes, the problems of the educational system in the Arab World most affect the teaching of Arabic itself. The language is still taught for the purposes of mystery rather than mastery, and its status as the language of the Quran, Islam's Holy Book, makes it difficult for potential reformers to challenge the existing programmes for Arabic directly. The tendency at Arab academic institutions has been to assume that students are competent enough in Arabic to carry out translation from and into it, but unfortunately, this is not necessarily always the case. In a discussion of German, Snell-Hornby (1992) reports that a new course in translation stipulated that students, native speakers of German, should do an intensive preparatory language programme in German prior to embarking on their translation courses *per se*. A similar requirement should be of greater urgency in Arab countries.

As noted above, translation played a vital role in the establishment and strengthening of the Arab empire and made Arabic a global language. For the Arabs, translation had two main objectives: (1) to enrich the Arab world with what the rest of the world had to offer; and (2) to enrich the rest of the world with what the Arab world had to offer. While MEAT achieved both objectives *par excellence*, MOAT has, however, fulfilled neither objective in any effective way. For historical reasons, both colonial and post-colonial, there are considerable differences, often difficult to reconcile, between the politics of translation across the Arab World in terms of state involvement, social awareness of the importance of translation, and the availability of trained and competently-skilled translators. The following comments about MOAT are in order:

1) Translation today is generally an *ad hoc* activity. It forms a small part of language curricula and remains without a clear and consistent policy regarding its status, and/or even the role it can constructively play within the teaching of languages. The teaching of languages in the Arab World is itself without effective policies, including the respective literatures and cultures of these languages (cf. Said 1993).

2) Translation is still seen as restricted to particular sections of society. Most of the books translated into Arabic from other languages, particularly English and French, remain directed at university students, and readers of romance and crime novels.

3) The quality of translation into Arabic has been sacrificed for immediate returns. University teachers and publishers make quick profits out of students who are required to buy textbooks. The teachers normally carry out the translations, but with no knowledge

of the norms, in the general sense of the term, of translation, nor of its ethics and its mission as a transcreating and transculturating tool.

4) Translation remains largely an individual task with no clear national or pan-Arab criteria for the choice of works for translation, the setting up of competent agencies, or monitoring bodies to follow up translation activities as projects (like any business projects that are supposed to yield good returns).

5) The low status of translation in the Arab World means that the quality of translators is, in the main, poor. Translators often do not even meet the minimum required command of their working languages. Furthermore, publishers and editors rarely check translations against original works. Publishers seldom subject translations to editorial or review processes; perhaps because the ultimate users of these translations are students of these translators-cum-teachers.

6) The *ad hoc* nature of translation in the Arab World is manifest in the fact that the same foreign works are often translated many times and often simultaneously into Arabic. This clearly shows a lack of appropriate co-ordination between the Arab states.

7) Although not directly related to translation *into* Arabic, translation *from* Arabic into mainstream European languages has not helped the situation much. This translation is essentially still seen as an exotic voyage which is carried out through a weighty component of representation in the target cultures (cf. Carbonell 1996; Said 1993). For instance, *The Arabian Nights*, mistakenly referred to as such in the West, is more famous in the West than in the Arab East. The attitude towards the exotic Arab World has led to a situation where the proportion of books written about this world in Western languages is in inverse ratio to the small number of books translated from Arabic. This attitude may have contributed to the low status of translation in the Arab World; a world feeling neglected and thus deciding to neglect. The victims here are both parties, the West and the Arab World, but above all the situation of translation in Arab countries.

The Arab nations and the various agencies operating under the auspices of the League of Arab States have set priorities and adopted resolutions and agreements to improve the status and situation of translation. But these remain doggedly ineffective. The reality for translation is that it is the least of this region's concerns. Translation programmes and initiatives remain isolated and without any lasting pan-Arab effects, a situation underlined as such in the United Nations report on *Arab Human Development* (2003: 67):

> Most Arab countries have not learned from the lessons of the past and the field of translation remains chaotic. In terms of quantity, and notwithstanding

the increase in the number of translated books from 175 per year during 1970-1975 to 330, the number of books translated in the Arab world is one fifth of the number translated in Greece.

The same report (p. 68) cites numbers that clearly show how the Arab world collectively translates less than what Spain, or Hungary, or Israel translates individually!

For over 40 years, the Arab states have been setting up translation and arabicization bureaux and agencies to co-ordinate efforts in, and unify use of terminology, and to streamline translation, at least in science and technology. Today, however, and despite the publication of a number of unified dictionaries, the gap remains as wide as ever between terms used across the Arab World. The unified dictionaries have turned out to be disunified. The problem remains that there are no clear policies that manage to integrate at a pan-Arab level the three ingredients of the triad, namely education, arabicization and translation (EAT). To deal with this triad effectively, the Arabs need strategic planning with clear key performance indicators to assess achievements.

The emerging situation is that within Arab academic institutions, there is not the required widespread will to configure translation training for professional work and to frame it as a social project (recall MEAT). The status of translation in today's Arab world can only improve if some, although preferably all, of the following points are seriously addressed—and as effectively as they were addressed by MEAT centuries before:

1) The teaching of the Arabic language should be reassessed in terms of its modern uses and the needs of its users within the context of globalization, and the requirements of the knowledge society and knowledge economy.

2) There should be a reassessment of the process of arabicization, with modernity and tradition seen as sides of the same coin in the process of decision-making for projects, institutes, compilation of dictionaries, etc.

3) A critical review of MEAT would certainly provide valuable insights.

4) There should be an appropriate pan-Arab assessment of translation vis-à-vis the population and the politics of sustainable development, by taking into consideration the social implications of translation as well as the educational planning and provision for translation.

5) In an age when expressions such as "the information (super) highway" and "cruising/surfing the internet", as well as "networking" and "social media" abound, there is a need for effective planning for the incorporation of information technology in any Arab translation project.

6) There is a need for an effective pan-Arab translation centre—a new *bayt al-Hikma* of translation that would house all aspects of translation and arabicization.

7) Arab academic institutions need to recognise the fact that translation is a collection of abilities brought into relation with each other by a central core of theory and good practice. In other words, translation is a discipline.

4. Conclusion

The great cultural shifts that have characterized the history of humanity have been made possible by translation. For the medieval Arab world, it was the new religion, Islam, which encouraged believers to do two things: to spread the new faith and to seek knowledge. This also included pampering and protecting translators and scholars. Within two centuries, the Arabs had managed to do both. They carved out a large empire and, at the same time, translated most of the major works of the time; thereby, as a consequence, creating in Baghdad in the east and in Cordoba in the west, centres of culture and splendour unrivalled in their time.

MEAT agents and patrons easily accepted the truism that cultures change and develop only if they come in contact with other cultures through translation. This is what, centuries later, Lefevere (1996: 55) so succinctly articulates: that translators are not merely passive conduits through which messages pass from one language to another, but act as active negotiators between cultures whose negotiations may, if they do not change the face of cultures all on their own, at least contribute powerfully to doing so. As such, not only are they worthy of study, but they also provide an incredibly fertile storehouse of materials for the study of cultural relations, acculturation, and multiculturalism.

As a culturally-motivated enterprise, MEAT managed to strike a balance between the universe of knowledge, as a human activity, and the universe of its discourse with its own cultural guidelines and discursive norms. For today's Arabs, it would indeed be beneficial to learn from MEAT. Projects and movements for translating cultures should be viewed and evaluated within the context of the cultures that trigger them in the first place.

For the Arab World today, translation remains "a formidable challenge and a vital requirement that necessitates the organisation and planning of efforts within the framework of an ambitious and integrated Arab strategy" (United Nations 2003: 67). However, the situation, state and status of translation in today's Arab culture is far from satisfactory, and would easily be recognised as such by al-Ma'moun.

References

Bassnett, Susan 1998, "Translating Across Cultures", in Susan Hunston, ed., *Language at Work*, Clevedon, UK: Multilingual Matters, 72-85.

Bassnett, Susan and Harish Trivedi 1999, "Introduction: of colonies, cannibals and vernaculars", in Susan Bassnett and Harish Trivedi, eds., *Post-colonial Translation*, London and New York: Routledge. 1-18.

Carbonell, Ovidi 1996, "The Exotic Space of Cultural Translation", in Román Álvarez and Carmen-África Vidal, eds., *Translation, Power, Subversion*, Clevedon UK: Multilingual Matters, 79-98.

Delisle, Jean and Judith Woodsworth 1995, *Translators through History*, Amsterdam & Philadelphia: John Benjamins Publishing and UNESCO Publishing.

Emig, Rainer 2001, "All the Others Translate: W. H. Auden's Poetic Dislocations of Self, Nation, and Culture", in Roger Ellis and Liz Oakley-Brown, eds., *Translation and Nation*, Clevedon and New York: Multilingual Matters, 167-204.

Faiq, Said 2010, "The cultural salad in/of translation", in Said Faiq, ed., *Cultures in dialogue: A translational perspective*, Antwerp: Garant.

—. 2009, "What Arabia lost in translation" in *The National*, 7 March, at www.thenational.ae/news/what-arabia-lost-in-translation.

Hatim, Basil 1997, *Communication Across Cultures*, Exeter: University of Exeter Press.

Khouri, Shahada, et al. 1988, *Al-tarjama: qadiiman wa hadiithan* [Translation: Past and Present], Sousse, Tunisia: Dar Al-Ma'arif.

Lefevere, André 1996, "Translation: Who Is Doing What For/Against Whom and Why?", in Marilyn Gaddis Rose, ed., *Translation Perspectives IX: Translation Horizons Beyond the Boundaries of Translation Spectrum* Binghamton NY: State University of New York, 45-55.

Nutting, Anthony 1964, *The Arabs*, New York: Mentor.

Said, Edward 1993, *Culture and Imperialism*, London: Chatto & Windus,

Snell-Hornby, Mary 1992, "The professional translator of tomorrow: language specialist or all-round expert?", in Cay Dollerup and Anne Loddegaard, eds., *Teaching translation and interpreting: training, talent, and experience*, Amsterdam: John Benjamins, 9-22.

United Nations 2003, *Arab Human Development Report 2003: Building a Knowledge Society*, New York: United Nations Development Programme and Regional Bureau for Arab States.

CONTRIBUTORS

(In the order they appear in the volume)

Judy Wakabayashi is Professor of Japanese translation at Kent State University. Her research interests are in the areas of Japanese language, the linguistic and cultural challenges of translating Japanese into English in professional and literary contexts, translation pedagogy, the history of translation in Japan and other parts of Asia, and conceptual and methodological issues relating to translation historiography, including comparative and connected translation historiography. Judy Wakabayashi is co-editor of *Asian Translation Traditions* (2005, with Eva Hung), *Decentering Translation Studies: India and Beyond* (2009, with Rita Kothari) and *Translation and Translation Studies in the Japanese Context* (2012, with Nana Sato-Rossberg).

Theresa Hyun teaches Korean Studies at York University in Toronto, Canada, having previously been a faculty member at Kyung Hee University in Seoul for a number of years. She has organized a number of international conferences and is active in international scholarly organizations. Her scholarly writing has focused on Korean culture, Translation Studies and Women's Studies. Her publications include *Writing Women in Korea, Translation and Feminism in the Colonial Period* and *Translation and Modernization* (co-edited with Jose Lambert), and a volume of original bilingual poetry, *A Cup of Tea at P'anmunjom / P'anmunjom eso ui Ch'a Han Chan*.

Kim Nam Hui studied German and Conference Interpreting (German-Korean) at Hankuk University of Foreign Studies (HUFS) in Yongin and Seoul, South Korea. She has a PhD in Translation and Interpreting Studies from the Department of Translation Studies, Linguistics and Cultural Studies at the Johannes Gutenberg University Mainz, Germany, where from 2007-2013, she taught courses including history, modern literature in Korea, comic translations into German, and history of interpreting. She also taught theory of interpreting and German as a foreign language at HUFS. Research interests include History of Interpreting, Translators and Interpreters in Historical Publications, and text linguistics. Kim works as a freelance translator and interpreter of Korean, German and English, and is a member of the German Association of Translators (BDUE) and the International Association of Conference Interpreters (AIIC).

Xiaoyan Wang is a lecturer in the School of Translating and Interpreting at Xi'an International Studies University (XISU). She holds an MA in Translation Theory and Practice (XISU, 2004) and an MA in Applied Linguistics (Nanyang Technological University, 2009). Her research interests focus on translation studies, translation pedagogy, meta-cognitive awareness in translation, the cognitive process of translation, translation processes, translation strategies, contrastive linguistics and translation, as well as translation practice between English and Chinese. Her publications include "On the '*Dao*' of Laozi" (2002), and "An Overview of Nida's Translation Thought" (2003).

Norhazlina Husin is a senior lecturer at the Academy of Language Studies, Universiti Teknologi MARA (UiTM) in Shah Alam, Malaysia. She is currently pursuing her doctoral studies in translation at the same university. Her areas of interest include sociology of translation and the translation of non-literary texts.

Rokiah Awang is a senior lecturer in the School of Humanities at Universiti Sains Malaysia (USM) in Penang. Her areas of interest include translation studies, news translation and translation evaluation.

Haslina Haroon is a senior lecturer in the School of Humanities, Universiti Sains Malaysia (USM), Penang, Malaysia. She completed her PhD in Translation Studies in 2001 at the University of Warwick, United Kingdom. Her areas of interest include translation history and the translation of literary texts. Besides writing and publishing on translation, she is an active practicing translator.

Rita Kothari is an author, translator, and Professor in the Humanities and Social Sciences Department at the Indian Institute of Technology (IIT) Gandhinagar. Her research and pedagogy span literature, sociology and cultural studies. She writes and speaks on issues of linguistic identity, identity politics in Gujarat, and hybridity in language. Her most recent publications include *Memories and Movements: Borders and Communities in Banni, Kutch, Gujarat* (2013), *The Burden of Refuge: Sindhi Hindus of Gujarat* (2007/2009), and *Translating India: the Cultural Politics of English* (2003/2007). She has translated *Angaliyat: The Stepchild* (2004/2013), *Unbordered Memories: Partition Stories from Sindh* (2009), and *Speech and Silence: Literary Journeys by Gujarati Women* (2006); and had co-edited *Chutnefying English: the Phenomenon of Hinglish.*

Srinivas Reddy lives in Ahmedabad and teaches at IIT Gandhinagar. He began studying Sanskrit with his grandfather, and later trained in classical South Asian languages and literatures at Brown University and the University of California, Berkeley. In 2010 he published *Giver of the Worn Garland*, a literary translation of Krishnadeveraya's Telugu epic *Āmuktamālyada*. He is also a concert sitarist and has given numerous recitals around the world.

Esmaeil Haddadian-Moghaddam is a research fellow at KU Leuven University in Belgium where he has also taught Persian. He holds a PhD in Translation and Intercultural Studies. His most recent research was on language and translation policy in Iran, as part of a European-funded project named TIME. His work experience includes the translation industry and media, language instruction, and higher education. His most recent publications include *Literary Translation in Modern Iran: A Sociological Study* (2014). He is the managing editor of the *Journal of World Literature.*

Ayşe Ayhan teaches courses on Translation Studies and Academic English in the Department of Translation and Interpreting at Yildiz Technical University in Istanbul, Turkey, where she is a PhD candidate, with a thesis on Translation, Migration and Identity. Her research interests include literary translation, translated Turkish literature, post-colonial translation studies and translation criticism.

Ahmed Ankit is Professor and Assistant to the President for External Relations and Cultural Affairs at Ajman University of Science and Technology (Ajman, UAE), where he chairs the Curricula and Study Plan Committee, and contributes greatly to the licensure and accreditation of academic programs. He holds a PhD from the University of Salford, UK, where his thesis was one of a few that focused on interpreting studies. He has been active in academia with a focus on teaching and research in Applied Linguistics, Discourse, Communication and Translation, and E-learning. He has presented papers at many international academic events and chaired a number of conferences.

Said Faiq, FRSA, is Professor of Intercultural Studies and Translation at the American University of Sharjah (UAE), where he was chair/head of department (2003-07, 2009-10), and director of the graduate program in translation and interpreting (2002-11). He is currently a visiting professor at the University of Exeter (UK). He has worked in Africa, the Middle East, and the United Kingdom: at Salford University (1990-2003, he was director of studies for undergraduate and graduate programs in Arabic/English translation and interpreting); at Leeds University (1996-1998, he was visiting lecturer in applied linguistics). He has served as a consultant to private and public organizations for educational and related sectors, and is an established figure in intercultural and translation studies and allied areas. His publications include *Culguage in/of Translation from Arabic* (co-edited with Ovidi Carbonnel and Ali Almana, 2014*), Beyond Denotation in Arabic Translation* (co-edited with Allen Clark, 2010), *Cultures in Dialogue: A Translational Perspective* (2010), *Trans-lated: Translation and Cultural Manipulation* (2007), *Identity and Representation in Intercultural Communication* (2006), *Cultural Encounters in Translation from Arabic* (2004).

INDEX